More Praise for

Barry Sonnenfeld, Call Your Mother

"The extraordinary thing about Barry is how many truly strange and amazing chapters he's had in his life." —Neil Patrick Harris

"Barry's memoir is amazingly honest and brazenly hilarious. Now excuse me, I need to take a shower and try to get some of those images out of my head." —Cheryl Hines

"Barry Sonnenfeld's memoir is not unlike many of his films. It's an incredible story about an unlikely hero. There is action, adventure, comedy, horror—and just a little bit of porn." —Kelly Ripa

"Hilarious, full of heart, and there are no typos." —Max Greenfield

"Anyone who has encountered Barry for any length of time has wondered how he came to be the way he is. The answer is hilariously, poignantly, and forthrightly told through various stories that resulted in me feeling nauseous, laughing out loud, blushing, and repeatedly saying under my breath, 'Oh my God, Barry.' Sometimes all of those things at once." —Allison Williams

"The most purely enjoyable memoir I've ever read. The content of this neurotic genius's life is fascinating, complemented by his rare gift of storytelling." —Patrick Warburton

"I couldn't put it down." —Marc Maron

"Hilarious." —Ryan Seacrest

"Writing a book this sharp, [Sonnenfeld is] puncturing the myth of the Director as God.... A wild account of his life and times.... Here we have not only a new entrant in the movie-director memoir genre but an even rarer beast: a book by someone in the entertainment industry who is neither self-aggrandizing nor self-important but uniquely, and painfully, candid." —*The Wall Street Journal*

"His utter lack of sentiment when it comes to his achievements makes for a tonic against the typical showbiz-dreamer's success story. It is also a very, very funny book.... Sonnenfeld is a portraitist with an ironic sense of humor some would call quintessentially Jewish, and he can't help but find the humanity and hilarity in the horror shows... uniquely insightful." —*Film Freak Central*

"A funny, wry, and thoroughly entertaining memoir. Sonnenfeld is, above all, a storyteller." —*BookPage*

"Sonnenfeld makes his debut as a memoirist with a brisk, funny recounting of his improbable rise to fame in the movie world.... Zesty anecdotes about family, marriage, and fatherhood combine with Hollywood gossip to make for an entertaining romp." —*Kirkus Reviews*

"A candid, sometimes dark, entertaining, anecdotal trip down memory lane from a Hollywood icon." —*Booklist*

"An extremely Jewy memoir." —*Jewish Telegraphic Agency*

"Sonnenfeld leavens his many struggles with a substantial dose of humor. He might have endured much, but *Barry Sonnenfeld, Call Your Mother: Memoirs of a Neurotic Filmmaker* reveals Sonnenfeld to be a survivor. It's also a testament to how the rivers of fate can push you in unexpected directions.... Sonnenfeld comes up with a wealth of entertaining stories.... Revel in the ruminations of a man whose youthful traumas seared but didn't scar him." —*Book & Film Globe*

Barry Sonnenfeld,

Call Your Mother

**Memoirs
of a Neurotic
Filmmaker**

Barry Sonnenfeld

hachette
BOOKS

New York

Hachette Books
Hachette Book Group
1290 Avenue of the Americas
New York, NY 10104

HachetteBooks.com

Twitter.com/HachetteBooks

Instagram.com/HachetteBooks

First Trade Paperback Edition: September 2021

Hachette Books is a division of Hachette Book Group, Inc.

The Hachette Books name and logo are trademarks of Hachette Book Group, Inc.

The publisher is not responsible for websites (or their content) that are not owned by the publisher.

The Hachette Speakers Bureau provides a wide range of authors for speaking events. To find out more, go to www.hachettespeakersbureau.com or call (866) 376-6591.

All photos and images courtesy of the author, with the following exceptions: pp. xiv and 316: *Men in Black 3* © 2012 Columbia Pictures Industries, Inc. All Rights Reserved. Courtesy of Columbia Pictures. pp. 29 and 275: *Addams Family Values* © 1993 Paramount. All rights reserved. pp. 52, 201, 235, 238, 239, 248, 253, 254, 258, and 264: *The Addams Family* © 1991 Paramount. All rights reserved. pp. 132, 135, and 136: *Raising Arizona* © 1987 Twentieth Century Fox. All rights reserved. p. 148: *Men in Black II* © 2002 Columbia Pictures Industries, Inc. All Rights Reserved. Courtesy of Columbia Pictures. p. 194: *RV* © 2006 Columbia Pictures Industries, Inc. All Rights Reserved. Courtesy of Columbia Pictures. p. 211: Image © National Museums Scotland. p. 283: *Throw Momma from the Train* © 1987 Metro-Goldwyn-Mayer Studios. All rights reserved. p. 289: *Get Shorty* © 1995 Metro-Goldwyn-Mayer Studios. All rights reserved.

Print book interior design by Six Red Marbles, Inc.

Library of Congress Cataloging-in-Publication Data
Names: Sonnenfeld, Barry, author.
Title: Barry Sonnenfeld, call your mother : memoirs of a neurotic filmmaker / Barry Sonnenfeld.
Description: First edition. | New York : Hachette Books, 2020.
Identifiers: LCCN 2019034038 | ISBN 9780316415613 (hardcover) | ISBN 9780316415637 (epub)
Subjects: LCSH: Sonnenfeld, Barry. | Motion picture producers and directors—United States—Biography. | Cinematographers—United States—Biography.
Classification: LCC PN1998.3.S616 A3 2020 | DDC 791.4302/33092 [B]—dc23
LC record available at https://lccn.loc.gov/2019034038

ISBNs: 978-0-316-41561-3 (hardcover), 978-0-316-41562-0 (trade paperback), 978-0-316-41563-7 (ebook)

Printed in the United States of America

LSC-C

Printing 1, 2021

Barry Sonnenfeld,

Call Your Mother

For Sweetie.

REGRET THE PAST
FEAR THE PRESENT
DREAD THE FUTURE

Contents

Contents

Foreword:
Spooky Action at a Distance

In 2011, I directed *Men in Black 3*, the third and final film in my *MIB* trilogy. It was a profoundly painful experience. Someday I might write about it.

Etan Cohen—not to be confused with Ethan Coen, Joel Coen's brother, who uses the same letters of the alphabet but puts the "h" in his first name, unlike Etan, who saves it for his last—wrote the screenplay. I co-wrote a pivotal sequence in which a character named Griffin the Archanan explains the concept of quantum mechanics to Will Smith and Josh Brolin—Agents J and K.

Griffin, played by Michael Stuhlbarg, is the last surviving member of the Archanan race and, as such, has the unique ability to see infinite potential outcomes of any action. I called him a "Quantum Mechanic." He is loosely based on me.

In the scene, set at Shea Stadium in the summer of 1969, Griffin offers Agents J and K a device to save Earth. He also provides them with proof of his quantum time–viewing ability by showing them the final game of the 1969 World Series, which won't happen for another three months.

The truth he reveals is that life is a series of accidents, and only the most optimistic of all possible outcomes would have resulted in me, Barry Sonnenfeld, making it to this point in life.

Wait.

That's not what Griffin says.

What he says is this:

There are so many futures and they're all real. You just don't know which ones will coalesce. Until then, they're all happening. Like this one: It's my favorite moment in human history. All the things that had to converge for the Mets to win the World Series. They were in last place every season until they won it all.

That baseball, for instance, thrown for the last out in Game 5, manufactured in 1962 by the Spalding factory of Chicopee, Massachusetts. It was aerodynamically flawed due to the horsehide being improperly tanned because Sheila, the tanner's wife, left him for a Puerto Rican golf pro that Sunday.

When that ball is pitched to Davey Johnson, who only became a baseball player because his father couldn't find a football to give him for his 8th birthday, it hits his bat two micrometers too high, causing him to pop up to Cleon Jones, who would have been born Clara, a statistical typist, if his parents didn't have an extra glass of wine that night before going to bed.

A miracle is what seems impossible but happens anyway.

That summarizes the story of my life.

Directing Griffin the Archanan. Men in Black 3.

I was at Shea that day when the Miracle Mets won the World Series, cheering on the home team with Judy Dakin, a zaftig Jewish girl I was in love with. We played hooky from Music & Art High School and took the 7 train out to Shea. At twenty bucks for the pair, Judy and I bought a couple of scalped tickets to history.

It's been a slow process, but over the past several decades, I've started to embrace another theory of quantum mechanics. I wonder if I have died multiple times and managed in each incident to move to a different multiverse—one where, instead of dying, I miraculously live on in a world exactly like the one I previously lived in, except:

My father managed to swerve the Caddy back into our lane and avoid a head-on collision with a tractor trailer.

I wasn't killed by muggers on 14th Street and Fifth Avenue.

I didn't die when my plane crashed at Van Nuys Airport.

And most recently, the elk I hit doing 70 miles an hour on I-80 forty miles east of North Platte, Nebraska, didn't kill me.

6:40 a.m., I-80 West, North Platte, Nebraska. HDR 9 exposures.

Or maybe there are no multiple universes and I'm just very lucky.

Of course, luck can be a subjective thing. There's the story of a Japanese man who was visiting Hiroshima on August 6, 1945, when the United States dropped the first atomic bomb on that city. He survived the nuclear explosion. Over the next three days, he managed to walk, bike, and hitchhike the four hundred kilometers back to his hometown of Nagasaki, whereupon the United States dropped an atomic bomb on *that* city. The man survived. So, are we calling this guy the luckiest man in the world—surviving two nuclear bombs? Or should we consider him the unluckiest—the only man on earth to be in the two places that have experienced the devastation of nuclear war?

I've been thinking about how it happened that I turned out the way I did, which, from certain perspectives, could be considered healthy and successful.

I am by all accounts one of the most neurotic people on the planet. Matt Lauer, on *The Today Show*, told me I was the most neurotic person he had ever interviewed.

Larry David—no slouch when it comes to neurosis—and I once had a shouting match, past Barry Diller and Donald J. Trump, across the power breakfast room at the Loews Regency Hotel in New York City, arguing about who is more neurotic. I was having breakfast with Chris Meledandri, pitching my idea for an animated movie called *Dinosaurs vs. Aliens*, which he wasn't interested in. I hadn't seen Larry, who was at the opposite side of the restaurant, when I heard his distinctive voice:

"Sonnenfeld. You claim you're more neurotic than me, and

there you are, having eggs with yolks, butter on your bread...and *bacon?!*"

"Extra crispy," I yelled back.

Larry and I only casually knew each other, but we were both friends of Cheryl Hines, who played Larry's wife on *Curb Your Enthusiasm* and acted in several films I directed. We had each asked Cheryl which one of us was more neurotic. Cheryl knew that whomever she chose as more mentally unstable, the other guy would be deeply insulted. But after a year's worth of pressure from both sides, Cheryl caved, announcing on *Late Night with David Letterman* that I was the most neurotic person she had ever met.

Somehow, I've managed to live an unusual and amazing life. Was it in spite of or because of what follows?

CHAPTER 1

Barry Sonnenfeld. Call Your Mother.

At 2:20 a.m., as January 28th gave way to the 29th, I knew my father was dead. It was 1970, and I was at Madison Square Garden with Judy Dakin. The next morning, I would discover she wore magenta satin panties.

At the time of the concert, we were students at Music & Art High School. I was a french horn player; Judy had gotten in on her piano skills. We were protesting the Vietnam War along with 22,000 other lovers of peace, not war, by attending the Winter Festival for Peace concert.

Jimi Hendrix and his Band of Gypsies were warming up for the second time. Earlier in the evening Hendrix had been on stage, tuned his guitar, walked around a bit, and then, not feeling the vibe, walked off in a huff.

It was a tad unsettling.

Other musical acts moved up in the queue, including Blood, Sweat & Tears; Richie Havens; the Rascals; Harry Belafonte; Dave Brubeck; Judy Collins; and the cast of *Hair*.

There was, of course, a moving version of "Blowin' in the Wind" by Peter, Paul and Mary.

I was eight weeks short of my 17th birthday and was living a life (if you call it living) full of contradictions. I had never been out this late without my parents, yet I went to the most progressive public high school in New York City. I was the shortest male attending Music & Art, though nine months later I would be six feet tall, still retaining my "short" weight of 108 pounds. I was exceedingly over-protected by my parents, yet to their credit, neither one of them wanted me to take on an iconic Jewish profession, like the law, medicine, or finance. My mother wanted me to be an artist and my father told me to decide what would bring me pleasure in life and figure out how to make money doing it.

As profoundly short as I was, every day I trudged a quite large Sansone full double french horn to Music & Art on the 104 bus, hoping to run into Rosaline Jacobowitz, a clarinetist who had a prominent blackhead on the right side of her nose crease.

My mother feared for my life on an hourly basis, yet the high school she had secretly worked the system to get me into was located at 135th Street and Convent Avenue, in the heart of Harlem, which, during the mid-'60s, was a very, very dangerous neighborhood.

For all her insanity, her fears, her lies, and her neediness, my mother, Irene "Kelly" (her maiden name was Kellerman) Sonnenfeld, was politically aware and outspoken. Kelly had attended Hunter College, and, according to my mother, her best friend at the school was future congresswoman and large hat wearer Bella Abzug.

I say "according to my mother" because Irene "Kelly" Sonnenfeld was a pathological liar, which was excellent training for working with certain film producers and studio executives down the road.

Mom was a liberal, hinting that she might have at one time been a communist. One of the worst days of her life was the day Adlai Stevenson died, and nothing could make her "go through the roof" more quickly than my Eleanor Roosevelt jokes:

So Eleanor and Franklin are taking a rare Sunday drive through the Hudson Valley. Franklin didn't like spending time with Eleanor, she was so self-righteous, but it had been months and he felt a little sorry for her. The sun was shining, the sky blue with hope, and they were sitting in the back of an open-air car.

Eleanor, feeling giddy, asked: "Franklin, notice anything different about me?"

Franklin, who was already having regrets about the drive, gives it a try:

"Um, new dress. Quite lovely."

"This old thing? I wore it at our wedding. And it's my 'feed the hogs' attire. Come on, Franklin. Look at me. Don't you notice anything different?"

"New gloves."

"Seriously, Franklin? These are my cow milking gloves. I've had these for years."

"Shoes."

"Oh come on, Franklin. These are my sensible shoes. I wore these the first time we ever met. And, also at our wedding."

Franklin, no longer wanting to play this game, looks at her with a sense of boredom, disdain, and dread:

"I give up, Eleanor. What's different?"

"I'm wearing a gas mask!" she exclaims.

"I am going to go through the roof, Barry. Not funny."
And then, Mom would sob.

At the age of ten, I announced I wanted to play the trumpet. Mom decided there were plenty of trumpet players, but very few good french hornists. She figured that the whole Vietnam skirmish was going to blow up into a full-scale war, and if I was a french horn player and was drafted (eight years down the road), I'd be in the army band instead of the infantry, and therefore less likely to be killed. Besides, Mom told me, both instruments were in the brass section, and after the war blew over I could switch to the trumpet.

Ten years old, but practicing to avoid the infantry.

With the possible exception of Pete Seeger, the Chad Mitchell Trio, and (somewhat suspect) Danny Kaye, no one tugged at my mother's heartstrings more than Peter, Paul and Mary. Since they were performing, and because the concert was called The Winter Festival for Peace, she let me attend.

"Okay, Barry. You can go. But you must be home by two. Tops."

The Garden event was huge. It was perhaps the biggest rally

against the war up until that time. Many hours into the concert, as thrilling and emotional as it had been, we were all aware that everything would be eclipsed by Jimi's performance, if he actually came back.

We were all expecting greatness, although with Hendrix, you knew it could go either way. He was having his addiction issues and there were rumors he wasn't happy with his band, but it was also a night of great hope. We had all come together, audience and musicians, to somehow stop a war. And Hendrix was going to bring us home.

The arena exploded in screams and cheers and poundings on the bottom half of our seats as Hendrix reappeared. He spent a long time tuning his guitar, adding to the tension. Jimi would stop and start, then go over to various Gypsies and whisper something. He seemed agitated and angry.

Okay. So that's the scene. He was ready. Though twitchy, it was evident that Jimi was pulling it together and something special was about to happen. Twenty-two thousand attendees leaned forward in rapt silence as Jimi nodded to his band.

We were about to witness history.

As his left hand started the motion to make contact with his guitar strings, breaking the tense silence, the following announcement echoed over the Garden's public address system:

"Barry Sonnenfeld.

Call your mother."

Three things happened at once:

1. A chant, which started in my section of the cheap blue seats, of "Baaaaareeee, Baaaaareeee, Baaaaareeee," began to gel in a rhythm and volume that only a Garden crowd could

achieve. It cascaded toward the more expensive orange and red seats below.

2. Jimi, feeling a disturbance—although I suspect the actual "Baaaaareeee" chant had not quite become auditory on the Garden floor—sensed yet another "something" was fucking with him and didn't get off to a clean start.

3. I, Barry Sonnenfeld, started to cry. I knew the only possible reason I was being summoned to call my mother was that my father was dead and I would be spending the rest of my life living alone with Kelly as a skinny, unappealing virgin.

By standing up, I effectively announced to my surrounding peaceniks that yes, I was, indeed, Barry Sonnenfeld, and that, yes, I was going to call my mother.

The chant grew louder.

Weeping, mucous pouring out my nose, I stumbled to a pay phone, put a dime into the slot, picked up the receiver—sticky from years of mustard, ketchup, and relish hands—and dialed my home phone number: WAdsworth 8-6160.

As it started to ring, I imagined the myriad obstacles that had lain in the path of Mom's attempt to reach me: from getting someone to actually answer the phone at the Garden, to convincing them that the issue at hand was so important—the death of an only child's parent—that Jimi Hendrix had to be interrupted. But Kelly's skill at manipulation, especially playing the helpless victim, was her strength.

My father, although a consumer of sixteen ounces of sour cream a night, was a healthy man. He did a tremendous amount of walking, calling on various lighting designers, architects, and studio engineers, trying to sell them lights and dimmer board equipment. Just the walk from the A train subway station to our apartment was a quarter of a mile. In spite of all that exercise, I knew that Nathan J. "Sonny" Sonnenfeld just had a massive heart attack.

Mom picked up the phone and not surprisingly, given the fact that my father was dead, was, like me, weeping uncontrollably.

"Mom. Is everything okay?"

"What?"

"Is everyone all right?"

"What are you talking about?"

"Dad. Is he dead?"

"What?"

"Mom. Who died?"

"I thought you did!"

"What are you talking about?"

"You said you would be home by two. It's two-twenty."

"But did they not tell you the concert was still going on?"

"Yes. Yes, they did. But they couldn't confirm *you* were there. Come home right now."

"Dad's okay?"

"Sonny? Of course he's okay. He's sound asleep for a change. What else is new?"

Mom agreed that it was too late to take Judy home, given that she lived in Laurelton, Queens, the second to last stop on the F train, and allowed that Judy could sleep on the living room couch, which in earlier years had been reserved for Cousin Mike the Child Molester.

An important aside: Mike was my mother's first cousin. Raul, a neighbor in my apartment building and my best friend growing up, and I called him Cousin Mike the Child Molester and shortened it to CM the CM. For several years in the early '60s, while he was out of work, Mike lived with us, sleeping on our living room couch. He kept Kelly company, driving her to malls and antique shops. He also molested Raul, several other neighborhood kids, a few of my cousins, and, yes, me.

But hey, back to the Garden.

As I was walking down the steep concrete steps back to my seat, trying not to sled down the gooey, gummy, sticky slide of stairs, I sensed something was very wrong with Jimi.

It was a disaster.

Hendrix had stopped playing, about a song and a half into his scheduled forty-minute slot. Before putting down his guitar and wandering off stage, he said something that sounded like, "This is what happens when Earth fucks with Space. Never forget that. This is what happens."

Peter Yarrow, the Peter of Peter, Paul and Mary, who was the MC and one of the planners of the concert, now gone so disastrously wrong, announced, "Ladies and gentlemen, please welcome the cast of *Hair.*"

A few minutes later, they, and the entire Madison Square Garden audience, minus Judy Dakin and me—who were snaking our way through Penn Station trying to find the A train to take us up to Washington Heights—were singing "Let the Sun Shine In."

The next morning, my parents went to work before Judy and I had our first class at Music & Art. Although it would be years before we went all the way, I did discover that morning that she wore wonderfully shiny magenta-colored panties. And that her kisses tasted like sour milk.

A few days later, Hendrix would tell *Rolling Stone* that, as he saw it, the Madison Square Garden disaster was "like the best ending I could possibly have come up with" for Band of Gypsies.

Eight months later, Hendrix was dead.

I blame my mother.

CHAPTER 2

CM the CM, Part 1

Cousin Mike the Child Molester.
4 x 5 Polaroid.

The punch in the gut happened in early April 2014, when Raul, my boyhood best friend, now a writer, published a piece in an online journal in which he talked about being molested as a kid.

Finding his email address, I wrote: "CM the CM?"

"Yes," he replied.

The next morning, I waited for Raul at the University Place Le

Pain Quotidien. I arrived early and ate two chocolate croissants before he arrived so I could impress him by ordering the healthy oatmeal choice. I hadn't seen him in fifty years.

Until early 1965, Raul had lived one floor below me in apartment 4A. In March of that year, he tried to burn down our building in an attempt to move far away from the child molester housed in our apartment. Although the building survived, he did enough damage to his apartment that his family was forced to move to the Upper West Side, putting five miles between himself and Cousin Mike.

Raul shared horror stories of how screwed up parts of his life were and how much he blamed my parents, Cousin Mike, and to a certain extent me for his years of molestation at the hands of CM the CM.

Somehow, although not without issues that still plague me, I had managed to live through the years of Mike's molestations without too much personal damage. But I was devastated hearing what it had done to Raul.

Upon leaving Le Pain Quotidien, I took the IRT up to my father's apartment to ask him why my parents allowed this to happen to us.

Dad was 94 at the time and, although he wore a hearing aid and used a walker, was still full of himself and his positive mental attitude toward all things Sonny. He lived in a cluttered apartment with his girlfriend, the multi Tony nominated lighting designer Jennifer Tipton.

Jennifer was twenty years younger than Dad. In some ways she was similar to my mother in that, unlike Sonny, she had taste. Poor Jennifer was surrounded by art purchased by my father and his second wife, now deceased, Honey Rose.

Sonny and Honey Rose's taste tended toward "Times Square Going Out of Business" art—dogs playing poker; quotes from the pope, Frank Sinatra, and Descartes that glowed in ultraviolet light; and badly printed Andy Warhol reproductions of dollar bills.

Sonny was always cold, and the apartment's temperature was old Jewish person hot. He wore a sweater. He offered me black coffee or tap water. I declined. I asked Jennifer if Dad and I could have a little alone time, and she offered up that she had to go to the bank. My father didn't deserve Jennifer.

Dad in his early 90s at the time of this photo.

I told Sonny about my conversation with Raul and asked if he had hated Mom so much he was willing to sacrifice all these kids as well as his only child to Mike's molestation just so my mother would have someone to hang out with, driving her to the Paramus Park Mall for the Magic Pan's Chicken à la King crepes.

Dad, with no irony, provided the following explanation:

"First of all, Barry, don't forget child molestation didn't have the same stigma back then that it has now.

"Second, also remember, Kelly was very upset because of all the affairs I was having, and I thought having Mike around would cheer her up.

"And third, I never thought Mike was molesting you. I only thought he was playing with your penis."

My ears started to ring.

"Huh?"

"I only thought he was playing with your penis."

"And that was okay with you?"

"Well. I play with my penis. It feels pretty good. Don't you play with yours?"

"But Dad. We were children! It was terrifying. It was sickening. What kind of parent allows a man to touch his son's penis?

"And may I point out, not that I want to continue this debate: you touching your penis is a decision *you* make. Would it still feel good if a man forced himself on you and played with your penis? Would that still feel '*pretty good*'?"

"I never thought of it that way."

"Okay. I'm going now."

That afternoon, I was meeting Jeff Price, a screenwriter friend from Telluride, at the New York Auto Show, something I used to do as a kid with my father and—because my story is full of dramatic irony—CM the CM.

I don't know what I was thinking, going anywhere short of a walk-in psychiatric clinic or a padded cell, but as soon as I got to the Javits Center, I collapsed against the side of a new blood red GMC Yukon XL, in profound sciatic pain.

Ever since I started to direct movies in 1990, I've had sciatica, which, according to Howard Stern, Emma Thompson, and my back doctor, the late John Sarno, is brought on by unconscious narcissistic rage. Sarno's theory is that I have profound rage about something or toward someone. My unconscious worries that if I express that anger, I will do irreparable damage to a relationship. The unconscious part of my brain's solution is to give me so much pain—from my lower back to my tippy toes—that every waking minute is laser beamed exclusively on the pain, thus preventing me from having the mental strength to express that unspoken rage, possibly ending a relationship.

I have sciatica in spades.

Jeff was looking for an upgrade to his current GMC vehicle and was very interested in the third row of the new Yukon, which, at the press of a button, would drop down the last row of seats. He wondered out loud if that meant he would no longer have to take the third row out of his truck and store it in the garage when he went elk hunting.

Jeff was asking the salesman a lot of questions—good questions if you were interested in a new SUV, annoying questions if you were having an emotional, existential crisis. I bent over as if about to vomit. The sciatic pain was at a twenty-five-year high. I told Jeff I had to leave immediately, taking a minute out of the Yukon XL discussion to explain why. He was pretty impressed I had even managed to show up at the auto show, although disappointed we couldn't explore a shiny 1989 Mazda MX-5 Miata, which he had mistaken for a 2015 high end Ferrari.

I waddled toward the distant cab stand, staggering from one identical looking car to another, desperate to get back to my wife, Sweetie, and our rental apartment at the Gehry building in the financial district of lower Manhattan.

Sweetie was out with friends. I spent the evening under a

blanket, shaking the bed with sobs. My entire life I had convinced myself that my parents, flawed as they were, loved me. Surely, they hadn't understood the full extent of Mike's torturous abuse. But I was wrong. They knew. My father had just made a stupid joke about the unthinkable crimes against little children, including his only child, without any recognition of the seriousness of those acts. My mother, father, and CM the CM should have been jailed.

CHAPTER 3

Depression Central

Weekdays, from 3:30 p.m., when she got home from teaching art at my elementary school, until she fell asleep, usually to Leroy Anderson's composition "The Syncopated Clock," which meant the start of *The Late Show* movie, you could find Kelly in the bedroom she shared with my father.

Rarely did she emerge.

Day or night she lay sprawled on her side of the king sized bed, a Princess Phone cradled between cheek and shoulder, a moist white hand towel over her eyes, tears running down her fleshy face. Kelly was in pain both physically and mentally. Her ankles were swollen, and "the space behind her eyes" ached. She was retaining water and surely about to suffer from an angina attack. Kelly's bedroom was her kingdom, melancholia her sword.

Depression Central.

While Kelly was on the phone lying in bed, her narcissism knew no bounds.

My mother craved the attention that neither Dad nor I would gift her. Mom's grandiose view of how the entire United Federation of Teachers (UFT) would collapse without her, to say nothing of PS 173M, where she taught art, could have gone without saying, although Kelly made sure it was said. Her sacrifices knew no limits—according to her.

I would try to sneak past her, only an elbow of hallway and our one bathroom separating me from the sanctuary of my bedroom.

"Ba?"

Stopping in the hallway, but not turning back:

"Yes, Mom."

"Come here for a minute."

I'd stand at the threshold to her room, squinting into the gloomy interior.

"Yes, Mom?"

"Oy. You don't want to know what is going on at your school."

"Okay."

"And you really don't want to know how much pain I am in."

"Okay."

"Would you go to the bathroom and get me a nitroglycerin pill? Just in case."

"Okay."

As I would turn to go:

"Ba. Don't worry. I'm sure my heart is fine. It's just in case."

"Okay."

"I just have to make some calls, and then we'll talk. Just bring me the pill."

As I walked away, she'd say:

"Barry. You know I love you."

"Yes, Mom. I do."

Mom's "You know I love you" wasn't a statement. It was a question: "Do you love me?" I acknowledged only the statement.

I spent most of the time after school in my room with the door shut. The flooring was strip oak, which gave me very specific lanes for my Matchbox and Dinky cars and tin soldiers purchased from FAO Schwartz and my collection of plastic dinosaurs bought at the Museum of Natural History. When Corgi came out with the Aston Martin from *Goldfinger*, I didn't leave my bedroom for weeks. It had an actual ejector seat and a tiny little plastic man that catapulted out of the car. The Aston also had front machine guns and a rear deflector shield, both of which were activated by little mechanical switches on the side of the auto.

Although I had a single bed, I never slept on the mattress. I would use queen sized sheets and blankets tucked in so deep and tight that I slept off the bed in a hammock-like cocoon. Tightly swaddled in that claustrophobic protective shield, hanging several inches off the floor and relatively safe from all the unseen evils that could attack me, sucking my thumb for comfort until the age of 13, I would attempt sleep.

Mom wasn't a cook. Most days for lunch, from 4th grade on, I made myself a sandwich of canned, cold Chef Boyardee ravioli stacked between two pieces of Levy's Jewish rye bread. On my 12th birthday, Mom announced I was old enough to use the stove without her help. From then on, I made myself dinner. I would chisel two of the three following Swanson TV dinners out of the top half of our ice encrusted fridge: fried shrimp, fried chicken, or all white meat turkey. There was a short time I experimented with Swanson's German dinner, which was their attempt at sauerbraten—slices of shiny beef in a kind of sweet and sour sauce, red cabbage, a strange potato-ish thing, and an apple-like dessert—but it was kicked out of the rotation pretty quickly.

Cooking these meals, although not exactly needing talent, did require following simple directions. According to my mother, pre-heating the oven was a total waste of time. That's probably why the pat of butter never quite melted into the whipped potatoes when I pulled off the turkey dinner's aluminum foil.

Aluminum foil, in fact, demanded most of my attention.

In the case of the white meat turkey dinner, the foil had to be kept over the mashed potato and pea corners, while the turkey was exposed to the full heat of our oven.

The fried chicken was a needy offering, in that the chicken had to start covered until the last ten minutes, when the foil was removed to crisp the bird. Any frozen food that demanded "steps" seemed like a traitor to the frozen foodness of it. I stuck mainly with the combination of fried shrimp and white meat turkey.

The secret to the fried shrimp dinner was to avoid the scalding hot cocktail sauce, substituting it with Heinz ketchup.

In addition to Kelly not believing in preheating, she was also not a fan of defrosting the freezer. Nor did she embrace the concept of moderation in temperature while cooking. We went through more salt than anyone in our apartment building—not for flavor, but to put out grease fires.

When my mother did cook, during perhaps a weekend evening when Dad came home for dinner, or if it was a special holiday, we would eat skirt steak, burnt in the lower broiler of our oven.

Mom's first step toward her version of a gourmet meal would be to wrap the broiler's grated, speckled, blue-gray, enameled, removable bottom tray in aluminum foil. This step was Mom's method of preventing the grease from going through the grates to the bottom holding pan, which would then require cleaning.

On the one hand, the foil kept the pan relatively clean; on the other, the pooling of the skirt steak's grease provided an extremely powerful fuel source for the inevitable fire.

Oblivious to the danger, since it was always Dad or me who put out the fire, she would place the skirt steak on top of the aluminum foil and set the oven to broil.

Meanwhile, on top of the stove, Kelly would melt a stick of butter in a pan before dumping in a can of Kelly's (no relation) Irish Potatoes. The blackening butter would sizzle and pop from the water in the canned potatoes. The splattering, burning butter bubbles would coat the top of the stove as angry streaks of black smoke and orange flames would come roiling out from the broiler, where inside the grease fire was working overtime.

It wasn't until fire totally engulfed the face of the stove that either my father or I, smelling the smoke from our bedrooms, would race into the kitchen, grab the cylinder of Morton's salt, open the bottom broiler, and dump half the container over the steak and grease, putting out the massive fire.

We would then stab holes in the aluminum foil to let the grease drip through the broiler's metal tray slots, as Tappan intended, even though this meant we'd eventually have to wash the tray. The next step was to peel the exceedingly oversalted steak off the aluminum foil and flip it.

By now the Kelly's potatoes were black on the bottoms and ready to be scraped off the pan and flipped over; all Dad or I needed to do was to add another stick of Breakstone's butter. While Sonny and I acted as combination sous chefs and volunteer firemen, Mom was back in her bedroom on the phone with various members of the United Federation of Teachers. Albert Shanker, the president, had called a strike.

There was a decade and a half during which Dad often ran out of money. Lapses in our electricity and phone service were common, as was my fear that we would be evicted. We could no longer afford meat from Lou the butcher, except on holidays. We pretty much gave up what little fresh food we previously could afford, although Kelly's philosophy was if you could buy it in a can, why bother with fresh. We also weaned ourselves off Swanson and onto cheaper frozen food, which often meant frozen potato dumplings.

Dad's fatherly counseling: "Decide what will bring you pleasure in life and figure out how to make money doing it," was sage advice, although in Sonny's case he managed the "bring you pleasure in life" part but rarely pulled off the "making money doing it" section.

Upon discharge from the army, he became a salesman for Century Lighting. I guess he knew his way around wires, since he was in the communications division of the infantry. Over the next decade, he became the number one salesman for the number one stage lighting company in America. He was like a son to Ed Cooke, the company's owner. Sonny and Kelly asked him to be my godfather. Sonny was making a good middle class living with an expense account that let him take his "clients" out for drinks and dinner on a nightly basis.

But Sonny's entrepreneurial nature, combined with an incredibly high sense of his own worth, made him believe he could do better on his own. He quit Century Lighting and with his life savings started Lighting and Electronics. Mom got a job as a schoolteacher, and Dad poured most of her income, as well as electric, phone, rent, and butcher money into his company. When L&E went under, he started his next company. Over twenty-eight years (you can go bankrupt every seven years), Dad filed for bankruptcy four times.

Several of these companies had a year or two of profit. He would take those gains and invest in Broadway musicals. Have you ever heard of the theatrical triumph *Bravo Giovanni*? I didn't think so.

Clearly, electricity and Swanson TV dinners were not things I could take for granted. And perhaps Kelly had her reasons for lying in bed with a wet towel on her face.

Century Lighting's #1 salesman wearing part of a lighting fixture.

Kelly would call me into her bedroom, lift the moist towel off her eyes, and say, "I have such a splitting headache."

"I'm sorry, Mom."

"Make yourself something nice for dinner."

"Okay. Thanks, Mom."

"I'll be in in a minute. I just have to make some calls."

"Okay. Thanks, Mom."

I'd start to head to the kitchen.

"Ba."

I'd stop in the long hallway that led away from the gloomy bedroom and raise my voice.

"Yeah, Mom?"

"I love you."

"Okay. Thanks."

As I walked toward the dining room and kitchen, Kelly would yell out, "Make yourself some pierogi."

I would push the kitchen's swinging door partially open, reach into the room with my right hand to turn on the lights before entering, giving the colony of bugs warning that a human was arriving. The room, suddenly bright, would send hundreds of cockroaches fleeing to their various hiding places.

Our kitchen was a science experiment. The first chore was to pull out the frying pan that was sitting in a cold-watered sink of dirty dishes and floating dead roaches. The deceased bugs had suffered a combination of Raid—sprayed over the dish water at the end of every meal—and the detrimental effect my mother's cooking had on all life forms. I would scratch the burnt butter and bits of blackened potato off the pan with a table knife, squirt some dish washing detergent onto the pan, swish it around with some tap water, wipe the pan off with a paper towel, and put it on the stove to get nice and hot before dropping in a stick of butter, just like mother taught me. I'd get the big kitchen knife out of the sink, dry it off, and start stabbing away at the freezer where the joys of frozen food lay beyond a cinched circle of ice.

Kelly "I'm feeling a little better" Sonnenfeld would enter the kitchen and decide to help me. She'd rip open the box and dump the absolute lead frozen-solid pierogies onto the pan, instigating insane screaming, hissing, and popping from the combination of angry burned black butter and pierogi-clinging ice crystals shooting out in all directions. Her work done, she'd leave the kitchen, announcing she still wasn't feeling that well and needed to go back to her bedroom, take a nitroglycerin pill, lie down, and continue her martyr-like phone conversations. Lee Frishberg was threatening to cross the UFT picket line.

Mrs. Frishberg was my 3rd grade teacher. Better than some, worse than others. Definitely not as banal as my 4th grade teacher, Mrs. Kremer, who bored me so much that I spent the year pulling

out single strands of my hair and scraping off the fatty root sub-
stance at the base of each follicle between my front teeth.

*Mrs. Frishberg's class. That's me in the top row, far left, a foot shorter than the
nearest short kid. At the bottom of the frame is the dimmer board my father built
for me. I lit all the school plays with it—a promise of things to come.*

Having retreated to my bedroom to play with plastic dinosaurs
and Dinky cars, I'd smell smoke. That was my signal to follow
the low hanging fog back to the kitchen, where I'd turn over the
pierogi, still white and frozen solid on top, but black and burnt
on the bottom. I'd scrape them over, add another stick of butter
along the outer rim of the pan, and go back into my bedroom. All
our windows were permanently painted shut, so smoke ribbons
floating through our apartment were the equivalent of a kitchen
timer.

Thank God we had no fire alarms.

"Ba. Dinner smells ready," Mom would yell from her sanctuary.

I'd open a sixteen-ounce container of Breakstone's sour cream, scrape the black tubes of pierogi off the pan, and dinner would be served.

Sometimes, on a weekend when Dad was home for supper, Mom would prepare burnt tater tots instead of burnt Kelly's (no relation) Irish Potatoes. This meant less top of the stove cleanup although more throwing matches at the broiler.

Both the broiler and oven, along with the top burners, required lighting matches and throwing them at holes while quickly backing away. The trick was to flee fast enough to avoid singeing your face from the huge fireball of ignited gas that would instantly detonate, yet not toss the match so fast that it would go out before making contact with the gas.

Tater tots were not necessarily a better textural option than the butter burnt balls of spud. The frozen taters were dropped on a sheet of aluminum foil and placed under the broiler, which was set to high. The tots were done at the same time the grease fire was salted out for the second time on the skirt steak. We'd peel aluminum foil off the meat and taters and plate our meal. The tots were particularly crunchy due to the combination of being blackened to a crisp on the outside—by both the broiler's raging flames and the skirt steak grease fires—yet frozen solid on the inside thanks to my mother's refusal to preheat an oven.

Ketchup helped.

Sonny usually came home around nine, having had "dinner" with a "client." He would enter the kitchen, turn on the light, wait for the hundreds of cockroaches to scatter, and make himself a second dinner. It was simple in its preparation, almost identical in its main ingredient, yet strangely diverse. Dad would take a bowl of Breakstone's sour cream and either slice up bananas topped with a fistful of brown sugar or add sliced cucumbers and salt to the Break-stone's. Sweet or savory, depending on the night. I'd sit with him and chat about the day, unless it was a basketball night, in which case we were in my room, watching the Knicks on the 12" black and white Emerson.

Nothing said "Kelly's fancy cooking" more than her Jewish Holi-days slow cooked brisket. Kelly would get an expensive cut of meat—which meant sending me to get it, since Lou the butcher was too nice to tell me we were hundreds of dollars in brisket debt—and then slather it with Yuban instant coffee. She'd then pull a large roasting pan out of the toxic dead cockroach swimming hole perhaps for only the second or third time that year. Into the oven it would go, along with cans of potatoes and canned baby car-rots. In order to facilitate clean up, the bottom of the roasting pan was lined with aluminum foil.

Over the hours of unattended cooking (Lee Frishberg was indeed going to cross the UFT picket line), the potatoes, carrots, Yuban, and whatever fat was in the brisket would caramelize, burn into, and become one with the aluminum foil, creating a new sin-gle elemental foodstuff. When dinner was served, Dad and I would scrape the choice strips of aluminum foil off the bottom of the bris-ket. There was a wonderful hint of burnt fat and blackened meat mixed into these cherished morsels of foil—like burnt ends at a BBQ joint but with a higher chance of giving you Alzheimer's.

When a Kelly prepared meal was particularly bad, Dad and I would look at each other and in unison say:

"Fisk?"

Fisk was the name of Dad's lieutenant who had been eaten by the starving Japanese soldiers on New Guinea during World War II.

"You guys are nuts," Kelly would scream.

Sonny. New Guinea. Looks like he
should eat some Fisk.

On weekends, Mom occasionally made hard boiled eggs. Dad and I were either bowling, at a Yankees game in the Bronx, or at his office in the Watchtower building in Brooklyn. The blueprint machine would give me wicked headaches from the ammonia, as he would look over plans for schools, offices, and stores, doing "takeoffs"—lists of lights, dimmers, and switchgear that he would try to sell to his customers.

Here's Kelly's recipe for egg salad:

1. Take a dozen eggs and put them in a slightly too small pot.
2. Add water and put on the stove to boil.
3. Return to your bedroom, lie on the bed, and place a wet towel over your eyes.
4. Call a UFT member and sob about how hard you're working and how no one appreciates you.

What you'll learn using Kelly's egg salad hack is that the longer you're on the phone, the more likely it is that all the water will boil out of the dozen egged pot.

At this point, what you're doing is frying hard boiled eggs. Eventually, and inevitably, the eggs explode. With a horrible report, they break apart, and, being contained by the walls of the pot, have nowhere to go but up, ending their trajectory when they hit the kitchen ceiling at 30 miles an hour.

Around five, Dad and I would come home from our father and son outing, open our apartment's door, and be instantly overwhelmed by the smell of World War II.

"Mom made eggs."

CHAPTER 4

White Shirts

Mr. Lichtenstein and Cowboy Barry.

Mr. Lichtenstein, my elementary school principal, called me the Little Professor. I exclusively wore white shirts, purchased at Best & Co., located next to St. Patrick's Cathedral at 51st and Fifth. My daily red tie, neither neck, bolo, nor bow, was an X with a pearlescent snap. The pants were gray wool. It was as if I was wearing a boarding school uniform except, sadly, no such luck. We lived across the street from my public elementary school, PS 173M, where less than coincidentally, my mother taught art.

Mom's first action upon exiting the Best & Co. elevator on the attic floor would be to crouch down and wipe my mouth with a saliva-drenched piece of lady cloth. Since I was painfully small, strangers would approach, lower themselves to my eye line, and pronounce me adorable.

Me, David Krumholtz as young me, and Julie Halston playing young me's mother. Addams Family Values *(1993).*

To this day, I can't enter a clothing store without unleashing shooting pains of sciatica—as my back doctor believed, the product of unconscious narcissistic rage.

From the time of my birth—April 1, 1953 (yes, I was born on

April Fool's Day, and there's nothing funnier than receiving a box of half eaten Godiva chocolates)—until I moved out twenty years later, Sonny, Kelly, and I occupied apartment 5J in a prewar building at 635 West 174th Street. The red brick fire-escaped structure was situated between Broadway and Fort Washington Avenues in Washington Heights, upper Manhattan. Henry Kissinger, Manny Ramirez, Alex Rodriguez, and Lin Manuel Miranda spent part of their lives in Washington Heights and represent the four immigrant tides that waxed and waned through the area over the past eighty years. The order of neighborhood immigration was German Jew, Cuban, Puerto Rican, and Dominican. Lou Gehrig lived most of his life in the Heights, very near our place.

Our apartment could have been a showroom for Design Within Reach. Although we had no money, we somehow had nothing but Danish modern furniture, including a Saarinen dining table and chairs and a living room filled with iconic Eames and more Saarinen.

We had several sculptures that were designed by a student of Alexander Calder, which Dad managed to turn into lighting fixtures.

Sonny had been walking past a shoe store going out of business, saw the owner chucking Calderesque sculptures onto the sidewalk, and bought them—fifty bucks for three. At the same time, he also bought a four-hundred-dollar pair of shoes for six bucks. Being the self-anointed greatest salesman ever, he tried to get the fancy footwear thrown in for free, but the store would have none of it.

Dad loved a sale. In this case, the shoes weren't extraordinarily cheap because the store was going out of business. The issue was that the left shoe had been in the display window for the last four years, receiving a daily dose of bleaching sunlight, while the right shoe had been carefully protected inside a shoe box in a dark store-room. If the pair of loafers had been rock guitarists, we're talkin' Edgar Winters and Chuck Berry.

Sonny lived for a deal. I could never convince him that it wasn't a bargain if we had no use for whatever he'd purchased, no matter how cheap the item.

"Chicken of the Sea chunk lite tuna. Six for a dollar!"

"We only eat Bumblebee solid white, Dad."

"Still. Six for a dollar."

One of the women I suspect my father was having an affair with was an artist whose sculpture he was lighting for the outdoor atrium of a Third Avenue office building. The sculptress gave Dad a small version of it, which looked like our Caddy's fender after a nuclear war. Mom built a little rock garden in our dining room where it was proudly displayed.

Lining the long hallway from our front door to the living room, two bedrooms, and bathroom were linen wrapped low cabinets surface mounted to the wall. Above them were four rows, roughly thirty feet each, of bookshelves filled with hundreds of novels. Behind the books and inside the surface mounted cabinets, hidden by various knickknacks, small sculptures, and my silver dollar collection, were empty bottles of booze.

The fact that my mother was an alcoholic wasn't a surprise, but someone's got to explain to me what's with the empties? Opposite the rows of books and empty liquor bottles were paintings and drawings, mostly abstract art. A lot of it quite good. Some of them, according to my mother, were painted (but not signed) by her, when she was on a Fulbright Scholarship after receiving a master's in art from the New School for Social Research. I cannot guarantee any part of the previous sentence is true.

*Kelly in front of the hallway of abstract
art and secreted booze.*

Our apartment's one bathroom was sacred. It is where my father read *The New Yorker* magazine's serialization of Truman Capote's *In Cold Blood*.

"Sonny. I need the bathroom," my mother would wail.

"Let me finish the chapter" would be Dad's automatic response.

The bathroom, via *The New Yorker*, was where I first fell in love with the dark, quirky humor of Charles Addams cartoons. It was also where my mother stored huge, pre-Costco sized boxes of Kotex.

Until I was in high school, I took baths in that bathroom wearing a bathing suit in order not to see myself entirely naked.

I would have been beaten up much more than I was, but whenever the Puerto Rican or Irish kids would see an easy mark, as they approached our group armed with rocks or eggs, I would point to myself and announce:

"Mrs. Sonnenfeld's son."

Not wanting to receive school demerits, they would mug one of my friends, although surely less deserving of a beating than myself.

As the art teacher, my mother was one of PS 173M's favorites. Everyone got an A, there was no homework, and you got to draw with Cray-Pas, a soft, waxy crayon that allowed you to smush different colors together with your finger. I will occasionally run into adults who, when hearing my name, ask if I am Mrs. Sonnenfeld's son.

"She was my favorite teacher."

"Yeah, I've heard that. You're just lucky she was your teacher and not your mother," ending what could have been a cloying conversation.

Cray-Pas Mona Lisa *by Barry Sonnenfeld, 1965.*

Sonny was also beloved. At camera and lighting conventions, or the Consumer Electronics Show in Las Vegas, which I covered a few times for *Esquire*, I'd be approached by some old guy, who spotting my name tag would bark out, alliterationally, "You're Sonny Sonnenfeld's son?"

"Let me guess. Sonny was your favorite salesman. He always brought you bread from Flakowitz. Corn rye and raisin pumpernickel. And when he was flush, bagels, lox, and cream cheese."

"What a great guy. How's he doing?"

"Well, Flakowitz moved from Long Island to Boca, so the bread gimmick is no longer. But he's still selling."

"Still selling? He's got to be close to 90!"

"Yup."

"Give him my best, will ya? I love that guy."

"Someone has to," I'd smile in response.

CHAPTER 5

Can't Be Beat

With the exception of J. Hood Wright Park and Fort Washington Avenue, our neighborhood had no trees. In the summer, heat waves rolled off the sidewalk and asphalt. There were only a few neighborhood playing fields—two in the school yard across the street and a couple in J. Hood Wright Park. If your group got a field early in the day, you had it until an older, bigger, less Jewish mob showed up, at which point the meanest kid would approach the scrawniest kid (me) and say the dreaded: "We challenge."

This meant that the interlopers were challenging the present tenants to a game—at which point the victor would gain control of the field.

"We challenge" really meant "Get off the field."

"Hey! Leave the ball!"

One unusually warm day in February, during a three on three basketball phase, we trudged up Fort Washington Avenue to 192nd Street, near Cabrini and Dyckman, about a mile walk, where Fort Tryon Park began. Unlike J. Hood Wright, it had a couple of basketball courts. We took a basketball and two shovels, since although it was warm for February, we were going to have to hack enough ice off the asphalt court to play half-court basketball. Two hours later, we were ready to go. That's when the Puerto Ricans showed up. Older, bigger, taller, stronger, and actually good basketball players.

"We challenge."

"Do we have to leave the ball?" asked Doofus, one of the more athletic members of our tribe.

"No," I said. "Let's play for the court. We cleared it. I'll play your best guy. One on one. To eleven."

The big guys laughed. My friends groaned.

"Barry. Let's go."

"Sure, little guy. Let's play."

I have two sports highlights in my life. This was one. I beat an actual athletic kid, a foot taller than me, eleven to nothing. I can't begin to explain what happened. Upon winning, I looked over at my friends, expecting hugs, congratulations, and manly nods of victory.

"Now can we go?" asked Schmidlap.

The other sports highlight is my continuous unbeaten streak in leg wrestling.

I am one of, if not indeed, the greatest leg wrestler in modern history. Leg wrestling is a game played by lower middle class kids of a certain age from a certain part of urban America.

Here's how it is done:

Two opponents lie alongside each other, hips touching. My head is next to my adversary's feet and vice versa. We count to three, each time raising our right leg so they meet as they face the ceiling (or sky if we're playing outside).

"One...Two...Three...GO!" On "go," which is the fourth time we raise our limbs, the legs wrap around each other. I try to flip my challenger over, while he or she tries to do the same to me.

I have never lost. Against my trainer. Our contractor. Will Smith. Neil Patrick Harris. Louis Hynes. Patrick Warburton. A tennis pro. A varsity soccer player. Manly cinematographers... Literally dozens of people, all much more athletic than me. I was particularly worried about Warburton because he's a big man, goes to the gym every day, and prides himself on never being beaten in arm wrestling. He was a piece of cake. So was Neil Patrick Harris, one of the most fit humans I have ever met.

Warburton about to be defeated.

During the making of a star-studded Macy's commercial, one in which I had to fire Donald Trump for bad behavior, I challenged Martha Stewart. Martha said she knew the game well, and could easily beat me, but declined to play.

On the last day of filming, Usher said he'd accept my challenge and would wrestle me at wrap. We put a furniture blanket on the ground; Usher and I took our positions. Martha, Emeril, Jessica Simpson, and dozens of crew members and cast circled around us.

Usher's entourage walked the perimeter, telling everyone, "No videos. No pictures. Put down your cell phones."

Usher wasn't so sure of himself, was he? "One. Two. Three. Go!" Our legs shot out on "go" and just grazed each other. We'd have to go again. I felt enough of his leg on the miscue that I knew it was as if I was leg wrestling a very thick log. Usher's leg was all muscle, all power, all self-confidence.

I however, had the advantage of all-encompassing angst, which cannot be beaten by physical strength.

"One. Two. Three. Go!"

This time we connected so forcefully that I flipped Usher 90 degrees as he instantly went from a lying down position into a flipped standing straight up stance. A shocked Usher reached out a hand and helped me up. He grabbed the furniture blanket, wrapped it around me as if it were a royal cape, and bowed deeply.

Martha Stewart, Chloe Sonnenfeld, and Usher before the takedown.

Sweetie has total faith in my leg-wrestling abilities, and has never doubted me, except for one match—and to tell you the truth, I didn't think I'd win either. Of the many competitive people I know, and we're including Will Smith here, they are all minor leaguers compared to Kelly Ripa. Kelly will not lose. In anything. She also knows how to leg wrestle, having grown up in New Jersey. Kelly and her husband, Mark Consuelos, are neighbors in Telluride.

We agreed on a date and a trophy was ordered. Sweetie and I talked about the possibility, probability even, that I would lose. She told me I shouldn't take the defeat too personally. Kelly worked out for hours a day, cared more about winning than I did, grew up leg wrestling, and we were playing on her home turf—her living room. I don't know this for a fact, but I believe Kelly trained for the event. Probably with Mark, who is a superb athlete.

Kelly and I laid down next to each other. Sweetie smiled at me. Unlike Usher, there were no rules about recording the event, and Mark had his iPhone rolling. "One. Two. Three. Go!" Our legs met. Kelly was instantly flipped and shocked. Sweetie and I both wept as we hugged each other.

"I want to go again."

"Kell. One of my rules is I never play anyone a second time. It's a no win for me."

"I want to go again."

"Kell…"

"I want to go again."

I was shocked as I heard myself say, "Okay. Just this one time. But never again."

"Babe," Mark said, gesturing Kelly over to his iPhone.

"I know his trick. Watch." They looked at the recording a dozen times, as I sipped some of Mark's fine tequila. Sweetie and I were now totally confident because here's the truth: I have no trick. I am totally unfit for walking, let alone leg wrestling. What I am, and nobody on planet Earth approaches this talent, is a totally nonlimber human. I have zero flexibility. My leg is a stiff, steel rebar rod of pain. My sciatica is so bad that my hamstrings and calves are inflexible tightropes of tension.

Kelly and I got down on the floor.

"One. Two. Three. Go!"

And...flip. Kelly was once again instantly tossed over her head by my unbending leg. Standing at my feet, looking down at me, Kelly Ripa was in shock. I grinned up at her.

The night, however, was not over.

"Babe. I know his trick. I can beat him," Kelly's husband declared.

Mark is a perfect physical specimen of a man. He works out, is totally chiseled, and very macho. He comes in second only to Kelly in competitiveness.

"One. Two. Three. Go!" And...Mark is standing up staring down at me. I don't know that Sweetie was ever prouder. I know I've never experienced the kind of validation I get from winning as a leg wrestler.

Certainly not as a film director.

CHAPTER 6

Miami Beach

L eave it alone."

"It's not on the station."

"It is."

"Sonny, you're nuts. It's driving me crazy. Do you not hear that?"

Sonny wanted to leave the Caddy's radio alone. Kelly wanted to give it another try. Both our Caddy and I were 10 years old, and even when new, not that we owned it then, the car was way over engineered for one built in 1953.

In addition to the broken five preset buttons on the AM radio, the receiver also had a "tuning bar." Press it, and the radio skips to the next station. Because this feature was also broken, touching the silver bar sent the cyan indicator strip across the radio from 540 toward 1600, unstoppable by any actual station it passed.

Kelly would gauge the speed the strip was heading toward WQXR and turn the radio off and back on hoping to nail it. The problem was when she got close.

"Kelly, leave the radio alone."

"It's not on the station."

"It is."

"Sonny, do you not hear that? Do you not hear that it is not on the station? Are you deaf?"

"Kelly. I am not deaf, and you've got to either give it a rest or accept that there's a little static on the station, not that Barry or I hear anything other than classical music."

"You're nuts. Do you know that?"

"Hey, Dad. How come you and Mom always fight in the car?"

"It's the only time we're ever together," Dad laughed.

We were taking our annual off-season drive from Washington Heights to Miami Beach, which was a thirty-hour trip.

Since we had no money, we didn't fly. In fact, Sonny drove non-stop to save the expense of a motel room somewhere in the Carolinas. Instead, Dad would pull over at various rest stops along the drive and "rest his eyes" anywhere from twenty minutes to an hour.

We started our trip at 4:30 a.m., to avoid New York traffic.

There were several distinct smells to the start of the Miami trip, some of them specific to the drive, others parental: Secaucus, New Jersey, smelled of chemical refineries—burning swamp, caustic smoke, fish, vinegar, and a hint of rotting Thai food—while the distinctive odor of leaking fluids and carbon monoxide reminded us that we were in a ten-year-old General Motors product.

Sitting between my parents, my small thin legs on the transmission hump or, more often, sitting on my mother's lap, I confronted the remaining two scents, one hideous, one sublime.

As much as Proust had his olfactory relationship to madeleines, I associated my mother's mouth stench with the sour smell of saliva mixed with a subtle blend of the A train in August.

Contrarily, I was keenly drawn to the smell of Dad's hair. He was starting to get a little male pattern baldness and engaged a hair treatment he called Glover's Mange. It was a perfect combination of citrus, tar, and lamb chops—my favorite food. I dreamt of lamb chops the same way others might daydream about Drakes individual coffee cakes with buttery crumble, Ring Dings, or a fine Devil Dog washed down with an egg cream.

There was always a lot of moisture surrounding Mom. She was either crying about something or salivating into a piece of cloth she'd use to dab my face so I could get a better smell of her horrible motherly mouth smell.

Mom used Dad's handkerchief, making him complicit in the torture.

I would look out the window, watching the rivers of rain crawl up the vent window and ask if I could sit in the back. Mom, her needy arms around my waist, would tell me that it was too dangerous back there, it was safer sitting upfront on her lap—in a pre-seatbelt, hard-dashboarded car.

Sonny did all the driving. Kelly didn't have a license due to, according to my mother, her father's epilepsy.

That's right. According to Mom, New York State did not permit the offspring of epileptics to drive.

She also, by the way, claimed that before she met Sonny, Kelly was engaged to a homosexual who killed himself right before their wedding.

As it relates to the driver's license, what's more likely is that Kelly didn't want one because she needed to manipulate others into spending time with her. She needed a chauffeur.

Either Cousin Mike the Child Molester or one of the teachers at PS 173M, be it Bernice Kramer, Sonny Slavotsky—or until she died of, according to Mom, blood poisoning from her red Italian shoes that leaked into a cut on her foot—Meryl Bunis, would drive her to the Paramus Park Mall.

Eventually, I became the designated driver. I guess New York

State felt that grandchildren of epileptics were of no risk to the driving public. And by the way, did Albert, my mother's father, actually have epilepsy? We'll never know.

The Paramus mall was very ahead of its time and had a magnificent food court so spectacular that it had both a Magic Pan and a Le Crepe. Kelly loved them both.

"What do you want, Mom?" The waiter's waiting.

She'd look up, moist eyed, "I guess just the split pea soup with sherry, and he'll have the chicken à la king crepe and the minced ham, the deep fried one with mustard sauce on top."

"Mom. I'm right here. I can order for myself."

"Is that not what you were going to order? The waiter's here, for Christ's sake. Why do you care who tells him what you want to eat? What is wrong with you?"

"Mom, why are you crying?"

"I love you so much."

It didn't matter if Mom was happy or sad. She cried.

Kelly had the same control of her tear ducts that Mariano Rivera had of his cut fastball. She was the master relief pitcher of the sob.

Once, having just released a single tear from her swollen lower eyelid, standing at the edge of the water in Hampton Bays, Long Island (or Shit Hampton, as I called it), I told her that if the tear reached the corner of her mouth I was leaving and not staying for brisket. As she stood in the shallow warm fetid bay, her pants rolled up slightly past mid thigh, I watched in amazement as the single drop defied gravity and rolled back up into her eye.

"What? What are you talking about?" said a dry-eyed Kelly.

It would turn out that this was going to be the last trip to Miami in the Caddy. About six months later, Dad mysteriously came into a little money and bought our first new car, a white 1964 Tempest with brown and tan striped vinyl seats. Sonny had bought the car in October '64, which meant the '65s were already on the dealer's showroom floor, so it was more like last year's model than it was new. But that was Dad. Although Mom still insisted I was safer up front with her and Dad, at least the Tempest had seatbelts.

At our first stop for Dad to "rest his eyes" somewhere between Delaware and Washington, DC, mom got out to "stretch her legs" and then "stretch out" in the back seat. I stayed awake most of the thirty-hour drive to ask Dad questions, in an anxious attempt to keep him awake.

Starting a hundred or so miles north of the border between the Carolinas were colorful billboards featuring "Pedro," a racist cartoon of a Mexican in a sombrero, telling us how many more miles we had to "South of the Border," a truly horrific theme park motel off I-95 with a miniature golf course, restaurants, a motel, a dilapidated amusement park, and—most interesting to me—a huge fireworks store.

Yearly, the signs gave me hope that we would pull over for a meal, although it was not to be. Instead, Dad would "rest his eyes" while Mom and I ate peanut butter sandwiches we'd brought from home. At least the racist signs meant that we were halfway to Miami. On the return trip we bought fireworks, usually a mat of Black Cat firecrackers, and a couple of 10 cent cherry bombs, one of which, more than a decade later, I would use to simulate a meteor heading toward earth in my student film.

As dawn was approaching for a second time, I knew Dad was tired so I kept up the questions. In the hint of a dark mauve predawn southern Georgia sky I realized we were drifting across the center line of the two-lane highway heading toward a rapidly approaching 18 wheeler.

Sonny was sound asleep.

"Dad!" I screamed.

Dad flinched as he woke up, jerking the wheel to the left.

"Dad, no!"

Sonny, who was now wide awake from what was a deep, deep sleep, realized his huge mistake and jerked the steering wheel to the right, past our lane, and onto the sand shoulder, at which point, just as you don't do on ice, Dad steered out of the turn, instead of into it. In spite of the car's weight and high center of gravity, we managed a 360-degree donut. With the dopplered horn of the passing truck adding to the cacophony of tire squeals behind us, we were headed down the road.

In our lane.

Facing the proper southerly direction.

Mom woke up with a start.

"What happened?"

"Nothing, Kelly. Go back to sleep," said Sonny, in a totally calm voice.

To save additional money, our reward for the drive was a five-day stay at a hotel on Collins Avenue that faced the hotels that faced the ocean. Since the temperature was in the fifties with strong gusty winds, we rarely left the enclosed concrete courtyard of our hotel.

CHAPTER 7

Fear of Flying

Every time I get off an airplane, I view it as a failed suicide attempt. I blame my mother.

The year after Sonny almost killed us driving to Miami Beach, Dad found a new business partner and suddenly, suspiciously, had money. Con Ed, Bell Telephone, and our landlord were all paid up. We no longer had to cross to the east side of Broadway to avoid Lou the butcher. We blew off pierogies and were back in the gourmand frozen food world of Swanson.

Over the years, my father would find new investors or sketchy partners to join him in the lighting business. Vince Lombardo was his second partner once Lighting and Electronics went bankrupt.

Sonny loved to tell the story about Vince, who was supposedly marked to be gunned down while driving up the Saw Mill River Parkway. Seeing the assailant, Vince took out his own gun and shot and killed the would-be assassin, his car careening into the parkway's divider as Vince continued his drive home to Westchester.

Before Vince, Sonny's partner was a Jewish mobster named Sid Green. Sid owned an electrical wholesale operation on Long Island. I believe Sid and Dad were both schtupping Sid's secretary. I suspect if Sid ever found out, he would have killed Dad and their mutual lover. Or at least Dad. I'm not sure Vince wasn't also diddling Sid's secretary. She was quite a looker.

Now that the Sonnenfelds were, relatively speaking, flush, Sonny decided to fly us to Florida for our annual vacation. I suspect he was still having PTSD flashbacks from the previous year's drive. I know I was.

The flight to Miami Beach was about to be my mother's and my first trip on an airplane. I was eleven.

It's common for one's first flight to engender some anxiety. Take that, then double down on the fact that Eastern Airlines was overbooked and had leased a plane from a Mexican airline called "Pan Americano." The plane was painted the festive colors of the Mexican flag, not exactly the reassuring Eastern Airlines "Wings of Man" logo I was counting on. Now add Kelly to the mix.

As soon as we were in the air she put a nitroglycerin pill under her tongue for her angina.

"Oy. I'm having a heart attack. I'll be okay."

Kelly was making sure I was completely aware how tenuous her hold on life was.

But the most frightening thing about the flight was my mother's recurring ability to bend people to her will. In the case of Pan Americano, as soon as we hit some turbulence, Kelly pulled off an impressive act of persuasion that predated the "Barry Sonnenfeld. Call your mother." episode.

In her first-time-flying panic, she managed to convince a barely bilingual team of flight attendants, and then pilots, that the only way to save her from dying was to drop mask: she couldn't breathe, her angina was out of control, and in a matter of minutes we'd lose her.

After an indecipherable, electronically futzed bilingual announcement intended to calm the passengers who were not dying of angina, but had the opposite effect, the pilots did indeed drop the oxygen masks. A hundred clear tubes, each one screaming airliner in severe distress, dangled from the top of the 707's cabin, their yellow cups swinging in the turbulence. My father on the aisle and me at the window pretended we were not related to the panicked woman sucking oxygen.

Ergo, this incident on my maiden voyage left me with a lifelong and profound fear of flying.

To this day, I know that if something doesn't alter my preordained progression toward death, I'm going to die in a plane crash. For decades, when flying from JFK to LAX on a Pan Am 747, or TWA's excellent Lockheed L1011, when, over, let's say Kansas, the pitch of the engines would drop a third of an octave from hmmm-mmmm to huuuuummmmm, and the plane would bank slightly to the right or left, I'd shake Sweetie awake:

"What's that? Why are we changing pitch? Why are we turning in the middle of nowhere? Something's wrong, and the pilot's not telling us."

"Nothing's wrong. Planes fly from one VOR to another. VORs are those bowling pin looking things that send a signal to a plane that locates it, and planes fly from one to another. They're not in a straight line, even over Kansas, so planes will change course to fly to the next VOR. We've talked about this before.

"Everything's fine. It's how planes navigate."

Sweetie, by the way, soloed on her 40th birthday, and would

have gotten her pilot's license if Hurricane Bob hadn't wiped out the East Hampton flying school days before her scheduled exam.

A side note: When Hurricane Bob hit the Hamptons, I was at Paramount Pictures, having a marketing meeting with MC Hammer, hoping he would write a song for the end credits of my directorial debut, *The Addams Family*. There were several surreal events surrounding that meeting.

First, while we were waiting for Hammer and his entourage to show up, the marketing team, the president of Paramount, and I were idly chatting about the hurricane back east. I offhandedly mentioned that it was a big deal for me, because my penis' name is Bob, and it was kind of cool to hear my penis constantly being mentioned on the news. The film's publicist, Kathy Orloff, was a friend of ours and called Sweetie after the meeting, saying I was telling heads of studios my penis had a name, and it was Robert.

"No!" Sweetie said.

"It's Bob."

By the way, Sweetie's vagina is named Christmas.

Secondly, in an unfortunate cultural misstep, our marketing team wanted Hammer to feel at home with us white folk, so they somehow got Aunt Kizzy's Back Porch, a soul food restaurant in Marina Del Ray, to open their kitchen early and cater our 9:00 a.m. breakfast meeting with sweet potatoes, collard greens, fried okra, ribs, and fried chicken.

The racial profiling didn't stop there. At the time, mid-1991, I owned two white 1962 Lincoln Continental convertibles. Each was a four-door, many-tonned car featuring suicide doors along with rolled and pleated turquoise leather seats.

Not unlike our '53 Caddy, the Lincoln was totally over engineered for its era, which meant that something was always wrong with it. If you wanted to drive one, you really needed to own two, because one was always in the shop.

Every day I would drive whichever one was working to Paramount, and without fail, as I crawled along Interstate 10 from Santa Monica toward the La Brea exit, an African American car enthusiast would drive past, giving me a thumbs-up.

Although these Lincolns were beautiful, resembling a very large bar of Ivory soap, they were such a nightmare to own that I decided maybe MC Hammer, a rich black guy, needed one of them.

As I parked the Lincoln in front of the entrance to our meeting, I could smell the fried chicken and ribs wafting down from the chafing dishes in the conference room above.

After our meal and a discussion about the song for which Hammer went on to win a big award, I walked Hammer to the lobby and casually asked him how many cars he owned. He told me twelve.

"I think it's about to be thirteen."

"Wait. That's not your Lincoln out front?"

"Yup, and I'm going to sell it to you for fifteen thousand dollars."

"C'mon. We're friends."

"Okay. Twelve."

"Deal. I'll pick it up same place tomorrow."

I had been expecting to continue negotiating, but Hammer hadn't taken my father's course in salesmanship.

The next day Hammer arrived in an emerald green Mercedes 560 sedan that had been customized into a convertible. He opened the glove compartment, and out fell a gun and an envelope with 120 hundred-dollar bills. I handed him the title and keys to the car and never looked back.

Hammer, my mother, and my father, on the set of The Addams Family. *My father is the man on the right.*

Back on the TWA flight to LAX, I was saying to Sweetie,

"Not this time. This time is different. I can tell. Plane engines don't change pitch in the middle of nowhere Kansas. Something's wrong, and this isn't good."

"It's all going to be fine. The huuuuummmmm will go back to a hmmmmmmm as soon as they reach their next coordinate. You'll see."

"I don't think so."

"Okay. Well, I love you, and I'm going back to sleep."

Eventually, the huuuuummmmm would indeed revert to a hmmmmmmm, and we'd land safely at LAX.

There was a period in my life when I thought I was rich and was going to be rich forever. I was sadly wrong, but for a while it was fun. I was a hot director and studios wanted to be in business with me. I had two deals—one with Disney, specific to films, the other with SONY for television shows.

My SONY deal was particularly brilliant because of one detail—the contract called for me to receive one hundred hours of "occupied" private jet travel per year. When the studio president realized the deal meant they were paying the equivalent of two hundred hours of plane rentals—given that they had to pay deadhead charges to get the plane back to its base—things took something of a downward spiral.

Because of my erroneous assumption of lifetime wealth, Sweetie and I accidentally bought a home in Telluride, Colorado, a town that is impossibly hard to get to from East Hampton, where we lived. The trip took an entire day, and that's only if United didn't cancel the connecting flight out of Denver. Unless of course, you had a hundred hours of occupied travel time in a private jet.

On February 16, 1999, Sweetie, our daughter Chloe, some friends of ours and I got on a Gulfstream II jet that SONY rented for some of my "occupied hours," flying between West Hampton, New York, and Van Nuys Airport near LA.

The plan was that everyone but me would deplane in Montrose, Colorado, an airport sixty-five miles away from our home with a much less scary runway than the one in Telluride—ironic that a fearful flier's nearest airport is the highest in America—and I would continue on to Van Nuys, where a *Wild Wild West* post-production meeting was scheduled with Terry Semel, the co-CEO of Warner Bros. I would then drive to SONY, who was paying for the plane, for a script meeting on *The Tick* that would eventually star Patrick Warburton.

Telluride airport. At 9,069 feet above sea level, it is the highest runway in America. Come in too low, you hit the cliff face. Too high, and off you go, into the wild blue yonder.

What I would find out much later was that the chairman of SONY Television was so furious about the deal he himself had made that he told his travel department to book me on the cheapest planes they could find. We were flying in a G-II, owned by Trans-Exec.

After dropping everyone off in Montrose, the pilot, copilot, flight attendant, and I jetted off to Van Nuys. The three crew members were in the cockpit, with the door between it and the main cabin closed, when 14,000 feet above Los Angeles the plane started to shudder and nose dive. From the cockpit, various warning beeps were being broadcast, some with what sounded like a lot of urgency. While the GPS map built into the bulkhead was showing a quick rate of descent, it was the vibrations, beeps, klaxons, and my view out the window that gave me a much stronger indication I was about to die.

I think the reason we're all afraid of dying in an airplane crash, or at least my reason, is the fear that you'll be aware your life is about to end for many minutes as the plane corkscrews toward terra firma. You're helpless to do anything about it, but you know it's going to happen. It's not like a car crash, which will happen almost instantly, or a disease, which can happen very slowly.

Nope. This will be me, knowing for the next twenty-one minutes and forty seconds, I'm about to die. How will I behave? Will I weep uncontrollably, snot pouring out my nose? Will I relive my life happily or think only of regrets? Or will I go total Quantum Mechanic and think about every single decision I could have made differently over my entire life that would have led to a reality in which I had not gotten on this plane? We're talking billions of iterations that could have prevented me from being, at this moment, about to die.

Here's what actually happened:

I folded my arms across my chest, put my feet up on the seat in front of me, and in a very flat, relaxed way, tried out different line readings of "And now I die."

I tried the line with the emphasis on each and every syllable.

"*AND* . . . . . . now I die."

"And *NOW* . . . I die."

"And now . . . *I* die.

"And now I . . . *DIE*."

All, I hope you'll agree, very solid choices.

Somehow, we found ourselves about a hundred feet above

and halfway down the length of the Van Nuys runway when the pilot decided to land the fucking plane. I had assumed she would do a touch and go, circle around the valley, and try again. I was wrong. The plane slammed to the ground way too far down the runway. The reverse thrusters spooled on and off in about a third of a second as we headed for the brick wall at the end of the runway. Amazingly, the pilot managed to do a U-turn, as we raced toward what would surely be our deaths, barely preventing the left wing from scraping the ground as it screeched through its 180-degree turn.

Sean, my LA assistant, who always rented Chevy Suburbans, had for some unknown quantum reason, decided on a Volvo this time around. As Sean backpedaled, watching the Gulfstream II scream toward him, he saw the plane's right wing clear the roof of the Volvo, which was parked on the tarmac, by an inch. If he had rented the Suburban, we would have taken out a wing.

As I sat calmly in my seat, having run out of line readings for "And now I die," the pilot, in whatever strange wisdom she had at that moment, decided the only way to stop the plane was to aim at, hit, and bounce over parked airplanes. Each time we pounded into and bounced over a series of Cessnas and Piper Cubs, assuming we would burst into flames upon each impact, I found new inspiration for my "And now I die" line. When we ran out of planes to perforate, we crashed through a fence and coasted across the Van Nuys Airport parking lot, destroying a Dodge Ram 3500 dually before groaning to a stop. The door to the plane was lodged against a pine tree—a surprising sight in the middle of a parking area.

At this point the door to the cockpit opened, and I witnessed three out of control human beings. In a total panic, pilot, co-pilot, and flight attendant pushed against the plane's door, not having the angle I had, which clearly showed the large immovable fir tree lodged against the plane's door.

February 16, 1999, memorialized on a mouse pad.

I felt there were bigger issues. I unstrapped the seatbelt, stood up, turned my body toward the back of the plane, and loudly cleared my throat. I had the crew's attention, so in a calm, what could be described as ironic, almost sardonic voice, pointed out the window and very flatly, which is the way I like lines delivered, said:

"Say. Are we at all worried about *that*?"

The "that" I was asking about was the copious amount of fluid pouring out of the left engine, which I assumed was high-octane jet fuel that would soon explode and consume the plane and us.

The pilot said something you just never want to hear from a pilot:

"Oh my God."

She fled to the back of the plane, trailed by the flight attendant and copilot. I've been in various situations where things have looked very, very bad, and in each case, I've gone very, very calm.

True to form, I stood there, waiting for instructions.

That is, until I realized I was alone on the plane. I walked toward the rear of the jet through the galley, stepping over all the glassware and china littering the floor, continuing on past the bathroom, where all the individual sized mouthwash, toothpaste, dental floss, and Chapsticks were spilled. I then ducked into the luggage compartment, where our bags were strewn on top of each other.

Looking out the compartment's door, which had been hastily opened by my panicky crew, I watched said crew fleeing the area as fast as possible.

News and traffic helicopters were circling the airfield. I witnessed Georgia, the pilot, now that she was clear of the potentially exploding airplane, ripping epaulettes off her shoulders so the aerial cameras couldn't identify her as the pilot.

I stood in the baggage compartment doorway, as the Van Nuys Fire Department surrounded the aircraft. The burly firemen ran toward the plane, and within seconds there were a baker's dozen of them looking up at me. I saw the fear in their eyes. None of them wanted to stand this close to a plane that was about to explode.

"Get off the plane!" they yelled.

Instead of being specific, which would have spun me into immediate action, their instructions were vague.

"Jump!"

I wasn't about to jump off a plane, my fear of flying being second only to my fear of heights.

Calmly, I said, "It's very easy for you to tell me to jump off a plane, but which one of you is going to catch me?"

"Get off the plane. Now."

"Get off."

Again, not specific enough. I realized I would have to be the guy in charge, so I surveyed the group and picked the fireman with the biggest mustache.

"You. You're catching me."

"I don't give a flying fuck," the fireman said without irony, although even in my mental stress, I found his phrasing particularly observant.

"Just get off this fucking plane! Now!"

As it turns out, I was about seven feet off the ground, and rather than a jump, all that was required was an awkward placing of my arms around the fireman's neck, a lean out, and a swing to the ground, as if he had just proposed, at which point we all ran as far away from the plane as fast as we could. The plane did not explode.

I was now late for my meeting at Warner Bros., so I declined to wait for the NTSB to arrive. I told a cop stationed outside some conference room at the airport that I was staying at the Hotel Bel-Air and they could contact me that night.

While still on the tarmac, I did call Sweetie and, trying to remain calm so as not to worry her, told her I'd been in a plane crash, but I was okay. She was in the middle of making nachos for our guests back in Telluride and assumed I was just being Barry.

"Good. It's like Garp."

In *The World According to Garp*, Garp and his wife are being shown the exterior of a house they are considering buying when a plane careens into it. Garp says, "We'll take it," his theory being that at least they can cross a plane crashing into their house off the list of things that could go wrong.

"No, Sweetie. It's not like *Garp* at all. I'm still going to die in a plane crash. It's just that I was in one, and I'm calling to tell you I'm alive, but the plane is totally ruined."

"Okay, Barry. Let's talk later. The nachos are burning."

It wasn't until I showed Sweetie the VHS tape my producing partner, Barry Josephson, had created of both the 10:00 and 11:00 o'clock local LA news, each featuring the plane crash at Van Nuys Airport, that she realized perhaps in this one case, I wasn't being overly dramatic.

By the time I got to Warner Bros., word of my failed suicide attempt had preceded me. The producer of *Wild Wild West*, Jon Peters, was a bit of an insane character. He was famous for going from being Barbra Streisand's hairdresser to one of the biggest producers in Hollywood. He wasn't at the meeting. As I arrived, I said to the various studio execs, including cochairman Terry Semel,

"I just want to remind all of you that if I die in a plane crash, Jon Peters gets final cut."

Without a second's hesitation, because the last thing Terry Semel wanted was Jon Peters, who told me in our first meeting he was a premature ejaculator, editing his movie, Semel called out to his secretary, "Jane. Get Sonnenfeld the G-V for his trip back to Telluride."

The Gulfstream-V was the brand-newest corporate jet at that time, and Warner Bros. had taken delivery of it three weeks earlier.

SONY was both relieved I was alive and thrilled that Warner Bros. was taking care of my flight back to Telluride, saving them some "occupied" plane hours. That evening, when I got to the Hotel Bel-Air, there was a bouquet of flowers from Trans-Exec, the plane operators who had tried to kill me, with a note that read,

"We apologize for your recent tragedy."

Maybe they knew something I didn't. Maybe, upon impact, I died and jumped to a different multiverse.

Years later, when I told this story on *The Late Show with David Letterman*, Dave leaned over to me during the commercial break and said, "Was that pilot's name Georgia by any chance?"

When I told him indeed it was, he turned white—which was hard because Dave wore a lot of orange makeup—and said, "Oh my God. She used to be my pilot."

The irony is that the flight attendant, who was of no help, sued Trans-Exec for trauma and settled for a large sum of money. I, on the other hand, sought no remuneration because the experience made me a much better flyer. Now that I know what to expect during my next plane crash, I'm somehow okay with it.

Addendum: While I was in the main cabin repeating my "And now I die" mantra, here is the NTSB transcript of what was going on in the cockpit:

The Safety Board Investigator In Charge (IIC) removed a Collins Model 642C-1 cockpit voice recorder, serial number 1846, from the airplane and sent it to the Safety Board Vehicle Recorder Laboratory in Washington D.C. The transcript began as the crew prepared for descent from cruise altitude at 1245:12 PST. It ended after the airplane overran the runway and the pilot turned off the electrical power at 1306:28.

Throughout the descent, no checklist items were heard.

At 1303:43, the copilot reported to Van Nuys tower that the airplane was approaching the San Fernando reservoir. At 1304:18 the captain remarked that it was, "one heck of a descent." The copilot chuckled and stated it should be interesting.

At 1304:28 a sound similar to a configuration alarm started and continued about 3 seconds. At this time a sound similar to landing gear operation began. The captain asked that the flaps be lowered to 20 degrees. The copilot responded, "flaps twenty," and followed that 8 seconds later with, "yeehaw." At 1304:58 the Ground Proximity Warning Sensor (GPWS) broadcast a sink rate warning. It repeated the sink rate warning three times, then repeated twice, "whoop whoop pull up." Eight seconds later a sound similar to the configuration alarm began and continued for 21 seconds. Simultaneously, the GPWS began to broadcast, "sink rate," which continued for 20 seconds.

The tower broadcast that the winds were from 130 degrees at 5 knots.

A sound similar to the configuration alarm began at 1305:44 and continued for 10 seconds. Eleven seconds later the captain called for flaps.

At 1306:01 a sound similar to hydraulic action associated with touchdown began and continued for 4 to 5 seconds. Seven seconds later he told the captain they weren't going to make it. At 1306:22 a sound similar to engine rpm decreasing began. The recording ended at 1306:26 when the copilot said they were hitting something.

CHAPTER 8

A Christian Bar Mitzvah

Every Monday and Wednesday afternoon, from three to six, between the time I was 11 until two weeks before my April 2 bar mitzvah at the age of 13, I was at Kenny Morrison's apartment.

The two years coincided with our make-it-yourself slingshot phase, manufacturing them out of heavy-duty clothes hangers, rubber bands, and strips of leather.

Firing at will from Kenny's sixth floor bedroom window overlooking J. Hood Wright Park, I nailed a kid sitting on the park wall, hitting his chest with such accuracy and force that he grabbed his heart as if a wasp had bitten him. Bobby was his name. He was a short kid who was a member of the Irish gang, not to be confused with the Puerto Rican gang, both of whom mugged us. As Bobby shot a look in our direction, we ducked below the window and crawled to the living room.

Mrs. Morrison was never the wiser as to why I was at Kenny's apartment, very specifically, on Mondays and Wednesdays from three to six. And Kenny never wondered why I was hanging out with him after school on those two weekdays, instead of with the kids in my building. That was until one afternoon when Kenny and I were huddled together in his bedroom, sneaking peeks at his father's *Playboy*. The door opened, and unannounced, my father, who had never left work this early except the day he passed a kidney stone, looked down at me and said, "Come on, Barry. Let's go."

For almost two solid years I had been playing hooky from Hebrew school.

There are three levels of Jewish tribes: Reformed, Conservative, and Orthodox.

My father was raised Orthodox. One of seven children, he was kosher until he was drafted. My mother was raised as a Conservative, although she never practiced. I was a cultural Jew, not a religious one, having no interest in what seemed to be a petty, mean, vindictive, judgmental, and insecure Old Testament God.

In my case, what made Judaism particularly painful was that Hebrew school was taught twice a week by Rabbi Baulmal, a bald man with a huge black wart below his left nostril. He was also blessed by God with baggy eyes and a bird's nest coming out of his nose and each ear. He looked more French bulldog than rabbi.

Hebrew school met in a windowless room in the basement of Temple Beth Shalom. The rabbi smoked White Owl cigars in a ventilation-free fire trap surrounded by kids under the age of 13. There were levels of smoke drifting around the room at different heights—like the clouds a 707 might descend through attempting to land on a stormy day at Idlewild Airport. We learned how to read the Hebrew alphabet and to phonetically speak the words. We didn't study what any of the words meant. When I say we, I mean everyone who didn't play hooky for two years. I couldn't take the smell, religion, or tedium.

Three times a year my father and I went to shul: Rosh Hashanah, Yom Kippur, and Passover. I disliked them all, but Yom Kippur, which some say is the holiest day of Judaism, was the worst.

For Yom Kippur we were at temple from around eight in the morning until sunset, although my father would go home in the middle of the day for a couple of hours to "rest his eyes." This is the holiday that Jews fast for twenty-four hours—from sunset to sunset. According to my mother the rules didn't apply to females.

The time at temple consisted primarily of old Jewish men hocking up phlegm.

Yom Kippur was especially tedious due to the hours spent raising money for the new temple. Beth Shalom was about to break ground on a modern holy shrine to replace our old, narrow, non-air-conditioned place.

As if the annual dues, tickets for High Holiday services, and the synagogue's tax-free status weren't enough, after the rabbi's endless financial plea disguised as a sermon, every member of Beth Shalom was called out to contribute money for the new building.

The cheapskates would yell "Same," meaning they were pledging a similar amount as last year. The big spenders would proudly boom "Plus ten," which meant they were giving ten percent more than the previous Yom Kippur. I tensed up when the rabbi got to Nat Schacter, who, alphabetically, was a couple of names before

Nathan J. Sonnenfeld. Schacter would phlegmishly clear his throat before pompously calling out, for all the congregation to admire, "Plus ten!"

Dad always found a trail to the bathroom a few names before Schacter, and I would sit, crouched low in the hard backbreaking pew, hearing, "Nathan J. Sonnenfeld!"

Silence.

"Nathan J. Sonnenfeld?"

Silence.

"Marvin Spitzer?"

"Plus ten."

What angered me most about Yom Kippur—and made me realize that the only reason to get bar mitzvah'd was for the twenty-five-dollar checks and US government E-bonds, which cost the purchaser eighteen bucks and took seven years to mature—was the many, many pages of prewritten, in very specific detail, apologies to God for the sins we had committed since the previous High Holiday.

I'm 11 years old, and I am literally reading out loud, I guess so God can hear me apologize, for coveting my neighbor's wife? Has God seen my neighbor's wife? Mrs. Carp is 80, deaf, and has a mustache. Plus, I'm 11 years old.

The last day I attended Hebrew school was a windy, bitter, cold afternoon. Rabbi Baulmal walked into his dungeon-like classroom smoking a cigar, his left arm bandaged from his elbow to his hand. His middle finger was individually wrapped, a symbol of what I thought about him and Hebrew school.

The rabbi lived in Riverdale, about a fifteen-minute drive up the West Side Highway from Washington Heights.

Two things happened the day before our lesson, both of which conspired to send the rabbi's left arm up in flames.

A toll booth had been installed on the Riverdale side of the Henry Hudson Bridge. It cost a dime. On the very same day, the rabbi bought a new Buick, his first car with a seatbelt.

The rabbi stopped his Riviera at the new toll gate and, realizing he needed a dime, reached underneath the seatbelt into his left pants pocket, whereupon he found both some change and a pocketful of strike anywhere matches for his White Owls.

As the man of God struggled to get a dime out of his pants, his hand stuck underneath his confusing, never before worn seatbelt, Baulmal became very conscious of the trail of cars honking behind him. The panicked rabbi made the soon to be hospital-visitation-inducing mistake of rubbing some of the strike anywheres together inside the dark, claustrophobic pocket of his slacks.

I can imagine the fascinated look on the toll taker's face, as he watched the rabbi's left side start to smolder and finally flame up, the religious leader's hand trapped in his trousers. I must say, it was so hilariously gruesome it almost made me believe there was a God.

A couple of weeks before my bar mitzvah, the rabbi realized he was about to be embarrassed that I didn't know a word of my haftorah.

He called my parents.

Busted.

Dad took me from Kenny's house right to Beth Shalom. The class was over, and the basement room stunk of Baulmal's stale White Owls. As we peered through striations of smoke and stench, I heard Baulmal say,

"What are we going to do with you, young man?"

"You mean about me not being able to read Hebrew and my being bar mitzvahed in two weeks?"

"Precisely."

He was a pompous ass.

"I guess I shouldn't get bar mitzvahed?"

"Barry," said my father, "we've already invited people and paid a caterer. You'll be getting gifts, and besides, your mother expects you to be bar mitzvahed. That's not an option."

The evening of my bar mitzvah I would discover the real reason my father wanted me to go through with the charade.

"Well, in that case, why don't I bring in my 3M Wollensak reel to reel tape recorder, the rabbi can read my haftorah into it, and I'll memorize it."

Which is what I did.

Here's where the event went a little south. Beth Shalom, by this point, was almost finished with their new building. They would be celebrating the first Sabbath in their fancy air-conditioned temple on Saturday, April 9. However, they had already sold their old building to an Orthodox sect, which was moving in Saturday, the 2nd, and didn't want us there.

The solution, and I know this sounds too good to be true, was that I was bar mitzvahed across the street from my apartment building in Beth Shalom's "Temporary Quarters"—which was a Catholic church. The rabbi and cantor (who does the singing at various Jewish holiday ceremonies and plays the hideous sounding shofar) entered the church the night of April Fool's, my birthday, and placed large burlap bags over the endless displays of crosses and crucifixes that looked down on the congregation.

Mr. and Mrs. Nathan Sonnenfeld
request the honor of your presence
at the Bar Mitzvah
בר מצוה
of their son
Barry
on Saturday, the second of April
Nineteen hundred and sixty-six
at nine o'clock in the morning
Temple Beth Sholom
Temporary Quarters
Broadway at 174th Street
New York City

Various people are given the honor of being called up to the podium to read passages from the Torah at a bar mitzvah. Usually the family picks uncles or fathers, or special friends. They check with the lucky participants ahead of time. My parents went a different way.

"And now we would like Joe Rabinowitz to come up and read the next portion of the Torah."

"No," called out a surprised Joe, who lived in apartment 6C and was the father of Amy, who had been in class with me from kindergarten through, as it would turn out, high school.

"Joe Rabinowitz. Please come up to the front of this, uh…"

The rabbi hesitated to find the right word, as he glanced around the burlapped crucifixes.

"…room."

"No," said Joe.

"You can't say no!" bellowed the blustering Baulmal.

"No. Thank you," said Joe.

"That doesn't work either. You are required, when you are called, to come up and read this passage. It's an honor."

"Not for me it isn't."

My mother walked back to Joe. They had a whispered conversation, during which Kelly was informed that Joe didn't read Hebrew. The rabbi, seeing this was going nowhere, left the podium and walked up to Joe. After a heated discussion, and a promise that Joe could read the words in English, Joe caved but was—with good reason—pissed.

Joe Rabinowitz, CM the CM, and Sonny. Hampton Bays, New York.

After pretending to read/sing my portion of the Torah, which was totally by rote, I then gave my bar mitzvah speech to the assembled guests, which was, and this is April 1966, a plea to end the war in Vietnam. It was ghostwritten by my mother. I can't imagine anyone thought the words were mine.

Although the new and improved Temple Beth Shalom's main floor wasn't ready for my bar mitzvah ceremony, the basement was finished enough for my big, cheap party as long as we didn't mind the spackle taped walls and kraft paper covering the floor. The event was in the evening, hours after my Catholic church appearance. It was an eight block walk from my apartment to the new temple, but Mom's legs were "bothering her," so Sonny drove. Kelly insisted I sit on her lap.

When we arrived at the shul, I jumped off Mom's lap as quickly as possible, since really, if a bar mitzvah represents a Jewish boy becoming a man, riding to his manly party on his mother's lap was just wrong.

I opened the Tempest's door, forgot Mom hadn't gotten out yet, and slammed it as hard as I needed to, closing the door on her leg. She should have walked.

For the entire party, my mother sat with her leg up on a chair, bags of ice taped around her ankle and calf. She was as much in heaven playing the role of injured martyr as I was in hell, playing the role of bar mitzvah boy.

My suit was shiny blue with a hint of green, as if lit by a mercury vapor lamp. The jacket had two inside breast pockets, and as the evening went on, they started to bulge as more and more envelopes with E-bonds or twenty-five-dollar checks filled them. My pecs were starting to look Schwarzenegger-esque. When we arrived home, Sonny and I sat on my bed, counting the loot. Over thirteen hundred bucks. A nice stash for a camera and an enlarger.

I would never see that money again. Dad took it, telling me we'd open a bank account the following Saturday. Unfortunately, he "lost" the manila envelope he had put the money in for safekeeping. Coincidentally, we could shop at Lou's again, and we no longer owed several months' back rent.

The most depressing incident, after the appropriation of my bar mitzvah gelt, was Sonny's theft of my silver dollar collection, hidden in the foyer cabinet that also concealed Kelly's booze. Both parents feigned surprise and dismay at the disappearance of my coin collection.

The sheer stupidity of the theft was that Sonny used my silver dollars *as dollars*. Each of the coins—in pristine condition from the 1800s—were worth a minimum of twenty bucks a piece. Dad showed up at the Con Ed building in Union Square and forked over twenty-two silver dollar coins to pay the electric bill. We now had electricity. Stupidly expensive electricity.

CHAPTER 9

"My" Dog

Circa 1968, Kelly came home with a dog. She named it Whisky. According to my mother, she found it "running around" the bus terminal—a recent addition to the Washington Heights skyline—located at 178th, between Fort Washington Avenue and Broadway.

Whisky, an intact male, was probably 4 years old when Mom decided we needed that specific dog.

Sonny never took Whisky out. Neither did Kelly, who would come home from school with a "migraine" and calls to make. I neither asked for nor wanted a dog, yet now I was responsible for one. Whisky was untrained, manic, and of course, being adopted by my mother, epileptic.

Occasionally, Whisky would have an attack outside Kelly's bedroom. My door would be closed, so I wouldn't have heard the thump of his convulsing body hitting the strip oak.

My mother would look up from her sanctuary, see the vibrating dog outside her bedroom, and say to whatever UFT teacher she was martyring to,

"Oy. Hold on a minute. Barry's dog is having a seizure."

She'd go into the kitchen, dig deep into the dead floating cockroach swarmed sink, reach around the silverware that had migrated to the bottom, grab a spoon, paper towel off the Raid, and schlep back to the area in front of her bedroom door where Whisky was convulsing in a pool of urine. As she bent down to put the spoon in the dog's mouth so he wouldn't swallow his tongue—or at least that was her thinking—Kelly would yell,

"Barry! Your dog needs you!"

She didn't have to yell. Even through my closed door, the rapid-fire chattering of dog teeth against metal spoon announced the poor animal's predicament.

As I reached the end of the hallway, there was Whisky convulsing, a Chuck Jones animated spoon in his mouth, the frequency of its movement creating a blur. I would bend down to this sad dog that we all hated, gently rubbing his dry, urine free flank. I placed my other hand around his snout, tightly closing his mouth, which stopped the horrific comedy death rattle.

As I looked to my right, I would see Kelly, sprawled out on her bed, a wet towel once again covering her eyes.

"I feel betrayed," she wept into the phone.

Whisky, appropriately, in Shit Hampton.

Once the quivering dog calmed down, I would get some paper towels from the kitchen, dry the floor and the poor dog's legs, and take him for a quick walk down 174th Street.

One late Saturday afternoon my father took Whisky for a walk, which was unheard of. He came home an hour later without the dog.

Eleanor Roosevelt

My elementary school did not prepare me for the two years of muggings I was about to experience at Eleanor Roosevelt Junior High. Fitting I should be attending a school named after my mother's idol. While in elementary school, I was Mrs. Sonnenfeld's Son—a designation that came with a "Do Not Mug" force field. At junior high, I was just another tiny underweight kid who carried mugging money.

Kelly did everything in her power to overly protect me. Fearing I'd be humiliated by attending any class related to physical ed, she arranged for my pediatrician, Dr. Rogatz, to send a harrowing letter to the principal, Mrs. Lorraine Addelston.

The doctor explained that I was his patient and was small and painfully underweight even for my diminutive height. He feared that if I were to attend the daily gym class, the exercise might lead to weight loss, which I could not well afford. Instead, he suggested, I be assigned an additional lunch period.

How my mother got Rogatz to write this letter is beyond me, but I'm sure there were some tears involved. Perhaps she stole his prescription pad and wrote it herself.

I had two lunch periods, and attended neither of them. Instead, due to my mother's UFT connections, I was assigned to the office of

Selma Lawrence, the vice principal. For two periods a day, I ran the AB Dick machine—the precursor to a copier.

This was a dream assignment: First, I didn't have to spend any time in the cafeteria, which smelled like vomit, bleach, and sweat; served inedible food; and was patrolled by Louis Rivera, who demanded mugging money. Second, Selma Lawrence's office was where every test got printed. This meant I usually viewed my own tests several days before I was given them, allowing me ample time to learn the answers.

In addition, the AB Dick machine used a carbon paper–like stencil, which was mounted on a roller. The roller then sent moistened paper across the stencil, creating an image. The liquid used to wet the paper was quick drying alcohol. By the time I spent a couple of "lunch periods" in Mrs. Lawrence's back office, I was as high as I would ever be until I met Sweetie, who taught me how to drink.

These faux lunch periods were perfection compared to the previous seven years of elementary school, where instead of eating with schoolmates, my mother insisted I spend that hour with her in the teacher's cafeteria, where Kelly would enlist the educators in a scenery workshop for the various school plays.

Kelly standing in the foreground, supervising her teacher scenic helpers. That's me in the deep background.

Eleanor Roosevelt Junior High School was opened the same year I matriculated. The building had cottage cheese ceilings and squares of blue and orange ceramic tile on the walls. Its aesthetic was very New York World's Fair.

The school was located ten blocks from my house, which was

enough distance to allow me to buy a monthly bus pass for a dollar. By the second day of each month, Louis Rivera had mugged me for it.

One spring afternoon, the kind of day you tie your denim jacket around your waist on the way home, I was in Ms. Lucatorto's geography class when we heard the school's intercom system come on. Whatever Mrs. Addelston was going to say was proceeded by coughing, throat clearing, thumps of fingers tapping the microphone, and an "Is this thing on?"

I yelled out to the class, "The room is bugged!"

"Barry Sonnenfeld. Come to my office immediately."

While everyone in Ms. Lucatorto's class was dumbfounded that I somehow knew our principal was spying on me specifically, I ran out of the room and burst into tears. "Barry Sonnenfeld. Come to my office" could only mean one thing: my father was dead. Earlier that week Sonny had made a surprise four o'clock appearance in our apartment, hours earlier than usual. Kelly, lying on their bed, a damp towel across her eyes, lifted a corner.

"Sonny? Are you sick?"

Surely Dad had a "dinner" with "a client" scheduled for that evening.

"Get off the bed, Kelly" was his ashen response.

Dad was experiencing his first kidney stone. He needed the entire bed to writhe around on. By the next morning, he had passed it and gone to work. But maybe it wasn't a stone. Maybe something was very wrong with him, and now, now he's dead.

By the time I got to the office, I was sobbing. The secretary led me into Addelston's inner sanctuary. Lorraine Addelston was a large masculine woman with a very manly haircut. It was died jet black, looking vaguely Asian. She wore a suit. She could have been married to my mother.

"Barry," she said, rising out of her seat to hug a weeping me. "What's wrong?"

"My father is dead."

"He's dead?"

"Isn't he?"

"How should I know?"

"But. You made that announcement. Why would you call me to your office unless he's dead?"

"Honey, calm down," she said, as she moved away from me, pulling tissues out of the Kleenex box on her desk—one for my tear drenched face, the other to wipe off some of the Barry snot and saline flowing down her breast.

"No one is dead. At least not that I know of. I need to get these papers over to Mr. Lichtenstein right away. Since you live across from 173, and your mother teaches there, I'm sending you home early with these papers. Give them to Mr. Lichtenstein as soon as you can."

"Um, Louis Rivera stole my bus pass, so it'll take a little longer."

"Louis Rivera stole your bus pass? That little shit."

Mrs. Addelston started to yell toward the outer office when I stopped her.

"Please don't call Louis down here. It will only make it worse."

"We'll see about that."

"Please don't," I said. "Don't make me cry again."

"Okay, Barry. Just go deliver those papers. Quickly now."

I don't know if Mrs. Addelston tried to call Louis Rivera into her office or not, but I do know that she didn't speak to him that day. I know because as I was racing with the important papers from JHS 143 to PS 173M, I came across Louis on the southwest corner of 178th and Broadway in front of the Dime Savings Bank. I guess Louis was taking a personal day.

"Give me your money."

"Okay, but then you can't punch me. Deal?"

"No deals. Just give me your money."

"Listen. Please. I'm on a mission for Mrs. Addelston," I said, hoping that would get his attention making him think twice about the mugging. "I don't have time..."

"Faggot. Give me your money."

I took out my mugging money—a dollar bill and four quarters—and handed the loot over to Louis. By this time, various old people that lived around the Dime Savings Bank stopped to watch the assault.

With his left hand, Louis took my money. With his right, he punched me as hard as he could, which was hard, directly into my chest. I collapsed on the concrete sidewalk and clutched my chest with both hands, dropping the intraschool papers.

Old people gasped and made "tsk tsk" sounds as they watched Louis walk away.

"Are you people nuts? No one says anything? No one tries to stop him from hitting me?" I screamed and sobbed at them. I picked up the important papers, scattered across the savings bank entrance, and cried my way to PS 173M.

The junior high school years were particularly lonely. At the age of 14, I had discovered photography, especially the street journalism of photographers like Lee Friedlander, Garry Winogrand, Robert Frank, and my favorite, Elliott Erwitt. Since my mother was hoping I'd become an artist, she suggested I take photography lessons from Herb Dreiwitz, who lived with his mother, Gertrude, in our apartment building. He was a 35-year-old gay Scientologist—an early adopter. Luckily, it took several years for his crush on me to manifest itself, and by then I was able to ward off his attempted kisses and respond to his love letters with kind rejection. I eventually told him *Dianetics* was a terribly written book.

Herb and I subwayed to the photography district on West 32nd Street, catty-corner to Madison Square Garden, and with the money I kept hidden from my parents purchased a used Leica M2 with a 35mm Summicron-M F2 lens from Charlie Pelish at Photoshop.

With Tri-X, Kodak's fast black and white film, I could place the lens' f-stop at an f/16 aperture, set it to 1/125th of a second, put the hyperfocal distance at four feet, and have everything from two feet to infinity in focus. This allowed me to bring the camera up to my face and take a photo without any delay required by focusing.

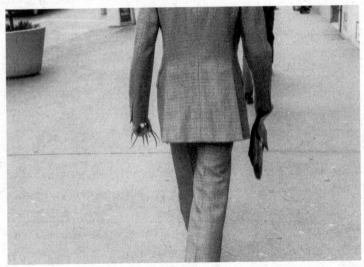

Perhaps my first alien encounter? Man with a plant hand, Fifth Avenue. Leica M2 35mm Summicron-M lens. Tri-X film. 125th of a second at f/16. Hyperfocal focus.

I wanted to develop the film and make my own prints, so I needed a darkroom. This meant tossing my bed and collection of empty Coke cans and building a four-by-seven-foot lightproof room in their place. I didn't have running water, but the bathroom was close and usually available, since Dad rarely did his toilet reading of *The New Yorker* until late at night or on weekends.

My mattress went in the narrow space between the top of the darkroom and the room's ceiling. I used an aluminum ladder to get into bed. Lying down, my head was only about eight inches from the ceiling, but luckily, I have a pinhead.

My empty Coke can collection, which spanned two different graphics eras (note bottom row). The roof of the darkroom was just under the molding, which left room for the mattress and me.

Spending years sleeping as if in a submarine has had a big effect on me: I love claustrophobic spaces. I sleep under desks on sets while waiting for the crew to finish lighting. On *A Series of Unfortunate Events* I replaced my office couch with a custom-built combination coffin/sofa that was lined in SONEX soundproofing material so I could meditate daily. Putting aside that the reason for getting an MRI is never a pleasant one, I love the experience. Talk about guided meditation. If I had the money, I'd own an MRI machine.

Couch/coffin/meditation chamber, door open. A Series of Unfortunate Events.

Several years after building my darkroom, my mother's aunt Esther gave me her used La-Z-Boy. I started to sleep in the recliner.

My developer of choice was Rodinal, which was a highly concentrated chemical distributed by Agfa. Using a pipette—a narrow glass straw—I would suck up eighteen milliliters of dark amber fluid from the brown bottle and mix it with sixteen ounces of water. Rodinal produced a very sharp, contrasty look. A year later, I went back to Photoshop and purchased a Leica F3.4 Super-Angulon 21mm lens with an auxiliary viewfinder. It became the way I saw things: wide angled and centered. Throughout my career as a cinematographer and director, I have always framed the images I photograph with very wide angle lenses and dead center framing.

Leica M2. 21mm Super-Angulon lens. Nova Scotia. End of world. 1972.

Junior high was depressing for yet another reason:
Charles Heckheimer.

My mother, still concerned about the Vietnam War, didn't trust I was way too skinny to be drafted and doubled down on the french horn as my savior.

In addition to playing in Eleanor Roosevelt's band and orchestra, All-Borough Band and Orchestra, and the All-City Band and Orchestra—both of which met Saturdays and Sundays in the West 60s—there was an additional music torture: twice a week after school I got on the 104 bus, transporting myself and my Sansone double french horn for lessons at Charles Heckheimer's apartment on Riverside Drive and 155th Street.

Heckheimer looked like a french horn player. He smoked a pipe and had a goatee. He was officious, self-involved, and rightfully impatient, given my lack of practicing. Everything about him screamed, "If I wasn't a french horn player, with these looks, I'd be a psychiatrist."

The walk from Broadway to Riverside Drive was three endlessly long, insanely steep city blocks. In the winter, the wind coming off the Hudson River was brutal. We spent two years working on one piece of music—Mozart's Third Horn Concerto—in preparation for my Music & Art High School audition.

Once again, my mother intervened. The local Washington Heights high school, George Washington, whose alumni includes Henry Kissinger, Harry Belafonte, Rod Carew, Alan Greenspan, and Manny Ramirez, was a nightmare. Louis Rivera was the Dalai Lama compared to the evilness patrolling the hallways at GW.

One of the amazing things about New York is its specialized public high schools. At the time, Bronx Science, Brooklyn Tech, Stuyvesant High School, Performing Arts, and Music & Art were as good as any private school in America. Kelly knew my attending George Washington would be like shipping me out to a deadlier Vietnam. So she set her sights on Music & Art.

M&A required an audition if you were applying as a musician. Of course, Mom asked her principal if he could intervene on my behalf. Mr. Richter, the principal of M&A, was good friends with Lichtenstein. It was arranged that my audition would be with Richter.

The day of the audition I sat in a tiny music room, horn on my lap. Richter was a small man with an important white mustache that matched his important white hair. If you didn't know the guy and had to guess his name, you'd say, "Richter?"

He walked into the music room and announced he was busy for the next half hour but would return. I spent the time warming up, running scales and rehearsing the concerto.

The french horn is a ridiculously hard instrument to master. The mouthpiece is very small in circumference and requires a very trained, muscle-memoried embouchure. By having this half hour to warm up, my lips were ready to go. I had never played Mozart's Third Horn Concerto one fifth as good in my life. I nailed it.

I had two music performance classes, a music theory class, and only one lunch period, since M&A had no gym. I also had five more periods of science, math, Spanish, English, and history. The faculty were hip and smart and treated the students as adults. The kids were hip and smart and treated the faculty as friends.

There was a lot of cross-pollination between the art and music students. One of my best friends, attending as an art major, was Liz Diller, who has since become a renowned architect. It's also where I met Judy Dakin, who, as my date, attended two of the greatest sports events in New York history—the Miracle Mets and the Knicks-Lakers playoff series.

M&A, where I spent three heavenly years, was a tropical island of intellectual and political energy surrounded by two dead seas of the worst education of my life. At the left end of the island was Eleanor Roosevelt. On the right—although I didn't know yet how horrible it would be—NYU.

The Button

Sonny

In spite of stealing my money and repeatedly exposing me to CM the CM, until I was 14, my father was my best friend. That changed on a breezy Saturday in early May. On the morning in question a couple of things went horribly wrong, both within a five-minute period.

Dad and I spent many Saturdays together while Mom lay in bed, the moist towel across her eyes.

My father and I had decided to head out to Yankee Stadium. The cool weather was perfect for a Yankees game, sitting in the upper deck of the old stadium. Dad offered to let me wear his hip looking bomber jacket from World War II. I'd never worn it before. It had two vertical zippers running down the front as well as hand pockets and a belt. Oh, and its former owner was, as Dad would say, "a Jap."

Sonny was an infantryman in the Pacific during World War II, working in the communications division. For some reason he was assigned to a unit of the Montana National Guard. He claimed it was because he was registered for the draft in New York but was in California when he was called up, so they compromised on Montana. I don't think that's how it worked. Dad was awarded a Silver Star, which is second only to the Congressional Medal of Honor. Before his death, he admitted that his multiple years in active combat were the best years of his life.

Dad hated the Japanese more than the Germans and was consequently one of the few Jews of his generation who would rather own a German car than Japanese. We never had German automobile money, so we're talking theoretically. His hatred toward the Japanese wasn't just because he spent several years in New Guinea fighting them. He loathed the "Japs" because they ate Lieutenant Fisk.

I never inquired how he ended up with a bomber jacket from a Japanese pilot, and he wouldn't have told me if I had. I once asked if he'd ever killed anyone in the war. Sagely, he said, "Answering that question is a no-win situation. Either you'll be disappointed I didn't or outraged I did."

The bomber jacket was tight on Dad and loose on me, but we were running late and the jacket was the easiest thing to grab. As I put it on, still in our apartment's foyer, I reached into the front zipper pocket. We both looked down at my hand in amazement, as it was holding a strip of condoms. Crestfallen, I looked up at my father.

"Your mom and I are planning a festive weekend."

Uh huh.

My parents and sex were separated by, I suspect, fifteen years, although I have always clung desperately to the hope that I was adopted. Finding those condoms broke my heart. It was the first time my father hadn't been my hero. I didn't exactly blame him. I wouldn't wish sex with my mother on Hitler, but like most children, I didn't want my father to be less than perfect, much less a liar and cheat.

As we waited for the elevator to arrive, Sonny made the huge mistake of trying to stay on topic, which was throwing good money after bad, not that he had much.

"Barry. Do you know how to give a woman pleasure?"

"Yes, Dad. I do."

"Do you know about the button?"

"Yes, Dad. I know about the button," I said, as I kept punching the elevator button.

"Well, inside a woman's vagina is a button, and if you rub, or press it, you can give a woman pleasure."

"Dad. I know about the button. Let's change topics."

"One other thing: Do you know when it's safe to have sex with a woman? I mean, so you can't get a woman pregnant?"

"Well, in your case, when you're wearing a condom."

"Right…yes…but if you don't want to wear a condom? Or don't have one with you?"

"That doesn't seem to be an issue with you, Dad."

"Do you know when? I mean, without a condom?"

"Yes, Dad. I know when to have sex with a woman so she won't become pregnant. Assuming I'm not wearing a condom. Please don't tell me."

And then he said it:

"The only time a woman can become pregnant is during her period."

I suddenly realized why I was an only child.

"No, Dad, it's kinda the opposite. See, when a woman is having her period, she's actually getting rid of that egg, and in fact, during a woman's period is practically the only time she *can't* get pregnant. Here's the elevator."

"Good to know," my father said.

We rode the elevator in silence.

My best friend. Miami Beach.

CHAPTER 12

The Flip Side

The day was not over.

After we watched Mickey Mantle hit two home runs, we returned to the Heights, only to sniff out Mom's science experiment of frying hard boiled eggs. After Sonny arranged for a kitchen ceiling paint job and I cleaned up the egg bits that weren't stuck to the kitchen's ceiling, Dad and I headed to the Chinese place for spare rib dinners with loads of duck sauce. Mom stayed home with a migraine, but as we left shouted, "Bring me back something."

My mother had several traits in common with Scott Rudin, the film and theater producer who hired me to direct my first movie, *The Addams Family*. Both had a very fluid relationship with the truth, and both were secret eaters. Neither Rudin nor my mother was what you'd call thin, yet both were rarely seen eating.

After dinner Dad and I decided we'd head over to Sloan's supermarket to take advantage of their excellent Sara Lee frozen cake section, which included the very rare German chocolate cake.

It was dark by the time we got to Sloan's, located on the dividing line of stickball versus softball neighborhoods. We heard a bang coming from the other side of Broadway that turned out to be a woman being violently thrown into the security grate of a closed candy store. A man in his 30s was yelling at her, stopping only to catch his breath and throw a punch.

"Wait here," Dad said.

Sonny ran across the six lanes of Broadway, screaming as he ran. He wanted this guy to be afraid of him before he got there.

"Aaaaahhhhhhhh!!!" he bansheed, as if charging up a New Guinea hill to bayonet the Jap who ate Fisk.

The perp turned and in a deep-pitched, threatening voice said, "This is none of your business."

The guy hoped to intimidate Dad, since he didn't quite know what this maniac was up to.

Dad turned toward me and yelled, "Barry. Go to that pay phone and call the police. Right now!"

I didn't have any change on me, but I walked over to the phone and pantomimed the call.

"Hey, man. We're fine. We're just having a little squabble."

"I'll keep him here. Why don't you leave?" Dad said to the woman.

"Thank you," she whispered as she rapidly backwalked away. Dad asked the man if he was okay.

"I'm cool, man. I'm sorry. Thanks for coming over. Thanks for stopping me."

Dad said that was fine, and once the light turned green crossed the street back to my side of Broadway.

We both turned as we heard the sobbing woman run back into the arms of her recently homicidal boyfriend. We stared in disbelief as he put his arms around her, giving his gal a long hug before violently tossing her, once again, into the security grate.

Dad sighed as a police car—someone with loose change had obviously made the call—pulled up in front of the conflicted lovers.

We walked into the supermarket.

Late that night, while Sonny and I were sleeping, Kelly secretly ate the entire Sara Lee German chocolate cake.

The next morning, according to Mom, Dad and I had left it at Sloan's.

CHAPTER 13

The Promise of Suicide

For three months in 1969, Madison Square Garden played an important role in my life. Obviously, there was the unfortunate "Barry Sonnenfeld. Call your mother." incident. The second event was as joyful as the Hendrix episode was devastating. It was mid-April 1970. I had turned 17 on April 1. The New York Knicks, having beaten the Baltimore Bullets in the Eastern Division Finals, earned the right to play the Los Angeles Lakers for the NBA Championship.

Several friends from Music & Art, including Judy Dakin, were planning to sleep out at Madison Square Garden near the head of the line to buy playoff tickets for the Finals, going on sale the next morning.

I knocked on my mother's bedroom door.

I heard her tell someone to wait a second.

"Come in," she sadly called out, pulling the moist towel off her forehead.

I peered into her dark, gloomy room.

"Mom. I'm leaving in an hour for the Garden. I'm spending the night with some of the guys on line at 34th Street. We're going to get good seats for the Knicks-Lakers series."

"Are you out of your mind?"

"No, Mom. I'll be with three friends. And probably about ten thousand other people. It's the only way to get good tickets."

"Well, you're not going, of course."

Mom then spoke into the phone's handset, cradled under her chin:

"I'm sorry, Bernice. My son has suddenly become an idiot."

I slammed her door and went back to my bedroom. I was a senior in high school. I had just turned 17 years old. And I had never, ever, in my life, spent a night sleeping anywhere without my parents. I thought about the consequences of disobeying and realized there were none. I put some warm clothes into a backpack and knocked on Kelly's door.

"Oy. Hold on, Bernice. My idiot son is knocking again."

"Hey, Mom. I'm leaving. I'm going down to the Garden."

"Barry. If you leave this house, your father and I will severely punish you."

"Go ahead."

"I am going to call your father."

"He can't stop me either, Mom. I'm seventeen and have never slept away from home and..."

"And you want to start now? This is the way you start?"

She was now crying.

"This is how you suddenly become an adult? By sleeping on the street with needles and drug addicts? This is how you start? You are stark raving nuts."

"Mom. The Knicks mean a lot to me. I need to do this. I'm leaving."

"Barry. Wait." There was a pause so she could wipe away her tears.

"Call me every hour. Without fail. Okay?"

"Okay, Mom."

I managed to spend the night outside the Garden without getting mugged or used hypodermic needle stabbed. The series between the Knicks and Lakers was historic. Many say it was the greatest NBA Finals in history. I was at Game 5 when Willis Reed, the Knicks' center, got injured, and somehow New York's small forwards, Bill Bradley and Dave DeBusschere, overpowered Wilt Chamberlain, who, in 1962, had famously scored a hundred points in one game against the Knicks.

I was also at the Garden for Game 7. No one knew if a still injured Reed would play. A moment before tip-off, Willis came out of the tunnel and hit a few short warm-up jump shots. The Lakers stopped practicing and stared at Reed. He lined up against the much taller, not injured Wilt the Stilt and scored the first four points of the game. They were the only points he would score that night. But LA was mentally defeated, and the Knicks went on to win the game and the championship.

Having been present for the Miracle Mets' World Series win six months earlier, I was now two for two in attended New York championship games.

The night of our MSG campout, disobeying my mother for the first time, Kelly realized she was going to have to up her game. Threats of punishment were now going to fall short. Soon after the Knicks' victory, with college talk in the air, she informed me that if I attended "sleepaway school"—others call it college—she would kill herself.

"And don't tell Dad."

I had dealt with this threat once before, and it was devastating.

I was 5 years old and fast asleep when my father gently shook me awake.

"Scoot over."

I untubed my body out of the self-made sleeping-off-the-side-of-the-bed hammock, and onto the mattress.

I rubbed my eyes.

"Barry. Your mother is very sad right now. She says she doesn't want to live any more. She loves you very much, and you should talk to her. Convince her that she shouldn't kill herself."

What?!

I walked into the living room. I was wearing red pajamas printed with firemen. I brought my coin jar with me. Mom, sitting on the couch that would eventually be co-opted by CM the CM, was surrounded by used damp tissues. Her eyes were red, her bloated face streaked with tears.

"Mom?"

"Barry. I want to die."

"Please don't say that, Mom."

"Barry. I'm not happy. I don't want to live. Your father and you should let me die. I'm just not happy. I want to kill myself."

I mean, really. Who the fuck does this? To a 5-year-old? I now suspect, sixty years later, that earlier in the evening, either my father had announced he was leaving her, and she went right to eleven, or that Kelly had just had it with my father's affairs. I'll never know for sure what brought on my mother's night of hell, but there was little Barry, right in the middle of it.

"Just let me die, Barry. I need to go. I don't want to live anymore."

"Mommy. Please don't do that. Please." I held out my coin jar. "You can have all this money. It's yours. Just don't do that."

I made her laugh.

Sonny, standing at the entry to the living room, stepped in, put his hands on my shoulders, and said, "Okay, Barry. Go back to bed. I'll be there in a few minutes to tuck you in."

Mom grabbed me and pulled me to her soaking wet face. As always, her breath smelled like August on the A train.

"I love you. You know that. I love you so much. Everything is okay."

I started to leave.

"Hey, take your money. I'm fine, Ba."

The next morning my mother and father treated the previous evening as if it never happened. But for me, I had been pulled into a vicious triangle that my parents desperately tried to keep intact for the rest of their lives.

Oedipus, Schmoedipus. As long as you love your mother.

CHAPTER 14

Yet More Promised Suicides

After the Knicks won their championship, in order to save my mother's life I agreed to live at home, not attend sleepaway school, and not tell my father why I had made this decision. I couldn't handle another night of suicide prevention.

I continued to sleep in either my aunt Esther's La-Z-Boy or the space between the top of my darkroom and the ceiling while attending NYU's University Heights Campus in the Bronx.

During the three years I was there I only took classes that met Monday, Tuesday, and Thursday, between the hours of 9:00 a.m. and 2:00 p.m. This meant that over three years, I took ninety credits exclusively in political science, since that's when those classes met.

I had so much free time I was able to put in seventeen hours a week as a clerk at the New York Public Library for the Performing Arts at Lincoln Center.

Barry Taylor and Judy Dakin worked at the library as well. Judy and I would occasionally make out in the freight elevator. On other occasions I believe she made out with the other Barry. I guess she had a thing for Barrys.

I despised NYU. I hated living at home. All I did was sleep and test my mortality by driving too fast in my used Oldsmobile Cutlass. Each school day I drove from Washington Heights, across the

East River viaduct to the Cross Bronx Expressway, merging onto the Major Deegan and exiting in the North Bronx. I'd find a parking spot on campus for my five-hour visitation and managed to not make a single friend in three years.

NYU University Heights was like college day camp. There were no dorms. On days I didn't work at the library, I was home by 2:30, napped until six, ate two Swanson TV dinners, and if there wasn't a Knicks game on television, fell asleep by 7:30. I slept as much as most hound dogs—although their lives were probably more fulfilling.

In the early spring of my sophomore year, I realized I no longer cared if my mother committed suicide. I drove up to Bard College on a day off from both NYU and my job.

The Oldsmobile Cutlass had a massive motor and a four-barrel carburetor. My windows were down, and I was at that age where I knew it was impossible to die. I passed cars on two-lane roads doing 90. I had brought my french horn and auditioned. I talked to smart, interesting professors.

Did I want to be a french horn player? They were looking for one.

Not really.

I wanted to be Jack Kerouac. To drive cross country and take photos and write stories about the people I met. The road. The landscape. Bard's admissions department told me they'd send out a letter of acceptance or rejection that same day. I left feeling invigorated.

Two weeks went by, and I didn't hear from them.

I was at the library when I called Bard's admissions department to ask what was up. I had an urgent, energetic feeling about the phone call.

"Mr. Sonnenfeld. When are we going to hear from you?"

"Well, I guess when I hear from you."

"You're accepted. I sent out a letter the same day you visited. We'd love to have you."

"Hi, Mom. It's me."

"Oy. I thought you might be Elena calling to apologize. Do you know I think she's having an affair with the principal?"

Kelly would have been much happier as a lesbian.

"Hey, Mom. Without telling you, a couple of weeks ago I . . ."

"If you think I found your acceptance letter to Bard College and ripped it up, I have no idea what you're talking about."

"Wow. Isn't it strange that you could be so specific about a letter you didn't see from a place you didn't know was sending it?"

"You're as bad as your father, and I'm not having this discussion."

"Mom. Without telling you I drove up to Bard College and had an interview. I called today since I didn't receive a letter that you didn't get to first and rip up. They've accepted me."

"So?"

"So, I'm going to transfer to Bard."

"And I will commit suicide, Barry. Between you and your dumb father, I have nothing to live for, do you know that?"

"And you would rather be dead than have me go to college away from home?"

"Absolutely."

"You would rather I be miserable for the next two and a half years?"

"Oh, stop it. You're hardly miserable. And, yes. I would rather be dead."

That night I made a deal with the devil. I agreed to continue at NYU, living in my recliner, if my mother would allow me to spend the summer away from home.

My buddy David Lindauer and I took out an ad in the back of the *New York Review of Books*, representing ourselves as "Geodesic Dome Experimenters." If someone would let us build a dome on their property, we would leave it up at the end of the summer for the landowner to keep. We received a response from an English professor at Brooklyn College, saying he owned a couple of hundred acres in western Massachusetts and would happily make that trade.

Now all David and I had to do was learn how to build a geodesic dome.

With instructions from the Whole Earth catalogue, a roll of 6 mil Visqueen, and eight hundred feet of three quarter inch EMT aluminum conduit, David and I managed to indeed build an eighteen foot diameter dome. It leaked horribly, and the mosquitoes were so bad that we rarely took off our mosquito-netting-masks.

David and I used the facilities at a nearby Howard Johnson's, where we also enjoyed their fried clam strips on a buttered bun. Some local hoodlums who also frequented Howard Johnson's started to threaten us so we were always cautious driving back to the dome, making sure we weren't followed.

One night, having sated ourselves with clam rolls and Howard Johnson's excellent fudge cake, our worst fear came true—our car was being followed. I stepped on the gas and drove the curvy two lane road as fast as I could, looking for our dirt road. I was doing 80 on a 25 mph road and put enough distance between us and the car following that I was able to crest a hill, screech onto our dirt road, and shut off our headlights before the thugs could see where we went.

Suddenly David shouted, "Take your foot off the brake!" It was too late. The Cutlass' brake lights had been illuminated, and the car that had been following pulled up behind us. Then it turned on its red, blue, and white strobe lights. I had never been pulled over by a cop before, let alone outraced one, so I didn't know the rules. I opened the driver's door, got out, and shouted, "Boy, are we glad to see you."

The cop pulled his gun and told me to put up my hands. After a long chat with David and me describing our assailants and explaining why we were living in the woods in a geodesic dome, the cops told us they'd talk to the local hoodlums. They were heading back to their squad car when the driving cop turned back to me and said,

"Does your mother know where you are?"

Blandford, Massachusetts. I'm on the left.

Near the end of my junior year at NYU it was announced that the school was selling the campus to Bronx Community College. All University Heights students had to transfer to the downtown campus.

I refused.

I told them that wasn't the deal we had agreed to. They made an offer: Attend any college I wanted, transfer the credits back to NYU, and still graduate in four years, with an NYU degree. It would be like a year abroad, but different.

The one political science professor I liked suggested I apply to Bryn Mawr. They had a great political science department. I figured, why not give Mom another chance at suicide. I didn't know it was an all-female school. I learned that at my in-person interview.

Arriving in the small town hours early, I decided denim jeans were the wrong attire and found a small clothing shop in the village. Deep in a dark basement corner were the few 27 waist 34 inseam pants. The pair of wide wale corduroys I chose seemed more intellectual than jeans. It wasn't until I wore them out into the morning sun I realized I had bought bright purple pants.

The dean accepted me during the interview. When I asked how I could attend an all-girls' school, she explained that since NYU, not Bryn Mawr, would issue my degree, they didn't care I was a male.

Being the only man at Bryn Mawr would be too weird. I had also applied to Hampshire College, in Amherst, Massachusetts, after becoming friends with Nick Ney, a Hampshire student, a couple of years earlier. I'd have an acquaintance right off the bat.

This was going to be a great year—"sleepaway school" and my mother kills herself.

Two birds. One stone.

Mom reneged.

Even without her self-inflicted death, at least I was going to spend my senior year not living with Sonny and Kelly. Between Nick Ney and my french horn, I was bound to make friends and meet women.

I received an aerogram from Nick. He was in Mexico, having fallen in love with a witch and former girlfriend of Carlos Castaneda. He wasn't returning to Hampshire.

At least I had my french horn.

CHAPTER 15

On the Road: Barry Does Kerouac

A year and a college degree later, I found myself back on Aunt Ester's La-Z-Boy. Other than knowing I didn't want to be a french horn player or a political scientist, I was a college graduate who didn't have a clue about the future.

I bent my legs, tightened my stomach, forced the chair upright, and walked across the room to the phone. I dialed the same phone number as I had when I graduated high school. I called Elliott Erwitt, whose photographs and humor I loved and who was listed in the Manhattan telephone book. I asked if he needed an assistant. He repeated the same words he had used four years earlier: "My stable is full."

I had no idea that fifteen years later I would marry his wife, but not during this chapter.

Taking my father's dubious advice to decide what would make me happy and then figure how to make a living doing it, I realized I loved, and would therefore make a living, as a still photographer and writer. I would drive cross country in my 1972 green Saab 96 and have adventures. I'd meet women who wore peasant blouses, no bras, and whose crystal blue eyes were magnified by their granny glasses. I would take photographs in the street style of Erwitt, Lee Friedlander, Garry Winogrand, and Robert Frank.

I'd take it slow and drive the back roads. My favorite book was Jack Kerouac's *On the Road*. I was going to be Dean Moriarty, letting my whim and the winds guide me. I would have no plans, no route, no schedule. My stories would be sold to *The New Yorker*. I would have exciting adventures and make friends with all type of folk and probably not get to California for months.

Of course, that is so, so not me. Four days after leaving the Heights, I was in San Francisco, speaking to no one, with or without a bra. The Saab briefly broke down in Cheyenne, Wyoming. As I lifted the hood, which hinged backward—the pivot point being at the headlights, not the windshield—some old cowboy yelled, "That's what you get for buying a Russian car."

Self-portrait. On the road. Sandals and socks.

The day I arrived in San Francisco I treated myself to a special Chinese lunch. I walked through Chinatown looking for authenticity. There it was. A second-floor walkup with only Chinese people enjoying what surely was the most Chinese of Chinese food. When I asked for duck sauce for my spare ribs, the waiter slammed a bowl of ketchup onto the Formica table and walked away, mumbling something indecipherable, thank God, under his breath.

That evening I parked on the sand at Pismo Beach. There were tents and cars everywhere. Fire pits were ablaze and music was blasting. There even seemed to be women not wearing bras. And sporting granny glasses. Watch out, ladies. I set my tent next to the Saab and was about to take out my 4x5 view camera and tripod—the closest thing I had to a puppy or a french horn as an attention getter—when a motorcycle roared past me and headed down the beach.

Saab. Pismo Beach.

What was I thinking? I couldn't sleep out in the open. Someone could run me over during the night. What if there were more guys on motorcycles? What if they saw my expensive looking camera? They'd grab my car keys and steal my gear and car. And slit my throat. I put everything back in the trunk, got in the car, angled back the driver's seat, crossed my arms, and tried to sleep. This wasn't working, since I was afraid to close my eyes. I drove to the nearest YMCA, where, due to the bathroom being down the hall, I was no less fearful.

Eight days after leaving on my adventure, I was back at my parents' New York City apartment. When I couldn't face any more time sleeping fourteen hours a night in the La-Z-Boy or on top of the darkroom, I headed back to Hampshire, spending the next six months living with my off and on again girlfriend. Although the previous year three of the straight women I had sex with at Hampshire had become lesbians, Julia wasn't one of them. Her situation was different: she had lost her sense of smell and was afraid she wouldn't know if she had body odor. Julia took five showers a day.

A half year of doing nothing was stupid, expensive, and deeply depressing. I was 22 and needed a job. I headed back to New York and rented the upstairs of a divorcée's house in Teaneck, New Jersey. A bedroom, bathroom, and no kitchen privileges. The dishes would pile up in the bathtub until I needed to bathe. There was no shower. Unlike Julia, I had a sense of smell and knew that every third day it was time.

I got a job as a lab technician at Frenchy's Color Lab in Manhattan. The only good thing about the job was that Frenchy's was across the street from Grand Central Station, where deep in its bowels lived the Oyster Bar. These were the years when I had an enviable metabolism and could on a daily basis sit at the lunch counter and order the fried clam dinner, followed by the oyster pan roast, which was a bowl of oysters "roasted" in heavy cream and butter. With the exception of lunch, my life was dreary and empty.

Frenchy's Color Lab was owned by a handsome French guy named Frenchy. He and his prick son Marcelle ran the place.

I was stuck in a small darkroom printing Cibachrome prints. The chemicals were so toxic that when mixing up a new batch, I was required to notify the staff so they could all leave the premises for two hours. I had no mask.

My coworker Terry was the expert chemist and printmaker who made the dye transfer prints used for all the Marlboro Man print ads. We hit it off and both knew that Frenchy was taking advantage of us. He would ski the Alps for three months in the winter and often take five-day weekends during the rest of the year. Terry asked if I wanted to go into business with him and open our own color lab. He'd put up the financing.

This would be the first of two offers to go into business that came my way. I can't imagine where I would be at this very moment if I had moved forward with either of those opportunities. I suspect where I would not be is in front of a Lenovo ThinkPad typing this memoir at my desk in Telluride, staring at the Colorado blue sky, a brutally shaken Belvedere in a martini glass patiently waiting for my arrival on our upstairs deck.

Brutally shaken Belvedere vodka in a martini glass. Jalapeno stuffed olive. Telluride, Colorado.

CHAPTER 16

NYU Graduate Film School

I spent the weekend debating about opening a color lab. Dad was out of town "on business." For some reason I agreed to have brisket with Mom. Kelly knew I hated my job and lived in fear I would "pick up" and move to Los Angeles.

"Look," Mom said, "you love photography. You love writing. Why don't you go to film school? Film is just a lot of photographs stuck together with words."

Wha?

"Your father and I will pay for it."

Really?

"Why don't you apply to NYU? It's the best."

Which meant "It's the closest to Washington Heights."

I was not a film buff. Growing up, I rarely had girlfriends, so the only time I went to the movies was with Dad, either at the Loews on 175th Street between Broadway and Amsterdam or the RKO Coliseum on Broadway and 181st. Mom only went to movies if they were at drive-ins. She couldn't deal with the cramped seats in a movie theater because according to Mom, her phlebitis might flare up.

Still, three years of film school paid for by my parents sounded better than poisoning myself mixing chemicals at Frenchy's. Or opening a color lab with Terry.

I showed my photography portfolio to Beda Batka, the Czech cinematography teacher, and was accepted into NYU Graduate Film School.

A few weeks later while Sonny was on another "business trip," Kelly and I sat at opposite sides of my parents' Saarinen table, peeling brisket, burnt potatoes, and carrots off aluminum foil.

"Mom. I got into NYU film school."

"I knew you would, Barry. You're so talented. I love you so much. You'll take out student loans, and when you graduate your father and I will pay them back."

"Wait. That's not what we agreed to. You said go to film school and you and Dad would pay for it."

"Never."

"Never did you say go to film school or never did you tell me you would pay for it?"

"Barry. Don't be ridiculous. I would never say such a thing. Look at your father. But you'll take out student loans, and when they come due, we'll pay them."

"You know film school was your idea, and you said you and Dad would pay the tuition."

"How could I possibly say that? I love you, Barry. Think whatever you want. But you're crazy. You know that."

In line to sign up for classes, I met Peter Exline, a tall, lanky guy who offered me a Bering Imperial cigar in a silver aluminum tube. The cigars cost a buck five for three, which was a step up from the forty-nine cents for five Hav-a-Tampas I'd been smoking since Hampshire College. Pete, a Vietnam vet, was married to a struggling actress and was living a few blocks east of NYU on 7th Street between Avenues A and B. This was 1975 and living across the street from Tompkins Square Park was like living across the street from Vietnam, though not as safe. We called Avenue B the DMZ. Exline told me there was an apartment available in his building—a one bedroom on the third floor for $238 a month.

My mother assumed when she offered up the ruse about paying for film school that not only would I stay in New York, but I'd also move out of Teaneck and back into my childhood bedroom. Discovering I was going to rent an apartment in possibly the worst neighborhood in Manhattan, she wept for days.

"I almost would have been better off," she told me, "if I had let you move to Los Angeles."

"Mom. I was never moving to Los Angeles."

"Now you tell me."

"Should I tell you all the other places I'm not moving to?"

"You know I worry about you."

"Yes, Mom. I do."

"Because I love you."

"I know you love me."

"Thank you," she wept.

"And by the way, I don't need your permission to move somewhere."

"No one is telling you where you can and can't move."

By now the tears are flowing.

"But the East Village? Are you literally trying to kill me?"

"No, Mom. Not literally."

Although I had little to no interest in film, I seemed to be good at cinematography. Technically, it was due to my years of still photography training, but aesthetically, film is not, in spite of my mother's proclamation, "a lot of photographs stuck together with words." In fact, in many ways it is the opposite. I loved how I could move a camera during a shot. I very quickly made it a character in the films I photographed.

I never could be an actor, but I found a way, only child of Jewish parents that I am, to make the audience pay attention to me, the camera.

When taking still photographs, the lens I used most often was the 21mm, which is extremely wide angled. Because almost everything is in focus, and the lens sees so much of the landscape, you have to tell the viewer where to look. My images were always center punched, and very symmetrical, which forced the viewer to look exactly where I wanted them to.

Sweetie. Center punched. Miami. Lumix FZ1000
27mm lens HDR 9 exposures.

As a cinematographer, not only did I use the 21mm as my standard lens, placing the actors and objects in the middle of the frame, I had an additional tool to force people where to look. I could dolly the camera, starting wide, and push in. The energy of a 21mm lens is very dynamic. I could be as close as five feet away from someone yet see most of their body and with just a three-foot push in on the dolly be in an extreme close-up.

I'M TELLING YOU TO LOOK RIGHT HERE!

NYU had a good concept for teaching film, which was "go make films." During the three-year program a student had to produce and direct five films, each one more ambitious in length and technique.

Since everyone had to make movies, we were always trading off roles to crew up. I'd agree to be the cinematographer on Pete's show, if he'd be the script supervisor on mine. Everyone worked in different capacities on different films, though I was often asked to be the cameraman.

What none of us knew when we enrolled was the first-year class was twice as large as the second and third years'. This meant that half the kids weren't going to be invited back for year two. After our first films were shown, letters were sent to 50% of the filmmakers—improve your films, or you're not coming back.

I did not receive the letter. My film was barely good enough. It was about a french horn player who moves to the East Village and loses his girlfriend. The girlfriend part was the only fictional element.

I was outraged. What kind of art school, after one project, issues such an edict? The day the letters were handed out I led a protest taking over the school. We were not going to leave the auditorium until Mel Howard, the chairman, explained how an art school could work this way. If NYU wanted to present itself as a trade school, then I was all in for their dumb rules. But judging an artist based on their first attempt was ridiculous.

Every time Mel spoke, I would scream a version of:

"Stop the lying, Mel!"

Mel would start to speak again, and I would scream:

"You'll say anything to get us out of this auditorium! Stop lying to us!"

Actually, he *was* trying to get us out of the auditorium. His friend, and one of my heroes, photographer Robert Frank had directed a documentary on a Rolling Stones tour called *Cocksucker Blues*. The Stones, having seen it, smartly refused to release it. That night Mel had invited some of his friends to our auditorium to see a double system work in progress print. Double system means that the picture and sound were not yet married onto a single piece of film, and there were very few venues outside of NYU that had the proper equipment to project the movie. Mel had invited the school to see it, as a method to sneak his friends Bob Dylan, Roger McGuinn, and Robert Frank into the theater.

Mel was running out of time, so he lied. He told us there was no set limit to how many students would be invited back for the second year. He said we had to trust the faculty to intuit who would succeed as filmmakers. He also agreed to set up a committee to discuss our grievances. We vacated the screening room.

That night after the movie, I saw Dylan get into McGuinn's Caddy. I made a snide comment to him about it being a good car to drive after a war—a nod to his lyrics. Bob offered up his middle finger in response.

It was June. The second semester was over, and the teachers had dispersed. Mel Howard suddenly remembered that of the students invited back, which not surprisingly was exactly half, he had forgotten to ask the "homeroom" teachers who deserved scholarships. Anyone whose name he remembered got a full scholarship for the next two years. Mel remembered my name but didn't remember why. I received a free ride the last two years although I was not a particularly worthy student.

Not so fast, Ensign Sonnenfeld. Although I was picked by Mel to get a scholarship, in typical NYU fashion, the school forgot to tell me.

My homeroom professor, Roberta Hodes, was an angry, acerbic, talented teacher. She was a former script supervisor on feature films and was painfully honest when she critiqued our scripts and films. She also let us infer that she had an affair with Marlon Brando during the filming of *On the Waterfront*, on which she was the script supervisor.

"What is this? A comedy?" she would literally spit out in vindictive frustration, a cigarette glued to her lower lip, an ash of such length it seemed like a magic trick—bobbing up and down in sync with her barks.

"Who cares about these people? Have any of you jerks led a life?"

We would sit in the school's auditorium/screening room, uncomfortably shifting in our seats, listening to Roberta berate our fellow student's film, knowing we were next.

We learned a lot.

Ken Kelch was another Vietnam vet, although Kelch made Exline look like a conscientious objector. Exline's favorite Vietnam moment was on Christmas, when his sergeant called the troops together and announced, "Catholic Mass is in tent A. Protestants in tent B. Jews, you're with the Protestants."

Kelch's favorite Vietnam memory surely involved killing somebody. He wore the same black T-shirt every day. On the front was a skull and crossbones with the words "82nd Airborne." The back said "Death from Above."

Kelch had been in whatever secret killing organization was above the Green Berets in manliness. He spent the war in Cambodia and Laos wearing no dog tags so if he was captured, he couldn't be identified as an American. We feared and despised Kelch. He was the opposite of anyone else in our school. He wasn't sensitive, worried, or in his early 20s. His films embraced violence and action, while the rest of us were making art films about living in the East

Village and being depressed. We lived on pizza and frozen food. He had lived behind enemy lines eating bugs.

Not like us.

The class we hated most was acting. It was taught by Marketa Kimbrell, a French woman who had a small role in *The Pawnbroker*.

Nothing gave us more anxiety than the thought of being picked to perform in front of the class.

When Kelch was called by Marketa to do an improv, we couldn't have been more thrilled. First, we were relieved we weren't picked, and second, let's see Kelch be a sensitive actor. This will be hilarious.

Kelch told us he was going to reenact the afternoon in Laos when his lieutenant was killed.

Not like us.

Kelch hid behind the couch, desperately yelling at his lieutenant to get back, get behind the couch. He watched in horror as his commander was shot. He raced out from behind the sofa, bent down, and gave his imaginary buddy pantomimed mouth to mouth CPR. He was failing in his attempt to save the officer's life, wailing in frustration between breaths.

"Don't die on me. Don't you fucking die on me!" Kelch screamed.

His improv came to a cataclysmic end when suddenly, shockingly, his best friend died, with the concomitant result of Ken sucking his imaginary lieutenant's imaginary guts into his mouth. He wept uncontrollably. So did the rest of us. Marketa hugged Ken, rocking him back and forth, but his sobs would not stop. The class was deeply saddened—Marketa had made Kelch seem human and vulnerable and made us feel sympathy for the man we feared.

Looking up at us, still hugging and rocking the sobbing vet, Marketa whispered "class dismissed." Now the only ones left to despise were the two TAs who ran the equipment takeout room, Vito Brunetti and Hale Aaron, who wore black gloves with open fingers.

Our directing teacher was Ian Maitland. An Australian. I have no idea where they found him, because unlike the other angry professors, Ian was nice. His classes consisted exclusively of watching movies. The greatest movie ever made, he taught us, was *The Sound of Music*. So not much help there.

Ellie Hammerow was the editing teacher. She also spent some years in the business as an actual editor, including cutting the pilot for *An American Family*.

She was short and had died jet black hair, probably cut with a bowl over her head.

As with all the professors, it was only after we shot our film that any teaching really began. In Ellie's case, that meant sitting in a small windowless editing room, just you and her, Ellie chain smoking, groaning, and oy-ing.

Ellie and Roberta were three pack a day smokers who hated each other. Ellie was a communist Jew, Roberta a Zionist Jew, who fought for the Israeli army. The only thing they agreed on was how lousy our movies were.

Beda Batka, the huge Czechoslovakian cinematography teacher, also a member of the chain-smokers' club, was as mean as Ellie and Roberta. He called me "Mr. Still Photographer." I was one of the two best cinematographers in the school, the other being Bill Pope, who lived in my building and went on to shoot *The Matrix* series, several *Spider-Mans*, and *Men in Black 3*, among many others. Beda knew I was good, so he picked on me. He had been the most sought-after cinematographer in Czechoslovakia until the political turmoil sent him on his way to the USA and NYU. Like our other teachers, with the exception of Ian, he was bitter, sarcastic, and mean.

I reluctantly admit this tough love must have made some sense, since my class at NYU included Bill Pope, Spike Lee, Susan Seidelman, Susan E. Morse (who edited over a dozen Woody Allen movies), Barry Fanaro (an executive producer and writer on *Golden Girls*), and Jim Jarmusch. Not bad for a class of about twenty-five students.

Because NYU hadn't informed me about my undeserved scholarship, I agreed to be Roberta's teaching assistant, which took care of my tuition plus paid $5,000 in salary, but required I stay on for a total of four, not three, years.

I met Roberta before the second year started.

"Why the fuck did you agree to be my assistant?"

"Well, Roberta, even though you're brutal and mean, I kind of think you're great." I lied.

"Jesus, you are so full of shit."

"Plus, I save twenty grand in tuition."

"But that moron Mel gave you a full scholarship."

"What?"

"Mel gave you a fucking scholarship. Full. Although, since you didn't take it, I'm sure some other undeserving schmuck got it."

I went to the new chairman, Laslo Bennedeck, whom we called "Eggs."

"Listen. There's been a horrible mistake. I was never told I received a scholarship. I don't have to work for Roberta."

"Sir," he said. "Nobody else will work for Roberta. Here's a proposal. Do it for these two semesters. Then for your third year, I'll give you a full scholarship and you won't have to stay on for a fourth. Will you do me that favor?"

"Eggs" was a Hungarian who directed *The Wild One* and the movie version of *Death of a Salesman*, which doesn't hold up, by the way. After a string of flops, he too found his way to NYU Graduate Film School. I agreed to his plan and spent a year being the target of Roberta's trash talk.

CHAPTER 17

Superman

My thesis film was *Superman*. This is years before the release of the Warner Bros. movie of the same name. My inspiration was the George Reeves television show and the beloved comic books. I was ahead of my time.

The film took place in a New York where Superman has stopped all crime. New Yorkers are fed up with the superhero. It's gotten to the point that he's policing jaywalkers. He's a bit like Mike Bloomberg, with a lot of rules for the good of the people.

Superman holds a press conference, but only Jimmy Olsen shows up. There's just no news to report.

"Where is everybody? I'm holding a press conference, and there's not a reporter in sight," says a distressed Superman.

"I'm here, Superman," says a fawning Jimmy, whose relationship to Superman was not unlike my mother's relationship to me.

"Well, here's some news. I quit. Let's see how long it takes before this town is begging for my return."

In a pique of anger, Superman storms off.

Unbeknownst to anyone, at this very moment, Lex Luther has turned the World Trade Center into an electromagnet. He is pulling a huge meteor toward earth and is about to demand a large ransom.

My Superman was played by a good-looking actor/body builder named David Orange. It was always a challenge to get decent actors for student movies. There was no pay, the days were insanely long and disorganized, and we didn't know how to direct. Still, we would put ads in *Variety* and *Box Office* magazine, and actors would sign up, hoping we would finish the film and they could get a copy for their "reel." Very few films were ever taken all the way to a print, since the cost of making one was substantial, and besides, what were you going to do with it?

David Orange résumé photo.

Having retired, Superman invites Lois Lane to his apartment for dinner. A piece of raw meat sits on a plate in the center of the table. Superman asks Lois how she likes her steak. As she speaks, he stares at the beef, cooking it with his X-ray vision.

Lois tries to be soothing, telling him how much he's loved and admired. Lois is sounding a lot like my mother. Superman, my alter ego, tries to avoid a confrontation by staring at the steak a little too intensely.

This was my first attempt at an "in camera" visual effect. I doused the meat with Ronson lighter fluid and put the camera flat on the table, the steak in the foreground with Superman staring at it in the background. I rolled the camera and had David Orange stare laser focused at the rib eye as Lois, off frame, continued to be more and more "helpful."

Superman, seething with anger, intensely staring at the meat, screams,

"Lois! That's enough!" at which point I threw an off-camera match at the steak. I was an excellent match thrower, thanks to my years of trying to light the oven without burning the hair off the back of my hand. Instantly, the steak, the plate it was sitting on, and my parents' expensive Saarinen dining table burst into flames. Success and failure. Great shot. Ruined the table.

Superman apologizes to Lois for burning her dinner. Being a bit horny from all that pent-up tension, he reaches for a box of low-grade Kryptonite condoms so his high-speed superhuman ejaculate won't kill her. She declines his advances.

Meanwhile, Lex Luther makes his ransom demand. Superman refuses to save New York unless he gets an apology.

No one apologizes.

During the movie, we've been intercutting between Superman's emotional crisis and the meteor heading toward Earth, accomplished with another in-camera visual effect. I slowly moved a cherry bomb—saved from a "South of the Border" stop a decade earlier—which had the rough surface of a meteor when filmed in extreme close-up, toward a large poster of Earth taken by the Apollo 11 astronauts.

We cut to the basement of Con Edison, the electric company that was often turning off power to my parents' apartment.

I've always feared incompetent people being in charge of my life—my parents, for instance—and in the utility's basement were two morons not doing a very good job of keeping their eyes on the electrical gauges. They don't notice a substation is about to blow, which, when it does, throws New York into a total blackout— another in-camera visual effect—killing power to the World Trade Center and shutting down the electromagnet that no longer pulls the meteor toward Earth. The city is saved.

The two Con Ed idiots are declared heroes. Jimmy Olsen promises he'll always respect Superman, even though he let New York down. Jimmy Olsen and my mother: Two peas. One pod.

Kidney Stones

It was my last year at film school, and I was in bed sound asleep with my girlfriend and fellow classmate, Debbie Reinisch. She hated me. At 2:30 a.m. I woke up, needing to go to the bathroom. Since Debbie's apartment was in the East Village, the toilet was a closet in the kitchen.

My urine came out "braided," to say the least. Then it stopped. Then it started again. Then I had to kneel at the toilet because I was throwing up. Then I was lying on the kitchen floor, having crawled out of the bathroom where there was no room to lie down. I was writhing around on Debbie's red linoleum floor groaning and making strange nasal noises, hoping to wake her up, which I eventually did. With a deep and put upon sigh, she reluctantly got out of bed.

"What are you doing?"

"I think I'm dying. Call the hospital. Call Bellevue."

"And say . . . ?"

"And say your boyfriend is writhing around on the floor, and it feels like someone took a huge sword and shoved it into his kidneys and out through his testicles and scrotum, and whatever invisible creature is doing this to him is slowly twisting it back and forth."

"That's what you want me to tell *Bellevue*?"

"I'm saying please. I beg you. Make the call."

Debbie called Bellevue. She only mentioned the writhing around and kidney parts. The hospital asked if it seemed like I was squirming uncontrollably, unable to find a position where I was comfortable.

"Uh. Yeah!" I affirmed.

The guy at Bellevue told her it sounded like a kidney stone, and there wasn't much to do about it. If I was still squirming in the morning, come to the hospital and they'd check it out. Debbie thought that was fair and left it at that.

"Call another hospital. I'm dying here."

"Call another hospital?"

"Maybe they're wrong. Maybe I shouldn't be in this much pain. I can't wait till tomorrow. Call St. Vincent's."

With a huge sigh, Debbie called St. Vincent's and described my symptoms, once again leaving out the part about the sword, my testicles, and my scrotum.

"Is he squirming around uncontrollably, unable to find a position where he can be comfortable?"

"Yeah. I guess."

"Tell him he's passing a kidney stone. There's not much we can do about it."

"I told you. You're passing a kidney stone," Debbie said, balancing the phone on her shoulder.

"Well, can I come to the hospital?"

"Not much they can do about it."

"Ask them if I can come in anyway."

"*Ask them anyway?*"

Let's pause here to discuss the concept of the silent schmuck. Rob Reiner was taught the phrase during lunch at The Ivy in Beverly Hills by New York playwright Herb Gardiner. Rob passed it along to me. Here's how it works. If you tell someone something, and they repeat it back to you as a question with a certain *intonation*, you're being given the silent schmuck. Or, if you tell someone something and their response is:

"*Reeeaaalllyyyy?*" with that same intonation.

A third iteration is the passive-aggressive sigh and eye roll. In any case, you're getting the silent schmuck. The schmuck is implied by the speaker and inferred by you, but it is...silent. So, when I heard Debbie repeat my request to:

"Ask them if I can come in anyway" with an

"*Ask them anyway?*"

What she was saying, and I was hearing was, "Ask them anyway? *SCHMUCK?*"

"They say yeah, sure, but they can't do anything about it, so let's wait until morning."

"*I HAVE A SWORD GOING THROUGH MY KIDNEY, THROUGH MY TESTICLES, OUT MY SCROTUM, AND IT'S BEING TWISTED BACK AND FORTH!* I can't wait until tomorrow. We have to go to the hospital. Now!"

Debbie grudgingly agreed to take me to St. Vincent's in her Pinto, the very same car that weeks later she would blame me for being towed away.

Debbie had over three thousand dollars in parking tickets, figuring since she had Illinois plates, they'd never track her down.

"Why are you picking me up in a cab?" she screamed when I arrived at the airport in a taxi. I had left her glove compartment open, and a parking cop, seeing her pile of tickets, had her car towed. Debbie went insane when she trudged to the "tow pound" and was told the car was worth less than the money due on the tickets. She had to abandon her beloved Pinto.

In any case, Debbie went to get the car and bring it around to the front of her five-story walkup, leaving me to get down the stairs by myself. Boy, did she hate me. I was in such pain I had to crawl. I couldn't stand up to put on clothes, or even reach for a coat. Over the next ten minutes, with Reinisch probably seething in her Ford, I lowered my naked self, filthy East Village step by filthy East Village step, down the five flights of stairs, down the concrete stoop, across the pebbled and dog excrement mined sidewalk, and, somehow, into her car.

Debbie drove silently to St. Vincent's as I produced a combination of wounded animal and moaning sounds.

"Oh God—don't let me throw up.

"Oh God—don't let me throw up.

"Oh God—don't let me throw up."

Reinisch crankily pulled up in front of the wide, endless steps of St. Vincent's.

"I'll park the car. Check yourself in."

And there I was, 3:00 a.m., totally nude, crawling up the steps of St. Vincent's Hospital. I got through the revolving door by laying on my side in a fetal position, then stretching out my legs as much as the sword would allow me, moving the forward door just enough until the door behind me would bang into my head. I then wormed my way forward and repeated this slinky action about forty times.

Eventually, I made it to the lobby, crawling on my hands and knees to the waiting room, where I promptly pushed two women off a bench. Cupping my hand around my penis and testicles, lying on the bench in a small fetal position, I cried out, "Give me morphine or kill me," until I passed out.

I woke up in the emergency room, two stoic black guys on gurneys on either side of me, due to a recent knife fight. They laid in silence as the doctors dealt with their wounded and bloodied bodies as I continued to moan my mantra:

"Give me morphine or kill me."

Luckily, the knife attack guys didn't know I had recently pushed their mothers off the waiting room bench.

Once again I passed out. When I woke, I was on a cold, flat table, curled up like a dying worm. An attendant told me I had to lie flat for the X-ray.

"No way. Can't do it."

"You want help or not?"

"Give me morphine! Kill me!"

"Not until the X-ray."

Somehow through my tears, I laid flat and still long enough for the picture taking. "Okay. Morphine."

"Not until you pee in this."

"What!"

"If there's blood in your urine, we'll give you morphine."

"But you said . . ."

"Ya gotta pee."

Somehow laying on my side, I managed to urinate onto the table, myself, and into the old, hard plastic beaker. In the vessel was urine and a small gritty rock that I assumed was from the St. Vincent's unwashed cup.

Typical.

I got my shot of Demerol, passed out, and when I woke up was pain free.

"Hey, guys. I feel much better, but I have to tell you—the pitcher you gave me had a piece of rock in it."

I saw one of the recovering knife attackees roll his eyes and realized what his silent schmucking peepers were saying: "That was your stone, fool."

The early morning sun was shining, and Debbie was angry. We drove back to her place in silence. I was wearing a paper bathrobe. A couple of weeks later, Reinisch made me take her to a wine bar on West Broadway to tell me she was no longer my girlfriend.

Debbie Reinisch. West Broadway. She told me I was no longer her boyfriend.

The second kidney stone, I knew it was coming—the strange, sharp jabbing in my kidney could only mean one thing. We'd been filming *Raising Arizona* for weeks in the heat of a Scottsdale summer. As the Coens and I were driving to the set I pulled the car over, making the risky decision to let Joel drive, curled up in the back seat of the rented Gremlin, and started to moan. The Coens were used to this and ignored me.

Only profound pain would allow me to let one of the Coens drive. Joel was once piloting our Gremlin, me in the passenger seat, Ethan in the back, when Joel looked in the rearview mirror and said,

"There's some real dumbass right on my tail, and he's been there for, like, five minutes."

Ethan looked back and said,

"Hey, Jo. That's a cop. He's got his flashers on."

"Do you think I should pull over?"

"Uh...yeah," I said.

Joel got a ticket for driving too slowly in the passing lane and refusing to yield to a police car. I became the self-appointed driver from then on.

When we arrived at the Dick Van Dyke Studios in the Carefree section of Scottsdale, the pain wouldn't go away. I needed to get to a hospital. The Coens laughed and begged me to ignore it. Debbie, who was the first assistant director on the film, recognized the symptoms but said nothing.

"C'mon, Ba. Just have a good vomit, and you'll be fine. Like the old days," said Ethan.

Left to right: *Joel, me, Ethan.* Raising Arizona.

I threw up on the set of *Blood Simple* eighteen times in forty-two days, and Eth was trying to bring back happy memories to avoid calling an ambulance. The problem wasn't shutting down production while I went to the hospital—we had insurance. The issue for the Coens was that we had a first-generation Motorola cell phone, the kind that looked like a white brick with an antenna and we had just gotten our first phone bill—$3,000 for the month. The brothers were freaked out by the amount and didn't want to spend the buck or so to call the ambulance.

"Hey, guys. I'm really in pain."

The Coens shrugged and called an ambulance.

The stupid ambulance driver refused to put on his flashers or siren. And in Scottsdale, if you're not making noise, you're stuck behind an old timer so short it looks like there's no one in the car.

I begged him to turn on his siren, but he said I wasn't an emergency. As we sat at a green light, waiting for some ancient person to wake up, I made a deal with the Lord. If the pain stopped, he could take my mother. God knew that wasn't much of a sacrifice, so the pain continued unabated. At the next light, it was take my father. Once again, not much of an offer. By the time we got to the hospital, Mom and Dad were dead and Sweetie had no limbs.

The stone wouldn't pass. They needed to operate. The surgeon explained he was going to take a "micro knife," cut the stone away from whatever it was stuck to, and then using a "micro basket" pull the stone out. Both devices were going in through my penis.

After the operation I woke up in a private room with a catheter inside me. This was an interesting twist. No one had mentioned the catheter. A nurse came in with a vial of pills that were salmon in color and huge. Circling the face of each pill were the following letters: UR A SPAS.

"Umm. Excuse me. Does this say . . . You're a spas?"

"Yes."

"Why am I taking pills that say, 'You're a spas'?"

"Because your penis is going to try to rid itself of the catheter by spasming it out."

"Ah."

"The pills reduce the body's desire to spasm."

Four hours later, a knock on the door woke me up.

It was a stripper in a pink gorilla suit, holding a boom box.

"Hi," I said, wondering where we were going with this.

"Hi. Do you know where I can plug this in?" said the pink gorilla, pointing to the boom box.

"So, who are you and why are you here, by the way?"

"Oh. Sorry." She opened up a card and read:

"Mike, Rusty, Kenny, Dennis, Earl, Brian, and Dave want Sheila—me—to cheer you up with a little striptease. Do you know where I can plug this in? It's the music."

"Sheila. Please don't take off your clothes. Okay? You see, the reason Mike, Rusty, Kenny, Dennis, Earl, Brian, and Dave have hired you to take off your clothes in front of me is, well, I have a catheter in my penis."

"Catheter?"

"Like a long, skinny needle."

"Uh-huh."

"And if you to take off your gorilla suit in front of me, I might, you know... You know..."

She looked at me as if indeed she were a pink gorilla.

"The boys' thinking, you see, is that it might be really funny to them, but incredibly painful to me, if, you know..."

Nothing.

"For me to get an erection, with a catheter in my penis. So, thank you and maybe some other time, but please, I beg you, do not plug in that boom box and do not...do not...remove your fur."

"But they already paid me."

Damn, she was professional.

"I'll have to give them back the money."

Professional and dumb.

"Here's the great thing! We'll pretend you did what they paid you to do. It will be our little secret. They'll laugh and laugh, you get to keep your money, and I won't suffer the pain of an erection with a catheter in my penis. Everyone wins."

"What's a catheter again?"

Rusty, Brian, and some other idiots, including Ethan and me, throwing rocks at an off-camera Coke bottle hanging on a cactus. On every film, tens of thousands of hours are spent this way.

Soon after Sheila gave me a cute backhanded pink gorilla wave goodbye, the Coens arrived. They pretended to be worried about my health but were actually concerned I had used up the film's insurance days. Since they assumed I'd get sick again, the boys wanted to know if I could come back to work tomorrow.

They promised a light day and said the crew had already set up a separate sitting area where I could relax while working.

The next morning on the way to the set the Coens were laughing their strange, dry exhalation of air laugh.

"Heh."

"Heh heh."

"Heh."

The scene we were filming was the last minute of *Raising Arizona*. The camera starts on a two shot of a young couple and pulls back, low to the table, the camera underslung, a 17.5mm Panavision Primo lens barely skimming the top of a Thanksgiving dinner. It continues to dolly back past a dozen or more people on each side of the table all dressed up in their Sunday best, until we land on Holly Hunter's and Nicolas Cage's backs, both with makeup and wigs to make them look old.

The shot was spectacular, the writing emotional, and I operated the camera from a "comfortable" toilet seat Mike, Rusty, Kenny, Dennis, Earl, Brian, and Dave had rigged up for me.

Heh. Heh heh.

The last scene of Raising Arizona, *the camera operated from a toilet seat.*

CHAPTER 19

An Actress Short, a Cum Shot Behind

What first made me nauseous was a little wormlike thing protruding from her anus. It was a stringy flap of skin or a vein—or maybe a gelatinous mucous membrane. I don't know what it was, but I do know it was disturbing. To be fair, she was not a professional actress but a tailor who had been recruited from her day job at Barneys to fill in on an emergency basis during our final day of a nine-day porn shoot.

There was also Marc Antony's penis, which had this squirrelly blue vein that ran down its lower half—the half near his mass of pubic hair. Sadly, Marc's vein was perfectly positioned to rub against the tailor's stringy thing, so each plunge of his penis into her butt created this horrible rubbing of vein against vein.

Sometimes his penis would push her veiny thing inside her ass and then pull it out again. Sometimes the veiny thing would just sit there, unmoved by a lack of friction. Occasionally, it would stay inside her butt for a thrust or two, then on the third or fourth thrust reappear. The membrane had a mind of its own. I was afraid something was going to burst.

*   *   *

I was less than a foot away from this God-awful activity watching through the viewfinder of a Bolex Rex V 16mm camera with a 10mm Switar f/1.6 lens. Until this surreal moment I had been able to deal with any event in my life, no matter how sad or dangerous or disgusting, by looking at it through a camera lens. This even included viewing my mother and her child-molesting Cousin Mike—CM the CM—sitting side by side in a Bellevue Hospital alcove waiting to find out if my dad was going to live or die after his massive heart attack.

Bellevue Hospital: Mom looking uncannily like George Washington.

Back on the set, however, the event was way too real.

It might have been the smell—a combination of bad perfume and fecal matter emanating from the dining room table on which this poor woman and hairy-assed man were having sex.

In any case, I was nauseous.

It was the last day of March 1979, and it was pouring rain. I was in a loft on 17th Street and Fifth Avenue, and it was the ninth and final day of my first paying gig as a filmmaker. Between film school debt, which my parents didn't pay, and buying a used CP-16R camera so I could call myself a cameraman, I was happy for the job.

Dick Masters of Mr. Mustard Productions owned the loft and was the producer and director of these films. He wore the same pair of blue bell-bottoms every day. Dick had dirty blond hair (because it was dirty) and a Fu Manchu mustache that made him look more friendly than frightening.

I came to my first day on the job wearing the baggy wide wale purple corduroys I had purchased years earlier for my Bryn Mawr College interview. The pants were more garish than Marc Antony's vein. In color.

I wore the cords because they were the loosest fitting pants I owned, and I didn't want the porn stars to see my erection. Ha! Not only did I not get an erection during those nine days of pornography, I didn't have one for the next six months.

It might have been the smell.

Or, it might have been the rubbing of vein against vein less than a foot away from me and what that action was to portend.

If you're trying to shoot nine feature-length pornos in nine days, you need a plan. Although I had only made student films, I offered up a suggestion to make the filming more efficient. Dick thought it was brilliant. We had a large poster board chart in the hallway that had every sex scene, in all nine movies, boxed out—Candy gets turned on by the dentist chair's Mr. Thirsty; Betty gets a job promotion from her boss; the Chinese food delivery guy has shown up at the wrong apartment, but the missus is hungry for more than egg foo young.

We had a black felt-tipped Sharpie hanging by a string. Shoot a cum shot, pull the Sharpie off its cap (which would remain swinging against the poster board), put a slanted line across the box—bottom left to top right—and call for the next couple.

All the rooms for all the scenes were prebuilt and installed inside Dick's loft. A kitchen, bedroom, and bathroom—where one sad night, our creative juices drained—Dick came up with the incredibly un-erotic idea of sex in a bathtub filled with fifty pounds of spaghetti and meatballs in a tangy tomato sauce.

You can imagine the problems: the pasta gets freezing cold in about thirty seconds, which does nothing for an erection; you have strands of spaghetti hanging from different body parts, not unlike Marc Antony's vein or the Barneys tailor's hemorrhoid; you have way too many balls in the tub, between meatballs and testicles; stuff that looks like dried blood is located in unfortunate locations on the actors' bodies, faces, and hair; there is little or no traction for the loving couple to get a good foot- or handhold for leverage, so it looks more like a wrestling match at the Special Olympics than a sex scene; and once again, there's the problem of smell.

There were more sets: a brightly lit roll of white seamless paper that was our "fantasy set," a dining room, living room, and a dentist's office. I think Dick thought the dentist's chair offered many possibilities for positions, although once again, Dick seemed to have no sense of the erotic. Given the amount of men that already think vaginas have teeth, do we really want scenes with women masturbating with Mr. Thirsty? And by the way, Mr. Thirsty is a sucker, not a Waterpik.

The walls of the sets were painted red, blue, green, and purple. Very porno. This is where my bright idea came into play: We would light a room and then shoot every scene for any of the nine movies that took place in that location. We'd shoot scene 3 of movie 1, scene 5 of movie 4 . . . so long as the scene took place in, let's say, the kitchen.

Porn actors came in and out of the loft all day, sat in Dick's office, and waited for their turn on the kitchen table. There was a stack of porn magazines, and for some reason the stars would all sit in this one old ratty leather chair, their legs swung over one of its arms, reading *Jugs*. No one ever sat in the chair in a normal way. I guess that's what made them porn stars. I once saw two of the actors making out in that chair, which was totally weird because kissing is not something they usually do.

Dick, the producer and director, was so proud of the idea of shooting out each room—as opposed to shooting each movie from beginning to end—that he stopped paying attention to the nature of the sex acts. Later when he edited the films, he discovered in one entire movie every sex scene took place on top of a desk.

Dick was a sensitive guy. He couldn't discuss money. We negotiated my fee sitting on either side of a calculator.

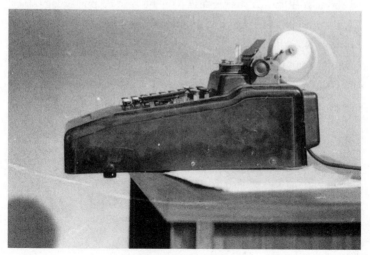

Dick's negotiating tool.

Dick would punch a number into a very old machine before turning it 180 degrees toward me, offering that much per day. I'd tell him he'd have to pay me an additional hundred. He'd blanch and make jabbing motions toward the calculator.

"Press the buttons. Press the buttons."

I'd have to punch in "+ 100," and spin the calculator toward him, at which point he'd shake his head glumly, tapping in some new digits.

I got $300 a day in salary, plus $3,600 in total for the nine days of camera rentals—the Bolex Rex V and CP-16 Reflex that I had just purchased with Mike, who was my connection to Dick. Mike was the lead cameraman, although willing to chip in as an "actor" when needed. In fact, it was a naked Mike that sad dreary night who, along with a cold, complaining actress, tried to swim upstream in fifty pounds of pasta and meatballs. Mike was a confused Catholic with a little blond Hitler mustache.

Mike did most of the filming with our CP-16. My job was to shoot still photos that would later be sold to porn magazines. That would be until the cum shot, at which point I'd put down the Mamiya 6x7 still camera, pick up the Bolex, and set the film speed to either 48 or 60 frames per second to get a slow-motion close-up of the ejaculation. Then before Mandy, "the paper towel" girl—who smelled exactly like the first whiff of a newly opened can of Campbell's chicken noodle soup—cleaned up the mess, I'd shoot some stills of the sperm, usually on the woman's breasts.

The stills weren't very good: we didn't re-light for them. The movie lights were usually gelled with "congo blue" or "canary yellow" or "flame red" sheets of plastic. Mike would use a small fill light—a Mole Richardson 750 soft light—to illuminate the area around the vagina, which in retrospect was totally the wrong way to go. Instead of adding just a little exposure in the area right around the insertion, the Mole Richardson 750 was such a broad source that it also lit up the poor woman's thighs and usually way too much of the guy's scrotum. It was truly the most garish, ugly thing you could ever imagine.

And then there was the smell.

Left to right: *Mandy the paper towel girl, Mike with the CP-16R, Dick with the Bolex, and two actresses in repose, waiting for a new roll of film to be loaded on our "fantasy set."*

We started filming at 10:00 a.m., which, considering photography had finished at six that morning, didn't give us a lot of sleep. I was the only crew member who went home. Mike; Mandy the paper towel girl; Eric, the weird Yugoslavian soundman and gaffer; and Dick would spend their few hours off in the loft stretched out in their clothes across various filthy set beds. I took the 14th

Street crosstown bus back to my apartment on 7th Street between A and B.

Each morning we would meet in front of the chart and see how many cum shots we had that day. If it was more than four, we knew we'd be there for at least twenty hours. We were averaging about five hours a cum shot, and here's why:

Dick would rehearse the scene with the actors. Then we'd take about ten minutes to shoot the dialogue. A couple of angles, and we'd be ready for sex.

Dick would tell the actors, "Here's what I'm thinking: Why don't you give him some head, then why don't we do some sixty-nine, then let's go...ah...doggy style," as if he was inventing some brilliant new order of sex scenes, "then you on top, then you sit on him. Wait! Lick her for a while after she gives you head.

"Now we're cookin' with mustard," he'd say.

Mike would shoot the various sexual positions, and I would shoot photos. After less than a half hour, Dick would announce, "We're ready for the cum shot, boys!"

You'd think this would be the easy part, but that isn't the case. Most porn actors train to maintain an erection but not cum. Because there are a bunch of angles and time required to film enough fucking to create a scene, these guys have somehow desensitized their members, and it's difficult for them to get their muscle memory working again.

Mike and I would sit against one of the plywood walls of the set painted some stupid color and prepare to nap. We also had a tower of twenty years' worth of *American Cinematographer Magazine*s that was over three feet tall. If we couldn't doze, we'd pull one out, start to read, and fall asleep but not before we dimmed all the lights on set, giving the poor guy a chance to get into it.

Occasionally, I'd have the perfect nap, one where I'd drool down my shirt, which on a porn set is the least disgusting thing exiting a human orifice.

There would often be false alarms.

We'd be awakened by a half-grunted, half-whispered "Okay" or "Ready." Mike and I would jerk awake, him grabbing the CP-16R, me the Bolex.

The lights would be brought up to full intensity. Mike would position himself farther away with a long lens, me up pretty close to the action just out of Mike's shot with the 10mm Switar, and Eric holding the microphone in one hand, which was stupid, given that all the audio gets dubbed and the sound of the Bolex running at high speed ruined the sound, and in the other the Mole Richardson 750 soft light, which was equally stupid.

Then...

Nothing.

No moan.

No ejaculation.

Just cursing, grunting, and silence. Perhaps an "Oy" under the actor's breath.

Mike would look at me, and together we'd whisper, "He's soft." We'd skulk away, dim the lights, sit back down against the wall, and sleep.

On the first day of shooting we had a premature ejaculator, which is a disaster in the porn business. I don't know how Dick found him; he even masturbated before we started filming so we'd get all the angles of intercourse we needed without blowing his ejaculation too early. During the first setup he announced he was ready to cum. Dick screamed, "Don't cum! Don't cum!" which if you've ever been in that situation you know has the opposite effect.

Neither Mike nor I was anywhere near the close-up required when he came. Dick was furious. The actress was furious—most of the women were double and triple booked, and she knew this would make her late for her next shoot.

We took naps while the guy recovered and regained his erection. Eventually, we shot the various sex angles—doggy style, her on top, missionary—and we were ready for the cum shot, which meant Mike and I dropped to our napping positions in the corner. Not only did this guy take hours, but the actress was so angry she was even less helpful than the customary no help that the actresses usually gave the guys.

The dynamic in porn is overwhelmingly feminist. The women are in total control and were aware of that every second. They flirt, they wear no clothes, they go to the bathroom and leave the door open—every single actress we worked with left the bathroom door open while she was in there. But most of all, they make the male actors suffer. They embarrass them. They don't help them cum. They lie there like a water bed, offering no resistance, no friction, to the poor guy's pounding, rubbing, or grinding.

The actresses would offer up comments: "Dick. He's soft... again."

Or:

"C'mon, baby. Let's get this over with," which is about as mean as you can get.

Samantha, a pretty brunette with red highlights, was particularly mean because she knew she was the sexiest actress we had. I looked forward to her arrival, which was about four or five times during the nine days. She had a sense of humor, and huge-nippled breasts, but was often uncomfortably mean to her partners. She would tell us a guy was soft even if he wasn't just to make him soft.

She also hated Ron Jeremy. Another reason I liked her.

Ron was the creepiest, hairiest person you'll ever meet. He had an incredibly long penis and a very short torso, which, due to what he could achieve with that physique, made Mike throw up. But Mike's retching wasn't until day nine—and not before I had thrown up due to the horrific outcome of Marc Antony's veiny penis' activity with the tailor from Barneys hemorrhoidal ass.

On the fifth day of shooting, Dick decided we needed a day out of the studio.

Probably it was the smell.

Open some windows, and let some of that fine New York fresh air from the photography district clean out the joint. That's what we needed.

Smell, by the way, is an underrated sense. If television was brought to you with smell, things would change a lot. It would probably put an end to war. Smell-o-Vision would put pornos out of business as well, although the industry would probably dub in some horrible sexy smell like vanilla to replace the odor of dry rot and excrement—similar to dubbing in the sexy, out of sync moans and "Oooooh, baby's."

We spent a day and night on location at a one-bedroom bachelor pad in the East 60s. The place was quite garish, and in fact was the inspiration, twenty years later, for the Worm Guys' apartment in *Men in Black II*. It had white shag carpeting and lots of black framed mirrors and chrome. There were raised or lowered floors, creating a sunken "love pit" in the middle of the living room.

It had a fake fireplace and a disgusting bathroom, the door to which Robin Byrd—then a porn actress, later a porn talk-show celebrity—kept open while sitting on the toilet. Unfortunately, the toilet had one of those squishy seat cushions that made a hiss sound whenever she sat on or got off the damn thing. She was on it a lot—the door always open and endless complaints coming out of her foul mouth.

Around three in the morning, she got furious at Mike and me.

147

A reinterpretation of the porno apartment designed by Bo Welch for the Worm Guys' bachelor pad, Men in Black II *(2002).*

The guy who owned the apartment thought it would be cool to have a porn shoot in his place, but he wouldn't give Dick permission to use his furniture for sex. Intercourse took place exclusively on the stringy shag carpet. There was nothing for us to lean against for our naps. Every space where wall met floor was filled with curves or stools or record albums. Mike and I ended up napping in the actual lying-down position less than a yard away from Robyn and whatever poor schmuck was getting absolutely no help from her but was—just the same—heaving and grunting and hard breathing while trying to maintain his erection.

Sometimes he would take his unhappy penis out of Robyn and play with it in his hands, talking to it, yelling at it, trying to stay hard, with Robyn storming off to the bathroom, making the toilet seat hiss, while yelling, "This is taking all night; this guy is terrible."

We had decided to give Eric the Slav the day off—he had burnt his hand holding the Mole Richardson 750 soft light the night before, yelling out in pain and dropping his other hand—the one holding the microphone—into frame at the precise moment we were shooting the cum shot. (Miking this moment made no sense, given that the sound of sperm fleeing the penis is not a dynamic one.)

Since we were on location, we used a couple of tota-lights, small units with a 1,000-watt bulb and a silver umbrella stuck into a slot in the fixture to bounce the light around the room. Between the tota-lights and the white cottage-cheese ceiling and white shag carpet, there was plenty of fill light, so we wouldn't need any supplemental "pussy" light. The insertion area would be bright enough. Eric got the day off. And for once thighs and scrotums weren't overlit.

So Eric was off, and Mandy the paper towel girl was running an errand, trying to locate an open Smilers to get chocolate chip cookies, coffees, and another roll of paper towels, which was difficult given that it was the middle of the night. Outside was raging the worst end-of-March blizzard the city had ever experienced. As a result, the only people in the loft besides the two sex combatants were Dick, standing up while reading *Jugs* in the white galley kitchen, and Mike and me, both curled up on the floor like newborns, a foot or so away from the grunting.

Mike and I started to snore while Robyn was trying to coax sad man into maintaining his erection. She went insane. She started to scream, waking us up from the blissful drool-filled place we'd briefly inhabited, shrinking the poor guy's penis down to a crepe of skin and scaring Dick, who was afraid we were going to wake up the neighbors and get kicked out before the cum shot. Or at least before Mandy the paper towel girl came back with the cookies.

Dick made Mike and me apologize to Robyn.

"Nothing personal."

"Just a bit tired."

"Excellent body."

"Amazing technique."

She calmed down and straddled our actor, who was stroking his member during Robyn's rage, desperately trying to keep it happy. As she bent down I noticed an errant bit of shag carpet had attached itself to her ass. A foreshadowing of things to come.

Eventually, we got the cum shot, although it was neither pretty nor joyful for any of us. He ejaculated on Robyn's tits. Mandy, back now for hours, slapped a paper towel on Robyn, did a quick wipe, and Robyn was out of there, leaving us to stand in the predawn Upper East Side trying to hail a cab in eighteen inches of overnight snow.

By day 9, back at the studio, we were an actress short and a cum shot behind. Mike, Eric, Mandy, and I napped against various walls. Marc Antony had his legs draped over the arm of the ratty office chair reading *Jugs*. And Dick Masters, of Mr. Mustard Productions, was out on a porn actress fishing expedition to find a replacement for the missing cast member.

He came back with a tailor from Barneys, located two blocks west of our loft. She seemed game, but being an amateur, her performance later that evening would lead to my sadness.

Dick made the catastrophic mistake of failing to change the sex acts her character was scripted to engage in. The specific sex position I'm referring to is the technically difficult "double insertion"—also known as the "double penetration" in some porn circles. A penis in her ass, a penis in her vagina, same time.

Dick once again came up with what had to be the least erotic mise en scène in the history of double insertions, which was having her lie face up on a wooden dining room table with the middle leaf removed. The man on top was in her vagina. The man under the table, Marc Antony, was in her sway-backed derriere. To get Marc close enough to the underside of the table to insert his penis into her rectum, Mandy placed a bunch of pillows from various prop couches and chairs and beds underneath him.

It was a disaster. He kept bouncing around on the pillows, which would separate in the middle, creating a Marc Antony "V"— his head and legs up on the separated pillows, his ass on the floor. Eventually, we built a box to corral all the pillows and pin Marc to the underside of the table, his head pressed hard against the oak. His hands reached around and clutched the table's surface, while his legs and ankles clung to the far end of the table. Marc looked like a desperate drowning soul trying to stay afloat on the bottom of his capsized boat. He could barely breathe and kept complaining about his stiff neck and back cramps.

His penis kept flopping out of the Barneys tailor's ass, and we'd have to stop the action to get it back in. Marc was in no physical shape (or position) to hang onto the table with one hand while reaching with his other to get his dick back in her rectum, so Mandy, working outside of her "paper towel girl" job description, lent a hand, delicately placing schlong into butt, at which point Marc would start his grotesque parallel-to-the-ground pull-ups.

The totally weird thing—yes, there was something weirder than a double insertion on a dining room table with a tailor from Barneys—was that the tailor was thrilled beyond belief. For the first time in nine days, we wouldn't have to dub in squeals of delight and screams of joy—although the soundtrack was ruined by Marc Antony's complaining and oy-ing.

Dick, feeling we had gotten all the angles he needed, was ready for the cum shot. Mike and I were heading back to dim the lights and take a nap when the guy on top of her—the one in her vagina performing the missionary position—said he was ready. This tailor from Barneys was really turning him on. We raced back with our cameras and quickly got a decent cum shot.

"We're cookin' with mustard now, boys!" Dick Masters of Mr. Mustard Productions once again proclaimed.

We had just saved many hours of sitting in the corner napping, drooling, and reading *American Cinematographer*. This wasn't going to be such a terrible day after all. We were merely one cum shot behind.

Mandy pulled the pillows out from under whiny Marc Antony once Dick resolved that he could have anal intercourse with the Barneys tailor on top of the table. The table's missing leaf was put back in, the tailor got on her knees, Marc stuck his veiny penis into her hemorrhoidal ass, and the two of them got at it with all the gravity and friction Marc needed. The tailor had lost all inhibitions:

"Oh God.

"Oh God.

"Oh God.

"Oh Gaaaaawwwwd."

Things were working out even better than we expected, except for the slight nausea I was experiencing from the vein to vein contact and the horrible smells.

"Oh Gaaaawwwwd.

"Oh Gaaaawwwwd," she squealed.

"Oh God, don't let me throw up . . ." I whispered.

Marc was ready to cum. We were about to set a new porn record of cum shot ready to cum shot achieved! I picked up the Bolex Rex V with the 10mm lens and ran to the set. Since 10mm is a very wide angled lens—the equivalent of a 21mm if filming in 35mm— you need to be close to the action. In return, there is a real sense of energy and a bigger than life quality to what the lens sees.

"Any time you're ready go for it, Antony!"

"Ready, Dick!" Marc declared.

The tailor was screaming with pure abandonment. Marc was grunting as if a furious grizzly.

And here, in all its profound sadness, is the truly horrible, horrible thing that happened when Marc Antony pulled his veiny penis out of the Barneys tailor's hemorrhoidal anus:

Imagine if you would, this woman's rectum and intestines as if it were a warm bottle of champagne stored at 98.6 degrees that had been shaken and shaken and shaken for twenty minutes.

Then imagine removing the cork.

Really, really, quickly.

I bet you can visualize what would happen. Being close to the uncorking, due to the requirements of a 10mm f/1.6 Switar lens, I was instantly covered in a fountain of warm, loamy, effervescent human excrement.

I immediately put down the Bolex, missed the cum shot, and started to vomit. I raced to the front of the loft and pressed the elevator button. I kept puking down my pants, and onto my sneakers, overlaying the Barneys tailor's excreta. I was bent over, holding my shirt away from my neck like a place kicker on the sideline, about to be called in with no time left to kick for the win.

Tears were pouring down my fecal covered face.

The elevator arrived.

Luckily, it was empty.

April 1 was a cold and rainy day. It was the kind of rain that wherever your coat ended, your pants from that point to your shoes were drenched. I stood on the northeast corner of 17th Street and Fifth Avenue, covered in the tailor's shit and my own vomit, arms outstretched to the heavens, looking like Willem Dafoe at the end of *Platoon*. It was too cold, windy, and rainy for people to pay much attention.

Besides, it was New York.

The chilling rain and Jesus pose—shit covered though I was—slowly calmed me down.

After fifteen minutes of street showering, I felt I was clean—at least physically.

Emotionally, I was scarred for life.

I was also freezing, and my career called. I got in the elevator, took a few deep breaths, and started to feel better. I made the mistake of looking down at my sneakers, where I spied a small brown speck on one of the tongues.

I started to dry heave.

The elevator opened at the floor-through loft. I knew Mandy the paper towel girl, pro that she was, would have cleaned up the Barneys tailor's "mistake."

"It's all okay. It's all okay," I chanted to myself.

What I didn't expect heading back to the set was the sound of Mike vomiting.

There's a joke that goes like this:

A pervert is brought before the judge. The prosecutor says, "Your honor, this man is accused of having sex with chickens, dogs, cats, sheep, cows, pigs, hamsters, rabbits, geese, giraffes, bears, ducks..."

The judge interrupts:

"Ducks. Eccchhh."

What upset Mike was not the human fountain of doody shooting out of the Barneys tailor's ass. He was fine with that. What got him all queasy was that after Mandy the paper towel girl cleaned up the sperm, vomit, and human waste coating Marc Antony, the Barneys tailor, the dining room table, and the Bolex Rex V, Dick decided not to wait for me to come back from my rainy adventure—I suppose he wasn't sure if I'd ever come back. Instead, he had Mike shoot the next bit of pornography, which was Ron Jeremy, the guy with the long penis and short torso, giving himself a blow job.

That was too much for Mike. He couldn't deal with that level of hedonism, strict Catholic that he was. He was off to the bathroom to wretch.

"Ducks. Eccchhh."

Mandy cleaned up the vomit from Mike's encounter with the short-torso'd, long-penis'd Ron Jeremy, we crossed off another box, bottom left to top right on the cum shot board, and at midnight we were down to the last cum shot of the entire shoot.

Sadly, all the vomiting and pooping had put us behind schedule. When we looked in Dick's office, the last two remaining actors had fled.

In retrospect, Dick was about to make another bad decision.

Dick convinced Marc Antony to stay for one more cum shot and, after taking her into his office for a long talk and I'm sure some back and forth action with the adding machine, convinced Mandy the paper towel girl to come out of retirement. That's when I discovered Mandy was an ex porn actress who had given up acting to devote herself to the technical side of the film business. She saw paper towels as her entrée into the glamorous world of porn cinematography.

Marc struggled. Mandy wasn't really into it and at some point during the hours of fucking realized she had made a terrible mistake. Marc kept complaining that Mandy was "dry."

"Dick. For God's sake, I'm chafing."

"Do you want us to put some hand cream on your dick?"

"This isn't fair to poor Mandy."

It was starting to get light outside. Dick gave up. He couldn't take Marc's constant drone of complaints. He stopped the "action," although you could barely call it that.

"I have been in this business for over twenty years, and I have never said these words, but here we are. We're going to fake the cum shot."

It turns out that faking a cum shot is some kind of porn sin. Who knew?

Everyone seemed devastated by this, but we were all really tired. And it would mean that we were done. It was time to take a shortcut. Mr. Mustard sent the whiny Marc Antony home. He then told Mandy to get some eggs and sugar. She got dressed, went down to the Smilers on 16th and Sixth, and came back with a half dozen eggs and a two-pound yellow box of sugar with a metal pouring spout.

Mandy didn't see the irony of being sent out into the cold predawn to buy the tools of her own sadness. Dick separated the half dozen egg whites into a bowl, yellow box spouted in some sugar, and made Mandy whip them into a viscous cloudy mixture with a shocking resemblance to sperm.

Mandy got undressed, her roll of paper towels just out of frame. Dick told Mike and me to focus on Mandy's tits—more genius direction from Mr. Mustard. Dick took a spoon and loaded it up.

"Ready? Roll cameras!"

Mike and I rolled. Dick snapped the spoon at Mandy. Egg white and sugar flicked off the spoon, landing between Mandy's left eye and nose.

"Cut. Sorry. Clean it up."

She took the roll of off-camera Bounty, snapped off a piece, and wiped her face. Dick tried again. As sad as the double insertion was, as sad as being covered by a warm liquefied fountain of shit was, and as sad as Mike's Catholic guilt vomiting was—nothing was as sad as Mandy having to clean up her own faked cum shot. Finally, Dick landed some sugar and egg white blend on one of her breasts.

"Cut."

Mandy paper toweled herself off and got dressed.

As I was heading for the elevator, having wrapped my porn career, Mandy came out of Dick's office with an Entenmann's white cake with chocolate frosting and a single candle. Mike, Mandy, Dick, and Eric the Slav sang happy birthday to me. It was April 1, and I was 26 years old.

Insult to Injury

The sun was coming up as I walked south on Fifth Avenue to the bus stop. My 26th birthday was off to a crappy start. My plan was to catch the 14th Street crosstown bus to Avenue A and 7th, walk the block to my apartment, and sleep until I turned 27.

As I waited for the bus in a deep depression, shivering in the early dawn, still a tad damp from doing the Willem Dafoe, two large, scary guys came alongside me, crowding either side of my body.

"Hey. You got a wallet?"

To add a night of insult to a morning of injury I was going to celebrate my birthday by being mugged.

"Yes. Yes, I do have a wallet."

"I've got a gun. Let me see your wallet."

In times of extreme stress or crisis, I become completely calm. It's the other 99.978% of the time that I'm an anxious mess. Not unlike my plane crash experience, if everything and everyone is out of control, I'll be the voice of reason.

"Okay," I said to mugger number one. "We have established I indeed have a wallet. That we have established. You should just know, as I reach toward the front right pocket of my pants, which is where my wallet is, since my father told me not to carry a wallet in my back pocket, which can lead to back pain and being pickpocketed, I am only reaching for my wallet. I am absolutely not reaching for a gun or knife, which I don't have. I am merely reaching for my wallet."

"Shut up and give me your wallet."

"Yes. I understand you want my wallet, but I want you to know I am absolutely no threat to you, or your friend."

"You promise, captain?" silent schmucked the up to now non-talking mugger number two.

"I totally prom . . ."

"Give me your wallet and shut the fuck up."

"Yes, that's what I'm reaching for. My wallet. And not a gun or knife."

"Man, I know you have no weapon. Just give me the fucking wallet."

"And here it is."

I gave the large, scary guy my wallet.

The guy on my other side, equally tall, large, and scary said, "You got a watch?"

"Yes. Yes, I do."

"Give me your watch."

"Okay. Here's the thing about the watch . . ."

"Man. I am going to . . ."

"It's on my wrist."

"I know it's on your wrist, motherfucker."

"I am telling you it is on my wrist so that when I reach across my body to get the watch off my wrist, you don't think I have a gun or a knife hidden up my . . ."

"I swear, man. . . ."

At which point the wallet guy says, "Jesus. You stink. Did you just shit yourself?"

"Ah. Well. No, I didn't shit myself, and yet . . . I do smell like shit. But here's the thing: you really don't want to know why."

"Hey. Are we suddenly having a conversation with this white boy?" said the watch thief to the wallet thief.

"Just give me your watch."

"Okay. Here goes. I am reaching across my body to . . ."

"Shut up and give me the fucking watch."

As I handed thief number two my Seiko, a westbound bus across the street from us stopped in the middle of the fast lane. The bus driver opened his window and stared at the three of us. Just stared me and the junkies down. It had the effect he was looking for.

The watch guy said, "I don't want this piece of shit. Take it back."

The guy with the wallet, after discreetly removing my few bills, gave it back.

"This is a piece of crap wallet. I don't want your fucking wallet."

The mugging took long enough that my eastbound bus arrived. The door opened.

I realized I had change in my back pocket. Although the wallet mugger had asked for my "wallet" and not my "money," was I really going to have a semantic debate with these guys?

If I got on the bus, they would know I held back some of my life savings. Although they returned my wallet, did they memorize the address on my driver's license? And even if they didn't, would they run alongside the bus from 14th and Fifth to 7th and A?

Now the three of us had two bus drivers staring at us. One on each side of 14th Street. I took as deep a breath as I could, given the way I smelled, and got on the bus, dropping some back pocket quarters into the change box. I heard the doors close behind me as we pulled away, leaving my assailants dazed and confused. The driver winced as remnants of the fecal fountain that had caked onto my clothes wafted into his nasal passages. I took a seat at the back of the nearly empty bus.

It took about six months, the same length of time it took me to get an erection, before I felt confident my tormentors weren't going to knock down my door in the middle of the night for holding back the fifty cents that was rightfully theirs.

CHAPTER 21

My Life Begins. I Meet Sweetie.

Sweetie. April 22, 1989. Our wedding day.

My life began the moment I met "Sweetie," Susan Ringo, my one true love, at an apartment on Central Park West. She was eight months pregnant.

I was there to be interviewed for a job by one of the world's great still photographers.

My idol.

Her husband.

Elliott Erwitt.

I had finished film school a couple of years earlier.

I was barely earning rent and food money and was struggling to pay the monthly charge on the student loans and 18% interest on my credit cards. No—Kelly and Sonny did not pay off my student loans.

Having given up porn, I was earning income from shooting industrial films with the used CP-16R 16mm camera I co-owned with Mike. Reeves Teletape and Rabbi Gelman Productions were both clients. I was a loss leader working for practically nothing if you rented my camera.

A semi-regular gig was as a cameraman for Howie Meltzer and his partner, Jon Klee, at Soleil Productions. Their main client was Michael Carson, who produced industrials for SONY Electronics.

When SONY was introducing a new Trinitron or Walkman to their sales force, they would take over a hotel and put on an extravaganza, with jugglers, comedians, and entire bespoke Broadway quality song and dance numbers. Many of these bits required a videotaped component, which for some unknown reason involved puppets. At least there were no mimes.

In August 1980, I was filming the puppets' introduction of SONY's latest Trinitron color television. Also on the job was Maggie, a sassy videographer who had plans to open a video rental company and wanted me as her partner. Maggie had business relationships with the Japanese, who paid cash and were willing to stake her/us to the new business. I had a crush on her and asked her out. We were back at my apartment when she told me she was a lesbian but would have sex with me one time anyway.

I asked her to give me a few days to decide about the video leasing business. Having finished film school several years earlier, the fact that my career consisted of SONY puppets and industrials for Rabbi Gelman was both depressing and barely lucrative. Maybe a video camera rental company was my future.

Friday morning, we were finishing the last of the puppet closeups when Jon Klee approached:

"There's a still photographer I did some lighting for a while back. He just bought some used 16mm cameras and doesn't really know what he has and what he needs. He's looking for someone to organize his stuff. You'd be great. Do you want his information?"

I was a weekend away from telling Maggie I'd go into the video rental business with her, but to be polite, said,

"Maybe. What's his name?"

"Elliott Erwitt."

As I've written, since the age of 14, I wanted to be a still photographer. More specifically, I wanted to be Elliott Erwitt.

The days I graduated high school, college, and graduate film school I had called Elliott, looking for work. Each time I got the same response:

"My stable is full."

It took a decade, but quantum mechanics had decided this Friday afternoon via Jon Klee of Soleil Productions, the time was right for my universe to merge with Elliott's.

"Speaking."

"Hello. Is Elliott Erwitt there?"

"Speaking."

Elliott asked me to come to his apartment on Central Park West that afternoon.

It was a sweltering late August day when I arrived at his non-air-conditioned flat overlooking Central Park. Spread across the enormous dining room table were half a dozen of his iconographic photographs. A very pregnant, very beautiful woman was sitting at the table. Placed in front of her were bottles of "spot tone," used to cover up little imperfections in a photo.

I silently gasped. Between the ages of 12 and 17, lacking dates, I would draw the profile of a perfect girlfriend. She had a pert nose that ski sloped up and long eyelashes. Although I couldn't draw, she was perfection. Since I only had illustrated my perfect girl's face, the pregnancy thing threw me off a little, but just the same, there she was, spotting prints.

Elliott introduced her as Susan. I assumed she was his assistant. He was nineteen years her senior, so it wasn't a totally dumb presumption. Elliott was a bit frantic. He needed those photos for a client, and they had to be "spotted" by that evening.

Susan said, "Happy to spot the photos, Elliott, but you have to keep an eye on Sasha." Sasha was their 3-year-old daughter, and Susan was Elliott's wife, but I didn't know that yet.

"Anything."

"Okay. Just keep an eye on her."

"Yes. Please, spot the prints."

Susan leaned over the first photo with a magnifying glass, put the tip of the spotting brush in her perfect mouth to make a superfine point, and began to cover up any bits of hair, dirt, or dust that might have been on the original negative. It's a tedious job, requiring a lot of concentration. Within a minute Sasha, who was indeed not being watched by Elliott, crawled onto the table and knocked over a bottle of spot tone, ruining a print. Elliott whined like hell about it, alternately blaming Susan or Sasha, but definitely not himself. He found a replacement print and took me to a back room that held several cases of 16mm camera equipment.

Elliott was a member of Magnum, the prestigious photo agency, and made his living as a still photographer. He had directed several terrific documentaries and wanted to make more.

Along with his writer friend Lee Jones, he had just sold a story to ABC's *20/20*. The segment for the show would document how the United States was exporting horses to Europe specifically to feed its robust horse meat industry. Elliott titled it *They Eat Horses, Don't They?*

I was being interviewed to not only organize Elliott's equipment, but if I passed the test, I'd come on as Elliott's camera assistant, second camera, and all-around schlepper for *Horses*.

Hours later, still sitting on the floor in the back room, all sorts of lenses, batteries, cables, film magazines, and filters spread out around me, Susan poked her head in.

"Want to stay for dinner?"

Elliott was very European—a Russian born in France and raised in Italy. Susan was from a small Texas town called Haslet, located between Denton and Fort Worth. Her father and mother both worked for General Dynamics. Her dad was also the mayor of Haslet.

Susan was "Miss Flame"—the beauty queen contest winner of Tarrant County's volunteer fire departments. She was also a Yucca Beauty at the University of North Texas, their Relay Queen, and runner-up to Miss Teen Fort Worth.

Not like us.

Sweet sixteen: Susan "Sweetie" Ringo.

I wasn't a gregarious guy, but I had a wry sense of humor that helped me get the job. I was reading Norman Mailer's *The Executioner's Song* and spent most days on the documentary chatting with Susan about it. We hit it off.

She borrowed my book.

At the end of filming, Elliott had been hired to cover the Cannes Film Festival for a magazine. He also thought it would improve the *20/20* piece to film some horse meat butcher shops in France. Trading in his first class ticket for two economies, he asked if I wanted to fly with him to Cannes. I'd be his photo and movie assistant. I needed to expedite myself a passport but was excited to go.

"Hi, Mom. It's Barry. Listen, I need to get a passport and was wondering if you knew where my birth certificate was."

"Why would you possibly need a passport?"

"To go to Europe. On a job."

"Who would possibly pay you to fly to Europe for a job? What's this really about, Barry?"

"Elliott needs to shoot some more footage for the *They Eat Horses, Don't They?* documentary, plus he's covering the Cannes Film Festival for a magazine, so he's hiring me to work for him on both."

"Barry, this makes no sense."

"Why is that, Mom?"

"Is Elliott gay? Why else would he want to take you to France all of a sudden?"

"Mom. First of all, Elliott is not gay. Second, if he were, he could do a lot better than me. And third, even if he was gay, does that mean I shouldn't work with him?"

"You're nuts, Barry. You really are. If you want your birth certificate, it's up here. You can come get it. But this makes no sense. You barely know Elliott, you speak no French, and you'll be flying over the ocean to somewhere. Do you even know what airline you're on? Please. This is a nightmare."

Our first stop was covering the film festival. I carried two cases of cameras, and slung over my shoulder was a four-step ladder for Elliott's high angle shots. On a slow day at the festival, we drove into town and filmed boucherie chevaline exteriors.

Elliott Erwitt on his ladder. Cannes, 1980.

For the next three and a half years, I was Susan and Elliott's young son. They took me everywhere, both socially and through work. During that time Elliott sold a limited documentary series to HBO called *The Great Pleasure Hunt.* Our on-screen narrator was Murray Sayle, a very funny Australian journalist.

Murray Sayle. Nairobi. The Great Pleasure Hunt.

We filmed outrageous ways to spend money in Europe, Africa, Asia, and America. This was pre–Robin Leach's *Lifestyles of the Rich and Famous.* The one-hour shows were always visually funny, often in ironic ways, like filming a black tie safari on Africa's Masai Mara, panning from wealthy types in black tie and evening gowns to black and white striped zebras reacting to the bourgeoisie.

Being with Susan and Elliott changed my life. I started to drink cocktails. I met interesting people. I took care of his movie equipment, arranging for Carnets—customs documents to allow us to move camera equipment and film across international borders—as we traveled over four continents for our HBO show. In addition to working as a second cameraman, I was now producing the show with Elliott.

I also became Susan's best girlfriend.

Susan had given birth to Amy, their second child, a couple of years earlier and was less willing to travel. A lot of Elliott's still photography work didn't involve me. He would travel on his own for weeks at a time, and I would hang out with Susan in New York. In order to maintain my role as best girlfriend, I kept up to date on all matters female through *Self* magazine.

"Have you and Elliott tried the new 'Today Sponge'? You know...for birth control?"

When I wasn't spending time with Susan and Elliott, I was alone. I had no real friends to speak of. Howie Meltzer's wife heard that someone had been murdered on my block in the East Village. She found an apartment for me at 160 West 71st Street, which I called the "Bagel Nosh Building," since Bagel Nosh had a storefront in it. A few years later, Bagel Nosh sold, at which point I lived in the "Hot and Crusty Building."

Howie's wife had heard about the apartment from an acquaintance. This person's friend was dying of cancer. I would move into the dying person's apartment while she was in hospice care and when she died I could hopefully convince the landlord to let me take over the lease. Possession, they say, is nine-tenths of the law. The arrangement was creepy, but many New York apartments are found through reading obits.

It didn't take long for this poor soul to pass on. Her parents asked if I could sell her stuff and send the proceeds to them in Kansas.

After bribing the super, the one-bedroom rental was mine. The night of the sales event, the apartment was crawling with her dear, dear friends looking for deals.

"Jen would want me to have this salad bowl."

"Actually, Jen is no longer with us, and her parents would like ten dollars for it."

I bought that salad bowl, and it sat under my apartment's north facing window. Every night I ordered the same Hunan Flower Steak and Capital Chicken takeout from Hunan Park Chinese Restaurant on Columbus Avenue and 69th.

Never was I disloyal to these two menu options. I would take the unused duck sauce, soy sauce, and Chinese mustard packets that came with the takeout and throw them in the salad bowl, which I called my "bachelor barometer."

On the rare occasion when I had a date, my first stop would be to bring the potential girlfriend to meet Susan at her apartment a few blocks away. After some chitchat, Sweetie would take me aside and say,

"Have sex. Don't marry."

I had been freelancing for Elliott for several years when the Coen brothers and I raised the $750,000 we needed to head to Austin, Texas, and make *Blood Simple*.

It was never the same with Elliott after I returned to New York. I was now a real cinematographer on an actual 35mm feature film, and that fact irritated the hell out of him.

Elliott, Susan, and I filmed one more episode of HBO's *The Great Pleasure Hunt* after I shot *Blood Simple*. It was a painful experience. There was a lot of tension, even though we were working in some of the most beautiful places in Europe and Japan.

Elliott and I bickered constantly. Susan and I were best friends, but she was Elliott's wife and felt caught in the middle. She didn't know whose side to take. It didn't help that she was missing her little girls, who had been left with her parents in Texas.

Blood Simple was released to glowing reviews after making its debut at the New York Film Festival. Many critics called out my cinematography, often mentioning me by name.

Around that same time, Susan told Elliott she no longer wanted to globe-trot. She fretted about leaving their young daughters with caretakers and wanted to stay home.

He didn't take the news well. He loved her and relied on her in many ways on his photographic assignments, often overseas. Eventually, Susan moved with Sasha and Amy to their weekend home in East Hampton to sort out her life.

Relationships are more complicated and more personal than this accounting implies. Although I was Susan's best friend, I was not privy to the intimate details of their marriage, nor its undoing. What I did know is that when Elliott informed their mutual friends, "You're either with me or with her," I asked, "Can I choose her?"

It was an easy choice.

Elliott and my friendship, already shaky, ended quite badly with the breakup of their marriage, especially after I sided with Susan.

Susan and I were together a lot in the Hamptons—she and her girls at her home in the village of East Hampton, me in my "starter house" a few miles out, off Springs Fireplace Road.

As weeks became months became years—Susan and Elliott were in divorce court for five years—some sexual tension started to enter the picture. Sex and the fear of it went unspoken for a long time. We were both concerned it could ruin our perfect friendship. One night as we were watching television (probably *The Miracle of Life* on PBS, a favorite we'd watched many times), I turned to her and said:

"Welp, here goes nothin'..."

We remained best friends.

And now we were lovers.

And Susan became Sweetie.

I can't help but wonder why I specifically pursued Elliott all those years. I could have called any of the photographers I admired—they all lived in New York. I only called Elliott.

If I had made one of a trillion, trillion other choices throughout my life, missing an elevator, opening up a color lab or video camera rental place, driving a mile an hour faster on the Saw Mill, stepping on a crack, I would not have been working for Soleil Productions on a SONY industrial and Jon Klee would never have suggested I call Elliott. Instead of being married to Sweetie for the past thirty years, I surely would be living with my mother, since whatever quantum reality kept me from meeting Sweetie would sadly be the same reality where my mother continued to live on forever, a phone cradled between her chin and ear, a damp towel across her forehead.

The Cash Machine

Sweetie was introduced to Sonny and Kelly at a Sunday brunch at Barristers, a luncheonette in Southampton, Long Island. The early '80s was an era before ATM machines. Dad vacillated between having cash and living without electricity. This weekend, my father had both. I called Sonny before lunch, asking if he could cash a $300 check since I was rarely in Manhattan to go to the one branch of the Amalgamated Bank of New York.

Surprisingly, my parents were a little cold to Sweetie. The issues, I'm guessing, were that Sweetie was five years older than me and had two kids. Oh, and wasn't Jewish, which, as far as I'm concerned, is a blessing. Jews are fine, smart, funny, and kind people, but Jews shouldn't marry Jews—no offense.

Near the end of an awkward first double date, I gave Dad my check for $300, and he reached into the breast pocket of his houndstooth sports jacket and pulled out a small wad of pre-counted $20 bills, folded in half.

I opened the fold and started to count the twenties to make sure there were fifteen.

"Barry?" Sweetie said, in a kind of kicking me under the table voice.

"What, Sweetie?"

"You don't need to count the money. I mean..."

I lifted my left hand to stop her and, with my right, made the international "give me" sign at Dad, suggesting he needed to give me something—which in this case, was twenty bucks.

Dad reached into his other breast pocket, where he had the missing twenty ready to fork over in case I was rude enough to count the wad of cash.

"Is this normal?" Sweetie asked the table.

"Oh, it's normal," the three Sonnenfelds replied in unison.

CHAPTER 23

Dolores

ank Danski was looking for a cheap non-union cameraman to film interstitial footage for a show he was producing on behalf of New York's local PBS station. I fit the bill. Although *Blood Simple* had been photographed, it would be over a year before it was released.

Here's an interesting Hank fact: Hank is a procrastinator. He has been married twice. Each wife gave birth to a child of his on the 59th Street Bridge, halfway between Queens and Manhattan.

Hank, his sound guy, and I flew to Atlanta to shoot a short film about Dolores French, a smart, red-headed prostitute. She was the media's favorite whore. If Ted Koppel wanted to get a working girl's perspective on legalizing prostitution, he'd call Dolores. She was friends with all the top Atlanta politicians—on a nonsexual basis, I assume. Dolores was an author and an occasional porn actress. But mainly, she was a prostitute.

The filming of Dolores consisted of a very tame talking head interview. I lit her to look sexy, draping her red bodices over various bedroom lamps. She wore an emerald green satin robe that revealed a lot of her natural, pendulous cleavage. Between the red lighting and her green outfit, it took on an unfortunate Christmas vibe, which wasn't really what we were going for. Lesson learned.

Dolores French

We filmed her shopping for lingerie, chatting on faked phone sex calls, and pretending she was setting up appointments with her johns.

When we were done filming, Dolores drove us back to our very crappy motel just off the interstate. She dropped the sound guy and Hank off first, then drove around the motor court to my side of the one-story structure. We had joked around during the day and wanted to hang out. She suggested we buy a bottle of vodka and chat in my room for a while. At some point, girlfriendless, several vodkas to the wind—poured into those cloudy plastic motel cups covered with waxy paper condoms—I was grilling Dolores for specifics about being a prostitute and asked how much she charged her clients.

"For you? A hundred."

"For me?" I stuttered.

"Isn't that why you were asking, Barry, darling?"

Um.

"Will you take a check?"

"Absolutely."

I pulled out my Amalgamated Bank of New York checkbook and wrote her a check. She smiled, put it in her purse, and went to the area of the motel room's sink. It was one of those places with a small bathroom not much bigger than a closet for the toilet and fiberglass shower and a separate space for the sink and towels against the back wall of the bedroom.

I laid on the bed, fully clothed.

She turned from the sink and walked toward me with a damp hand towel, the kind my mother might place across her forehead when she had "a splitting headache." Not really what I wanted to be thinking about.

For services rendered.

A couple of hours later, Dolores French was my girlfriend. I gave her my phone number and said if she ever was in New York to call me.

Three days later, Dolores phoned.

She loved me.

She needed desperately to be with me. She was calling from a pay phone in a department store because when she told her boyfriend we had sex, he threatened to kill me, but I shouldn't worry.

She was heading to Berlin next week for a sex show and prostitute convention, but she would route her ticket back through New York if I'd pick her up at JFK.

Uh, yeah, I would.

We'd drive in my very small 1972 Honda Civic out to my "starter home" in East Hampton.

I was 29 years old, skinny, practically a virgin, and barely making a living.

Yet, a serious, no kidding around good-looking prostitute, after a few hours of sex, was in love with me. It was quite an ego boost.

Waiting at JFK on the other side of immigration, I had no idea what to expect. Scores of travelers from her plane had glided past me, with no Dolores in sight. If she was on the flight, would she be in "business attire"? And if so, what version of "business attire"? Corporate executive or whore? Would she look at me and make a U-turn back into customs?

Different planeloads of passengers departed. Still no Dolores.

Then she made her appearance.

It was business attire.

That is, if her line of work was playing the role of a hooker on a Cinemax softcore porn movie.

I got a whiff of Dolores before I saw her. I was facing away from the security doors when their opening wafted the scent of a very aromatic perfume into the waiting area.

Its fragrance said, "I'm a whore, and later Barry Sonnenfeld will be having sex with me."

Ms. French had traveled from Berlin to New York in a dress that barely covered her breasts. Her chest was adorned with a series of very colorful feather boas wrapped around her neck yet somehow managing to not cover any seriously important cleavage. Her lipstick was ruby red. Her eyelashes were long.

Boy, she was wearing a lot of rouge.

And a lot of perfume.

She smiled and stuck out her tongue as she approached me, arms opening for an embrace. Over the course of the next two minutes, Dolores' red lipstick transferred from her full lips to mine.

Dolores had arrived at JFK on a summer Friday night, which meant a three-hour drive from the airport to the Hamptons. She was getting hornier with each slowly passing Long Island Expressway exit and frustrated that the drive was taking so long—she really wanted to show me her newly pierced nipples.

At some point, between where the LIE came to an end and the additional hour drive to my home, Dolores, having reapplied her lipstick for the occasion, performed an act that I suspect is still illegal in certain southern states, especially when the person who is being acted upon is driving a car.

The next evening, Dolores and I were going over to Susan and Elliott's house. Elliott had a 16mm projector and rented movies from the MOMA film department to project in his East Hampton home. Since I lived nearby, I was often invited over for movie night, mostly because they needed a free projectionist.

Dolores insisted that we have sex one more time before heading over to the screening. She was already wearing her best fuck-me outfit, was doused, almost bathed, in fuck-me perfume, and had applied a slightly excessive amount of fuck-me glitter on her face. We had a quickie on the sunken living room's couch.

This is who Dolores fell in love with, BBQing
in the Hamptons.

When we got to Elliott and Susan's, the rest of the assembled guests had already arrived. The party included Steve Ross, Warner Bros.' CEO; Ted Carpenter, a noted anthropologist; and his partner, Adelaide de Menil, of the Menil Foundation. As Susan took me aside to brush glitter off my face and hair, she mantra'd:

"Have sex. Don't marry."

"Believe me."

Dolores was seated next to Ted.

He put out his hand for a shake: "Ted Carpenter. Anthropologist."

Shaking it, Dolores countered, "Dolores French. Prostitute."

"I guess we're both in the people business," Ted replied.

*   *   *

A week later I drove Dolores back to the airport. She promised her Atlanta boyfriend was not going to kill me. She would "take care of it." For the next year, I was Dolores' New York boyfriend. I have very fond memories of the Chelsea Hotel. Eventually, the long-distance relationship wore on us, and I had fallen in love with another woman. We parted as friends.

CHAPTER 24

The Coens

In the winter of 1980 I was at a pre-Christmas party thrown by Hillary Ney and her husband, Dick. They were from Darien, Connecticut. Her father, whom the Coens and I called "Whispering Ed," was president, chairman of the board, and CEO of Young and Rubicam, at the time the biggest, waspyish ad agency in the world. Ed had three kids; they all were, to various degrees, wacky. I was invited to the party because I was friends with Hillary's brother, Nick Ney.

I met Nick at the Republican and Democratic National Conventions in Miami in 1972. I got to be a page for NBC through Cousin Mike the Child Molester, who worked at the company as their party planner. Nick was hired because one of Whispering Ed's biggest clients was Gulf Oil, the sponsor of NBC Nightly News' *The Huntley–Brinkley Report*.

When Nick and my Eastern Airlines plane arrived in Miami, we had to sit on a hot bus for a half hour, waiting for transport back to the terminal from the tarmac because Nick had dropped his clear hippie glasses out of his shirt pocket and into the plane's toilet. We were waiting for a mechanic willing to stick his hand into the shit receptacle to pull them out. Eventually, some hero did the deed. Nick and I hit it off.

Hillary and me, 1978.

So here I was at a party in a Soho loft, hosted by Hillary and Dick. Every attendee except me and one other guy was very rich. All of them, upon their parents' death, would inherit Pennsylvania coal mines and Caribbean islands.

Not like us.

Across the room, I saw a tall, gangly guy with curly, unkempt hair who seemed equally uncomfortable and Semitic. A tad Howard Stern–ish. Like me, he also wasn't wearing Prada black. His name was Joel Coen, otherwise known as the taller Coen brother. He knew Hillary from Simon's Rock, a boarding school they both attended in Massachusetts. Joel had attended NYU undergraduate film school, and although I had recently gotten a degree from NYU's Graduate Film School, the two programs had no overlap and, in fact, were rivals.

Joel and I had very different feelings about film. He loved them and, along with his brother, Ethan, had been making home movies in Minnesota since they were 8 and 5.

I had attended NYU with little interest in film and had used graduate school as a method to stay out of the job market for three years while managing to build up a large debt of student loans and credit card bills. By the end of the three years, although hardly a film buff, I had discovered I was a decent cameraman.

Recently, Wim Wenders' *The American Friend* had been released. Joel and I talked about the masterful job that Robbie Mueller, the Director of Photography, had done on the movie. It seemed we shared a mutual aesthetic about cinematography.

Joel explained the Coen brothers' plan for breaking into the film business. After NYU, Joel had spent a year at UT Austin's graduate film school because his wife at the time was attending school there. He hated the program but got a good feel for Austin. He and his brother, Ethan, wrote a taut, small thriller set in Austin around very specific locations he knew well. Now he was back in New York, having recently divorced.

Joel was working for Edna Paul, an editor of low-budget horror movies. Sam Raimi had just filmed *Evil Dead*, and Edna was cutting it. Sam gave Joel his advice on how to finance an independent feature: Write a script and film a trailer as if it were a finished movie. Use the trailer to raise the money.

I told Joel I owned a 16mm movie camera.

"You're hired."

Over the next several weeks we met at the brothers' apartment at 280 Riverside Drive, which was below street level. There was a grated window where we watched passing shoes.

Joel and Ethan would pace while I usually laid on the floor with a wet towel on my face—was I already becoming my mother?

"What if we tracked on the back of the boots?"

"Outside or inside?"

"Road or wood floor?"

"How do we get out of the shot?"

"Dotted line of the road."

Joel and Ethan were like a human version of a school of fish, or a flamboyance of flamingos that hypnotize you on YouTube videos. How do those fish and birds know who's in the lead and when they should turn on a dime? That's what it was like watching Joel and Ethan pace.

Joel would follow Ethan. They would turn on their mark. Now Ethan is following Joel. It all makes sense, but suddenly Joel turns, and instead of Ethan, who was behind Joel, doing a 180 to take the lead, on this particular turn Ethan continues to pace, going behind Joel, letting Joel stay in front.

Or not.

It would go on for hours, and the tension, at least for me, of never knowing what psychic communication those two brothers were signaling was fascinating and gave me a headache, hence the wet towel across my eyes.

A different version of their psychic communication would happen on the *Blood Simple* set. After a take with an actor Joel would mumble, "Cut," and Ethan would say, "Hey, Jo," and Joel would say, "I know. I'll tell him."

We needed the trailer to raise $750,000. The thinking was that doctors, entrepreneurs, and lawyers who might invest couldn't read a script and know if it was commercial, nor could they tell if we knew what we were doing, but show them a trailer, and two things happen:

First, a trailer is something everyone is an expert on.

"I'd go see that movie." "That looks exciting."

Second, the trailer showed we could produce something that looked professional.

"It looks just like a trailer you'd see in a movie theater," said my chain smoking dentist, Dr. Yeshion.

A quick aside about dentists. When I was five my dentist died on me. Took a bow into my lap and stopped breathing. My parents, who were always short of money, took this as a blessing, insisting that the world of dentistry was too traumatic for little Barry. When I was fourteen, at which point I had fifteen cavities, my parents made friends with dentist Bob Yeshion of Riverdale. He did my dentistry for free but was bitter about it, so he smoked the entire time I was in the chair. When Bob told my parents I needed braces, Kelly insisted they would ruin my french horn embouchure—although the real issue was cost.

I was in my early fifties, sitting in the waiting room of Chloe's orthodontist when my adorable 11-year-old dragged her doctor by the hand into the reception area.

"If you think I need braces, look at my dad!" said a very excited Chloe.

Hours later, we both left the office with braces. For several years we'd have back to back appointments so Chloe could pick the colors of my rubber bands.

Since I wasn't sure we'd raise the $750,000 for *Blood Simple*, I thought at least I'd have something great looking for my reel—the résumé of film footage I'd use to get more work. The nine feature-length pornos weren't going to help. I convinced Joel and Ethan that in spite of my owning a 16mm film camera—and the reason I was hired—we should film the trailer in 35mm.

A 35mm Arriflex IIC, with a motor too loud to be used for filming with sound, was cheap to rent. If we rented it for one day, the Friday before President's Day weekend, we could pick the camera up Thursday for Friday's rental; film Thursday night, Friday day and night, Saturday day and night, Sunday day and night; and, since Monday was a holiday and Ferco, the rental house, was closed, return the camera Tuesday morning. For the cost of a one-day Friday rental, we had the camera for five nights and four days.

We designed the trailer to require no actors, just bodies. It had no dialogue. Just music, sound effects, and title cards. We tied a two-by-six-foot piece of lumber to my Oldsmobile Cutlass' front bumper, mounted the camera on it, and ran a long cable from the camera to Ethan, smoking in the passenger seat with a battery on his lap. Joel was in back, also smoking.

We drove up the Henry Hudson Parkway, the Saw Mill, the New York State Thruway, and Route 17 to the all night Big Apple Diner, where we'd stop for coffee. Filming started around 11:00 p.m., when traffic thinned out, and we'd film until predawn. The Oldsmobile straddled the middle of the road, the yellow dotted line under the lens. We were lucky and never got pulled over.

We built a sheet rocked wall in Hillary's loft. The idea was to have the camera track in on the wall as bullet holes shot out, sending beams of light in various directions. When *Blood Simple* was released several years later, the bullet hole sequence was the iconic scene that most reviewers mentioned.

Of course, we couldn't afford bullets or professional movie "squibs" (tiny bags of gunpowder). Those were way beyond our ability or finances. Instead, we used a drill to cut one and a half inch circles out of the sheet rock. We then put these plugs back in, added a thin layer of plaster over all the plugs, and on the back side inserted large screws into each plug with a number.

As the camera tracked toward the pristine wall, a film school friend of Joel's was waiting on the other side with a big mallet. I would yell, "One! Four! Two! Seven! Six! Five! Nine!" as if I actually knew where each number was located. At each call the mallet would hit the appropriate screw with such force and the plug would shoot through frame so fast, it was invisible to the camera. In its stead, a beam of brightness from the twenty small lights called inkies aimed at the plugs would suddenly appear.

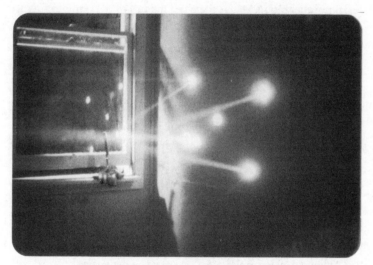

Perhaps the most iconic shot from Blood Simple.

When we viewed the footage at the lab the following Wednesday we were flabbergasted. It looked great. Joel edited the footage down to trailer length, adding sound effects and music. In a stroke of luck, Edna, the horror film editor, convinced Lee Dichter to mix the sound elements. Lee did it for free because he wanted to get out of commercials and into features. He went on to become *the* New

York sound mixer, working on Woody Allen's, Nora Ephron's, and the first *Men in Black* films.

It took us a year to raise the money for *Blood Simple*. Ethan quit his job as a statistical typist at Macys. Yes, Griffin the Archanan in his speech to Agents J and K at Shea Stadium says Cleon Jones would have been born Clara, *a statistical typist* if his parents didn't have an extra glass of wine before going to bed. In any case, Ethan, who had been making an additional fifty cents an hour since he was one of the few people willing to spend eight hours a day typing serial numbers, quit Macys to spend his full time trying to finance our show.

Joel was done with his job on *Evil Dead*. I was the only one who had any money and would often pay for our late-night meals at a diner on 66th and Broadway. After pretending to look at the menu, which we had memorized, Joel and Ethan would sheepishly say, "Hey, Ba. Can we get the freshly squeezed orange juice tonight?"

I always said yes.

One of my jobs was as the production manager on a music video for Ritchie Blackmore's "Rainbow." I suggested some prop people—there is always smoke in music videos, which is the purview of the prop department.

"Anyone can do smoke. We don't need an expensive prop person. Just move one of the production assistants to smoke," the video's producer declared.

I really thought that was a bad idea, so as a self-fulfilling prophecy I put Joel in charge of smoke. I had hired the brothers as PAs to pick up food supplies, run errands, and make phone calls. It meant hundreds of dollars in salary for the week, and maybe a few meals I wouldn't have to buy them.

Joel was a lousy production assistant—on his first day he got two parking tickets and couldn't find a coffee maker. I assigned the coffee maker job to Ethan and told him, "Look, at the end of the job they're going to let me have the coffee maker. Buy a decent one."

He returned from Canal Street with the cheapest Mr. Coffee he could find.

"I couldn't do it, Ba. It seemed to me that coffee is coffee. And this one was six bucks."

During the first rehearsal of Ritchie Blackmore's song, as the smoke was getting quite heavy, the producer smugly sidled up to me.

"I told you anyone could do smoke."

We looked over to see Joel in a frozen daze, mesmerized by the Rosco Fogger, the device used to make smoke, which was presently a melting mess of metal and black plastic engulfed in flames.

Yes, Joel made some great smoke. Unfortunately, it was highly toxic, since if you don't put any smoker "juice" into the device—a step Joel somehow skipped—the heating element uses the machine itself as fuel. An hour later, after the crew was evacuated and the stage aired out, Joel was demoted back to making coffee with the lousy Mr. Coffee machine and we got a real prop guy.

During the year of *Blood Simple*'s fund-raising, Joel spent most of his time in Minneapolis, where the boys grew up. He was armed with a list of the biggest donors to Hadassah, the Jewish women's hanging-out-together society. Ethan and I continued in New York City, bringing a 16mm reduction print and projector to various dentist investing clubs, rich friends of parents, and other assorted people with money. Whispering Ed did not partake of the opportunity. My parents' rich friend Lou McAuliffe invested. Lou had been married to Meryl Bunis, the UFT member who, as previously reported, tragically died of, according to my mother, blood poisoning from the red dye in her Italian shoes. Lou, now a widower, had designed a cheaper spray pump for plastic bottles and was a multimillionaire.

Fifteen thousand dollars got you a point. Fifty points, or $750,000, represented 50% of the show. The other half was controlled and doled out by Joel and Ethan as they saw fit—to themselves for producing, writing, directing, and editing; to the actors; and to me.

We raised the money. It was time to head to Austin.

Left to right: *Ethan, Fran McDormand's shoe, Joel, and me. New Year's Eve during the filming of* Raising Arizona.

CHAPTER 25

Blood Simple

Joel, Ethan, and I had never been on a film set before our first day on *Blood Simple*. I had never been a cameraman on a feature, nor worked in the camera department of a real movie in any capacity. Joel had never directed anything outside of student films and home movies, and Ethan had never produced. We simply declared ourselves filmmakers.

The canon of Joel and Ethan's youthful Super 8 work included *Lumberjacks of the North*, *Henry Kissinger: Man on the Go*, *Advise and Consent (a Super 8 Reinterpretation)*, and *Ziemers in Zambezi*, which was their Super 8 remake of *The Naked Prey*.

None of their previous work really prepared them for the road ahead.

We spent three months in Austin in pre-production, then filmed *Blood Simple* in a couple of months, alternating five- and six-day workweeks.

The catchphrase "For a Day or a Lifetime" has appeared in various Coen Brothers and Barry Sonnenfeld films. The stationery at the Hotel Earl in *Barton Fink* and the side of the camper in *RV* both exclaim, "For a Day or a Lifetime." It was the slogan of the Telegraph Hill Apartments, located just off Interstate 35 a few miles outside of Austin, where we lived for twenty weeks—more than a day, less than a lifetime.

From the movie RV: "For a Day or a Lifetime." Added bonus: an eight-foot image of me.

Each day of pre-production began at Denny's, where the boys and I ordered the Grand Slam Scrambled: two scrambled eggs, two sausage links, two pancakes, and two strips of well done bacon. Denny's had a community bulletin board at the front of the shop. We were intrigued by a photo of a missing person by the name of Clinkscales.

This teenager was also on a carton of milk, which for a while had missing kids' photos on them.

After breakfast, the three of us spent a few hours with an architect, a storyboard artist, and a local production assistant—a Slav named Andreas Laven. He seemed smart enough, so we made him our script supervisor. He had long blond hair and a face that screamed, *"I am a professional killer working for the KGB. I hate you and don't get your stupid ironic jokes. I also don't like working for Jews."*

We would sit around the architect's living room, designing shots for the movie. The process was as overproduced and control-freaked as the rest of the film. Joel, Ethan, and I had already shot listed all the camera angles at 280 Riverside Drive in New York the previous months. Now we were refining those shots based on our actual Austin locations.

Andreas, the never-before-employed-as-a-script-supervisor script supervisor, would write notes; the architect would draw a floor plan, a bird's-eye view showing where the camera was located and where the actors stood.

The storyboard artist would draw an illustration of what the camera was supposed to see. In bedroom scenes, he would draw Abby, the character played by Frances McDormand, naked, a blanket half covering her cleavage. This wasn't something we had requested, so we always hid the storyboards from Fran.

Below the floor plan and illustration, the bottom third of each sheet of the page was for lighting, camera, or editing notes.

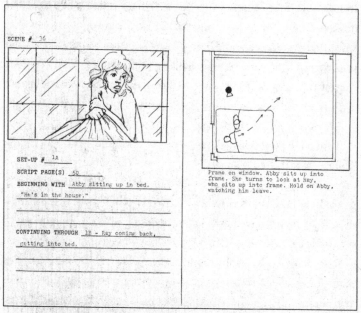

SCENE # 36

SET-UP # 1A

SCRIPT PAGE(S) 50

BEGINNING WITH Abby sitting up in bed.
"He's in the house."

CONTINUING THROUGH 1B - Ray coming back,
getting into bed.

Frame on window. Abby sits up into frame. She turns to look at Ray, who sits up into frame. Hold on Abby, watching him leave.

Typical page of Blood Simple*'s overproduced storyboard.*

The boys and I came up with nicknames for a variety of shots: Someone's point of view of a place that didn't have a person in frame was called a "Clinkscales," based on the missing Austin kid.

An insert, which is a close-up of something—a doorknob, a piece of paper, the back of a boot, a bullet—was always called the "Larry Kasdan Panty Insert," based on a specific shot in Kasdan's film *Body Heat*.

In the film, William Hurt throws a chair through Kathleen Turner's front glass door, enters her home, and pins her to the floor, and as the two breathe heavily, Hurt yoga positions her up and pulls off her panties. Larry then cuts to an insert of a section of carpet next to the lovers, slightly high angle, where we see Kathleen Turner's panties enter frame and drop to the rug. The Coens and I loved the shot.

We did, however, feel the angle was too steep. It would have been more filmic if the camera was right on the ground so that the panties broke frame from above, dropping directly in front of the camera's lens in extreme foreground. Larry had placed the camera high, looking down. The visual problem was that as the panties fall toward the carpet, the lingerie gets smaller, since the panties are now farther away from the lens, creating a less dynamic "money shot."

Years later Larry and I became good friends.

When I felt our friendship was on solid ground, I brought up the "Larry Kasdan Panty Insert," suggesting the camera should have been sitting on the carpet. To my surprise, Larry agreed. In fact, he told me he wanted the camera exactly where Joel, Ethan, and I thought it should have been, but Richard Kline, ASC, didn't want to spend the extra time to light it from what was clearly a better angle.

The rest of a typical pre-production day on *Blood Simple* was spent location scouting, which was always dreary. Endless hours in a car, getting out and asking someone where the bathroom was, then looking at a location for Ray's or Abby's home, which might have a great exterior on a great street but the rooms were too small, the ceiling too low, or the neighborhood too loud. We'd then schlep back in the car to the next location. This tedious process went on for many weeks and is, to this day, my least favorite part of filmmaking.

Thanks to a Los Angeles astrologer, the Coens and I were extremely lucky. Although we were very well organized, we were total novices. The night before our first day of filming I had the assistant cameraman bring the Arriflex BL3 to my apartment to show me where the on/off switch was.

For me, the single most important crew member was the key grip. Grips are the guys that build things. They also lay track for and move the camera. Our grip would have to figure out how to execute all the outrageous, self-conscious shots Joel and Eth and I had designed. Without a great key grip, *Blood Simple* would have been less of a movie.

That's where the astrologer enters our picture. Tom Prophet was one of the best grips in Los Angeles. Unfortunately for Tom, his wife's astrologer told her that Los Angeles was about to have a major earthquake. Mrs. Prophet insisted they leave town pronto. Tom had shot a movie in Austin, remembered loving the city, moved there, and opened a not successful sheet rock business that he shut down to join our show.

One of the most self-conscious shots was in a scene in which Fran McDormand's character finds herself in the back room of Julian Marty's (her estranged husband) bar. She looks around the room as we cut to various Larry Kasdan Panty Inserts, such as dead fish on a desk or a battered safe dial, while at the same time dazzling the audience with a Clinkscales of the empty back room of the bar, where the rear door's glass window has been broken.

Tom built a special rig that would allow Fran and the camera—both mounted on a mini scaffolding of pipes, couples, and elbows—to maintain the same distance and angle to each other as they descended through space. The rig would pivot ninety degrees to rotate the background, while the relationship between the camera and Fran remained a constant. At the beginning of the shot the back of the bar is her background. As both camera and Fran pivot, it feels like she and the audience are falling through space, our collective stomachs going queasy. The end of the shot has her head landing on a pillow. We then pull back in a different location—her loft, as the audience wonders if any of what she saw was real or a dream.

The moment becomes more surreal when Abby sees her husband sitting across the room, since the audience knows Marty is dead.

When we asked Tom how he designed this one-off specialty rig, he proudly told us he had seen blueprints for a similar sex device in *Hustler* and was hoping we'd let him keep the rig at the end of the show.

Setting the angle on Tom's sex machine.

At some point one of our cameras, the new Arriflex IIIc, started recording a double image of every frame—the second overlaid image a ghostly version of the original. The lab couldn't figure out the problem, and we surely didn't know what was causing the issue, so Arriflex sent Euie, their most Germanest technician, to Austin to suss out the situation. We showed him several angles of the double exposed footage of Marty, played by Dan Hedaya, being shot by his rival.

His prognosis was instantaneous:

"Yes. I see the problem," Euie pronounced.

"Yes. Yes. To me, it is not realistic. You show the one man aiming the gun at this angle, almost at his head, yet in the next shot, the other man is killed in the heart area, down here. This is not to me realistic."

Joel scowled in my direction.

"No. Euie. We mean. The camera. What is causing every frame to be double exposed?"

"Of this I have no idea. It is a mistake, no?"

"Well, yeah. It's like a really big mistake."

"I suggest you use a different camera."

Until my mid-30s, my stress indicator was vomiting. Although I'm still a sympathetic vomiter—if I see, smell, or hear it, I'm there—my anxiety barometer over the last thirty-five years has evolved from vomiting to debilitating sciatica.

The first day filming *Blood Simple*—the first day I had ever been on a movie set—we were shooting a scene at a strip club. Joel, Ethan, and I pulled off the road on the way to work so I could throw up. We got through the day on schedule.

The next morning we filmed the opening credits scene. Abby (Fran McDormand) and Ray (John Getz) are driving Ray's car in the rain at night. The camera was in the back seat looking out toward the rain pelted windshield, with Ray and Abby silhouetted in the foreground—it didn't matter what car we used since we never saw its exterior. We wanted the two actors close together in the frame and used a small Fiat.

The exterior of Ray's car was an Oldsmobile, although over the year of post-production, when we needed a car for an insert, we also used a Volvo and a Buick. Each auto was a different color. No one has ever noticed.

The Fiat was parked in a garage whose walls were covered in a black fabric called duvetyne. The prop person, whom we would fire after two days of filming, was sitting on the roof of the car with a Hudson sprayer and a spray wand, sprinkling the windshield, simulating rain. A grip with a two-by-four rocked the underside of the car to imply movement. I had a series of small lights on a dolly draped in black to match the dark garage. They would dim up in brightness as the lights would dolly past the lens, simulating a passing car.

The aforementioned prop woman was a disaster and had to go. She was full of silent schmucks and was incompetent. It was due to her firing that the Coens and I created the concept of giving a crew person a cake when being let go—our version of "swimming with the fishes" but less violent. Throughout the three films I did with the brothers, and then as a director, "giving someone a cake" is code for firing them.

Another bright idea from *Blood Simple* I continue to embrace is to start filming on a Thursday or Friday. There is always a crew member you immediately realize has no place on your show. By not starting on a Monday, you're not stuck with the slug for too long. A day or two, tops—then the cake. You've got the weekend to find a new person and bring them up to speed.

Film sets love sheet cakes. Here's one Scott Rudin commissioned. It's on the set of The Addams Family *the day after I shut down production by fainting.*

After wrap on the second day I drove the Coens to our production office, where there was a 35mm projector set up to watch the strip club dailies from the first day of filming. The boys and I were about to see the first footage shot by any of us in our professional careers. The projector rolled, and there was an image. The angles looked great and the acting was fine. I stopped the screening, left the room, and threw up. All the pent-up tension—was I good enough to be a cinematographer on a feature film?—exploded from the depth of my stomach.

Unfortunately, the film lab had printed the footage too bright, making it look like bad porn, which, I admit, was my oeuvre.

My camera notes to DuArt, the film lab in New York, had been "MAKE LOOK NICE." Once I changed it to "MAKE LOOK DARK," the dailies started to look great. Still, I threw up every third day.

On almost all feature films a specialist—the camera operator—is hired to physically operate the camera. The Coens couldn't afford an additional crew member, so on the three films we did together it fell to me to badly operate as well as be the cinematographer.

Unfortunately for Joel and Ethan, when we started to work together the cost of a video feed from the camera to a television monitor was too expensive, so I was the only person who witnessed the photography in real time through the camera's viewfinder.

By the way, video playback was invented by Jerry Lewis.

Joel and Ethan relied on my bad operating, not knowing what I was filming until the next night at dailies. One entire scene was shot in Maurice the bartender's bedroom with Debbie Reinisch, my ex-girlfriend and our first assistant director, sitting against the back wall—walkie-talkie attached to her hip, headphones over her head—fast asleep. In every take. The scene couldn't be used, though Joel and Ethan thought about leaving it in the movie and giving Debbie credit as Maurice's girlfriend.

I am easily distracted, assuming whatever is going on nearby is surely more interesting than what I'm doing. To avoid distractions while operating the camera I had a large piece of black cloth that I put over my head. Joel, Ethan, and I would often call for my "schmatta"—Yiddish for piece of cloth—when we were ready to film. Tom Prophet assumed "schmatta" was East Coast film lingo he had just never been privy to.

Tom's "Would you like me to put on your schmatta, sir?" always made me smile.

I was wearing my schmatta, filming a close-up of Fran, when the camera tilted down Fran's body, from her face toward her feet. Since the storyboard called for the camera to remain on Fran's face, Joel and Ethan thought I was calling an audible but were confused by how I thought they could use the shot. The tilt was not actually my idea, either. I had fallen asleep. It was based on this shot that Joel tried to convince me my memoir should be titled *Asleep at the Eyepiece: The Barry Sonnenfeld Story*.

We finished the film on time and on budget and headed back to New York, where Joel and Ethan spent a year editing the footage. Their cutting room was in the National Film Building at 1600 Broadway. At the time, De Palma's editor Jerry Greenberg was on the same floor cutting *Scarface*. It was the rare afternoon that either Joel, Ethan, or I went to the seventh floor's bathroom that Jerry Greenberg wasn't in there.

"Greenberging" became our code word for taking a shit.

Joel himself spent a fair amount of time in the bathroom. Ethan and I suggested his biography should be titled *Between Two Stools: The Joel Coen Story*.

The brothers struggled to finish the film. We needed additional coverage in certain key scenes, which ended up being filmed in the backyard of my "starter home" in East Hampton. The house was built by New Sunshine, a local developer, on a quarter acre plot in the blue collar section of town. It was one of three models to choose from. Mine came with a "love pit," a sunken area of the living room for socializing. For a short time, I dated a Catholic girl. After sex, often on the couch in the love pit—the same one Dolores French and I commandeered—she would announce:

"That made me very sad. I feel so bad at what we just did."

She also mentioned, while watching *Taxi Driver* on my 25" RCA—at the time a large television—that the color of the New

York City police uniforms was exactly the color she wanted for her bridesmaids' dresses when she got married.

"Have sex. Don't marry," advised Sweetie.

There is a key moment in *Blood Simple* when Ray, the boyfriend, buries a still alive Julian Marty in an open field late at night. Joel and Eth felt they needed additional angles to make the scene more horrific.

Joel and I buried Ethan behind my starter home.

We dug a deep hole, put Ethan into it, covered him with dirt, and as I shot over Joel's legs (in Ray's clothing) Joel shoveled more and more of my yard onto the writhing pile of hidden Ethan.

Joel and I figured Eth probably could still breathe under all the detritus, since the pile of dirt was still moving.

At some point, Joel wanted a shot of the dirt mound not moving and yelled, "Hey, Eth. Stop struggling."

Ethan couldn't hear Joel under what was now quite a mound of soil and continued to frantically move around the dirt.

"For Christ's sake, Eth. Stop moving."

The frantic underground action continued.

"Eth. Don't move. Stop moving."

There was no change in Ethan's performance.

"Cut. Dammit," Joel snapped.

Joel dug a little hole with his hands, estimating where Ethan's head might be. He guessed right, and with a half dozen scoops of earth we were looking at a vignetted Ethan face.

"Hey, Eth. I just want some footage of the grave with no movement. We'll cover you up again, but don't move."

"Hey, Joel."

"What, Eth?" Joel said, slightly annoyed.

"Never mind."

"Hey, Eth. Just tell me."

"Well, I'm just thinking... If what you want is the grave with no movement at all..."

"Good point," laughed Joel. "Hey, Ba. Help me lift him out."

Ethan prepares to be buried. My backyard. East Hampton, New York.

Many months into post-production, I visited the editing room and saw they had cut out a dynamic shot that would become one of the critics' and fans' favorite moments. The shot takes place at Marty's dance hall. The camera is low to the top of the bar. As

Maurice the bartender chats up an actress (Fran's stand-in), the camera tracks toward them, scraping along the bar. Halfway down the long bar top is a drunk guy passed out in the foreground. As the camera approaches, we boom up, just scraping past his prone head, continuing our path toward the eventual two shot of the actors.

"Why'd ya cut out the shot?"

"Eth and I thought it was too self-conscious."

"You're picking on that shot?" I whined.

"The whole movie is nothing *but* self-conscious shots. You might as well not release the film if you're going to take out all of our fancy film school stuff."

The Coens put it back in.

A rare image of Joel in the cutting room—as opposed to the bathroom.

The boys were eventually done editing, and we had a screening for our investors at the Bombay Movie Theater on West 57th Street in Manhattan. It was pouring rain that night, and the theater leaked. But that wasn't our biggest problem.

The investors hated the movie. More than a third walked out before it was over. Of the ones that stayed, most weren't even polite in their post screening criticism.

Though devastated, Joel and Ethan submitted *Blood Simple* to the New York Film Festival, where it was accepted.

The Coens and I were leaving our local Greek luncheonette on the Upper West Side when I looked at my watch:

"Hey. I think the film festival critics' screening of *Blood Simple* is like right now. Just across the street at Lincoln Center. Let's go stand in the back of the theater and watch a couple of minutes."

"Please, no, Ba. Haven't we seen it enough?" said Ethan, lighting a cigarette.

"C'mon, Ba. Anything but that," Joel moaned.

"I know we've never had a good screening, but maybe the critics will get it. C'mon. It will be fun."

As we walked through the lobby toward the auditorium, we heard laughter.

And as we got closer, more laughter.

"Wrong theater," Ethan shrugged.

"I think we're in the right place," I said.

"Wrong time," said Joel, as we heard a huge laugh.

Joel, Ethan, and I opened the door in the back of the theater. We were greeted by another laugh from the critics. Staring down at us was a perfectly projected print of *Blood Simple*, large and beautiful. Finally, an audience liked our film. Luckily they were all film critics.

The entire cast and crew of Blood Simple. *Far right bottom row are the three grips, Tom Prophet next to Joel, who is next to me in my Shady Brady cowboy hat. Farther down the row with cigarette in his mouth is Andreas the Slav. Behind Joel and me are Debbie and Ethan. Photographed with a Toyo 4x5 Field Camera.*

CHAPTER 26

Big

I was desperate to be hired as the cinematographer on *Big*. The producer, Bobby Greenhut, was the best in New York, producing many of the movies filmed there. If I could get in his good graces, maybe I could work in my hometown more often. Greenhut had a wicked sense of humor. When describing Gordon Willis' very dark lighting on the movies Greenhut produced for Woody Allen, Greenhut quipped, "Gordon Willis lights for radio."

I had been the cinematographer on two low-budget Coen films—*Blood Simple* and *Raising Arizona*—as well as Frank Perry's independent movie *Compromising Positions* when I went for an interview. The Coen Brothers movies had gotten a lot of attention, so David Gersh, my agent, was able to arrange a meeting with Penny Marshall, *Big*'s director.

I arrived at *Big*'s office on 57th Street and was escorted into a room I could barely see into due to the harsh direct rays of sun coming through the window, backlighting Penny's cigarette smoke. Sitting behind Penny was a man who smiled at me but neither introduced himself nor spoke. He was dressed in blue New York Giants football gear down to his blue sneakers. He looked like a Smurf.

He grinned a lot.

I assumed the guy was Penny's cousin who was either mentally challenged or at least shy and a tad off. In the foreground Penny started to tell me about the look she wanted for *Big*: When the kid is a kid, the camera should be low and naive. When he is transformed into an adult, the camera should be higher and more sophisticated. I listened and tried not to interrupt. I *really* wanted the job.

This is what I knew: steadfast rules of cinematography never work. What if we want to be low angle, looking up at adult Josh to see a building behind him, but we can't because low angle is only for young Josh? What if we want to be high angle, looking down at young Josh, as he reaches for a can of Kelly's (no relation) Irish Potatoes, but we can't because high angle is only for adult Josh?

It was great that Penny had thought about how to tell her story visually, but I knew it wasn't going to work out the way she saw it. And I wasn't sure how to manifest a camera's naïveté or sophistication. Should I lie and say everything she suggested was brilliant and I would love to execute her vision? Should I disagree to prove I wasn't a yes man but risk losing the job?

Penny put out one last cigarette and mumbled,

"Well, whaddaya think?"

Here's what I said:

"Would it be okay if I just make it look nice?"

Penny turned to the Smurf in the back of the room and in an over the shoulder mutter said,

"Nice would be good."

The blue guy got out of his chair, put out his hand, and said,

"Nice meeting you. We'll be in touch."

"Nice meeting you, too. Hey. Who are you?"

"Bobby Greenhut," Greenhut chuckled as he led me out the door.

I had blown my interview.

"Would it be okay if I just made it look nice?" doesn't inspire confidence, although truthfully, most films fall short.

I was working on a SONY industrial for Howie Meltzer and Jon Klee. We were prelighting the stage for tomorrow's puppet work when my cell phone rang.

Cell phone rang? In the mid-'80s?

I was an early adopter of technology. A decade later I had a monthly column in *Esquire* called "The Digital Man," where every month I reviewed gadgets. In the mid-'80s, I was answering a Panasonic EF-6151eb, which was about a foot square and six inches deep. The handset was attached to the huge body (mainly battery) with a coiled cable. The antenna rotated so you could lie the beast flat or upright.

Panasonic EF-6151eb

"Hello?"

"Sonnenfeld? This is Greenhut."

"Hi, Bobby. What's up?"

"I was walking to work this morning, and I realized we start filming in ten weeks and we still don't have a cinematographer so I said to myself, 'Why not just hire that idiot Sonnenfeld?'"

"Ya know, Bobby. Thank you very much, but I don't want to be hired on those terms."

"What are you talking about? I'm offering you the job."

"Not as that idiot Sonnenfeld. If you want to hire me, let's have another interview so you can hire that really smart guy Sonnenfeld."

"Are you serious?"

"I want another interview."

"You know, Ba, you're a little nuts. All right. Can you come up to the office right now?"

I was done pre lighting and made my way from Mother's Stages, an old mansion in the East Village that had been converted to small soundstages, up to 57th Street.

As I got off the elevator and into the production's bull pen, Greenhut came out of his office and yelled across the room,

"I just got off the phone with the studio. They said hire the cheapest cameraman you can find."

"That I can do. As long as I'm not the idiot Sonnenfeld."

"Great. You're hired, Not Idiot Sonnenfeld. C'mon. The location van is waiting for us. We're scouting Rye Playland."

"Not with me."

"God. Now what, Not Idiot Sonnenfeld?"

"Bobby. I can't go scouting with you. We don't have a deal. If I go out to Rye Playland and say something you don't want to hear, like we'll need X amount of lights, or if I give Penny all the reasons why the location won't work, you'll fire me before I'm even hired."

"Jeez, you're tough. Hold on."

Greenhut went back into his office and came out three minutes later.

"Okay. I just spoke to Gersh. We've got a deal. Get in the van."

A few weeks later, 20th Century Fox shut down *Big*. Barry Diller, the chairman, didn't want to make the movie with Penny's first choice for the lead, Robert De Niro. He wanted to wait for Tom Hanks, who had just started another film. I went to LA and shot *Throw Momma from the Train* with Danny DeVito while Hanks fulfilled his previous commitment.

After finishing *Throw Momma*, I was back in New York, starting to work on *Big*.

Penny and I liked each other as people, but she truly disliked me as her cinematographer. We came from very different ways of working. Her expertise was acting and comedy. My strength was visual storytelling. It could have been a dynamic partnership, but that's not what happened.

Penny didn't like to make decisions and wanted as many options as possible. I came from film school, where each eleven minute roll of film, from raw stock through developing, cost several hundred dollars. For a film student, the solution to the enormous cost of making a movie was to pre-plan the edit and make every decision before you started to roll very expensive film.

Penny wanted a million different angles and would shoot many, many, many takes of each. I discovered just how much Penny didn't like to make decisions on the first day of filming, which was a one-night shoot at Rye Playland. We were filming in the summer, and our nights were relatively short.

The scene involved Tom Hanks and Elizabeth Perkins. During pre-production we filmed two hair and makeup tests with Elizabeth so Penny could decide if Perkins should be a blonde or redhead. Normally, these choices are made many weeks before filming so the wardrobe and makeup people can select outfits and makeup that complement the chosen hair color.

The evening before our first day of filming, Greenhut called Penny and me into his office.

"Pen. We start filming tomorrow night. What's it going to be? Blonde or redhead?"

"I don't know," Penny whined.

"Barry didn't do a good job shooting the tests."

"Well, Pen. You're going to have to decide," smiled Greenhut.

"Okay," Penny mumbled.

"We'll film it both ways."

So, the first night of *Big* we filmed every angle of the scene with Elizabeth as a blonde and then a redhead. Because of the time required to switch out wigs and change her makeup for each hair color—for every camera angle—we decided it would be faster to film every shot of Elizabeth as a blonde, then go back and refilm every single setup except for Hanks' close-ups as a redhead. We had a million tape marks on the ground with notes for where the camera was, where each light was, so we could quickly redo every shot.

During the filming of *Big* I discovered how Depends adult diapers worked. I rarely leave the set, and I don't think any crew member should either. It would drive me crazy when I needed an additional light or wanted to add a piece of track to a dolly move, and I'd ask, "Where's Rusty? Where's Dennis?" and some crew member would say, "In the bathroom, sir."

"Sir" is crew code for asshole, by the way.

I knew the boys were really on the pay phone with their broker or taking a quick nap, and I wanted to put a stop to it. Making the crew wear diapers might be the solution.

One weekend about halfway through the show I went to my local East Hampton IGA and bought a box of Depends adult diapers. I took off my pants and underwear, put on a set of Depends, and, thank God, stepped into the bathtub and peed. That's when I discovered what Depends don't do. It turns out they're not designed for full-on urination, so much as an occasional dribble. As the urine rapidly cascaded down my leg—those were the days—I said to myself, "Good to know."

Another example of Penny's indecision was in the now famous scene of Hanks and Perkins taking a limo ride through New York. The night of filming there were three grip and electric crews rigging three different cars with lights and cameras.

"Penny. You've had all of pre-production and eight weeks of shooting to decide. Is it the Subaru, the Corvette, or the limo?" Greenhut asked, as he pointed at three cars lined up in a row.

Penny had liked the Subaru XT because it had a colorful dashboard. She liked the Corvette because it was a convertible, and Josh, Hank's character, would have liked a Vette. And, finally, we had the limo.

"What does Barry think?" asked Penny.

"The limo."

"Okay. The limo," Penny mumbled.

Then she added:

"Just remember. I said it was a bad idear."

"Wait. Pen. Which would you prefer?"

"No. No. You said the limo. I'm just saying it's a bad idear."

Before I could respond, Bobby put his arm out in front of me to stop any further discussion and announced:

"It's the limo, guys. Stop rigging the Vette and other thing."

For Hanks' company's Christmas party, Penny asked the prop person to have caviar, knowing Tom would be brilliant in how shocked and disgusted he was by the taste. She also asked for baby corn, so that Tom could pick up the little pickled appetizer and eat it like it was a corn on the cob. Penny really knew where a joke was. She just didn't like making hard decisions and didn't like my visual style.

Penny and I got very little sleep. After filming for at least fourteen hours, we would drive to DuArt, our film lab, stand in the lobby for twenty minutes waiting for the elevator—every film lab in New York had shockingly slow elevators—and then watch literally two hours of 35mm projected dailies. Many people slept. Greenhut had a party-size red cup of Dewars handed to him at the screening room door. After dailies—sixteen hours into our day— Pen and I would be driven back to her apartment, where we discussed the angles for the next day.

While sitting in her living room trying to explain the shots I was suggesting, Penny would get three phone calls from people who had seen the previous day's dailies in LA. Jim Brooks, a producer on the show and Penny's friend, would tell her she needed more tight close-ups. Sara Colleton, a Fox executive assigned to our movie, would call and tell Penny she needed more wide shots. Finally, Scott Rudin, Fox's president of production who later produced my two *Addams Family* movies, would tell Penny to do whatever I suggested. I would get back to my apartment hours after midnight to get picked up at six.

Early Monday morning of the second week, we were setting up for a shot in young Josh's neighborhood in New Jersey, when Penny's driver arrived with her daily breakfast of a dozen White Castle hamburgers and a carton of Marlboros.

Penny, burger in her mouth, cigarette attached to her lower lip, squinted past the haze of smoke and mumbled,

"I tried to fi-a you this weekend, but they wouldn't let me."

"Who wouldn't, Pen? Who wouldn't let you fire me?"

"They wouldn't."

"Pen, you should have any cameraman you want. If you don't want me, you should get someone else. I'll understand."

"No. They said I can't fi-a you."

"I'm sorry, Pen."

"I called Danny. He says you're good, but I don't think so."

DeVito and I loved working together on *Throw Momma from the Train*, and he was a fan of my visual style. Danny was a friend of Penny's, so it made sense she would have given him a call.

"I don't know what to tell ya, Pen. I'm really sorry."

"No. It's okay. It's just that you're not very good."

Somehow, we got through another eleven weeks of filming. On schedule. There are dozens of stories too painful to tell, so I'll only give a few more.

Hanks' character works at a toy company. Robert Loggia's character was the president of the firm. We filmed the scene where Hanks meets cute with Elizabeth Perkins using a big crane—a twenty-three-foot giraffe with a remote head. The camera pulls Elizabeth and Robert down a hallway as they chat. Then the crane starts to pull away, booming up higher and higher. As the camera comes to a stop, high angle tilted down, we see Hanks walking along the opposite corridor, ninety degrees from Loggia and Perkins. At the intersection they crash into each other. Loggia falls, Perkins' papers fly everywhere, and the romance is on.

Between the beginning of the shot, when Perkins and Loggia are walking and talking, until the time they crash into Hanks, there is no coverage. The shot plays out as one continuous piece of acting. If anything goes wrong before the crash, call cut, because you can't use the take. Plain and simple.

Penny, as was her want, was on take 15.

Loggia limps up to Penny and says, "Pen. I love you. And I'll do whatever you need. But I'm an old man. I can't keep crashing into Tom. I'll give you one more take, then we have to move on. End of story."

That day, Sweetie, whom I was not yet married to—that would come at the wrap party for the Coens' *Miller's Crossing*—and Amy, her younger kid, were visiting the set. Amy was seven at the time. We all had headsets fed from the sound department so we could listen to the acting. We were standing next to Penny, watching the shot on a television monitor, the image fed from the movie camera.

We rolled film, and the actors started the scene. Almost immediately, Elizabeth screwed up a line. The take is no good. It can't be used in the movie. Loggia has said he won't fall again. Obviously, we should cut and start a new take. But Penny doesn't call cut.

"Penny," I whispered. "Call cut."

"Huh?"

"Perkins messed up her line. You have no coverage. We can't use this take.

"Loggia said he wouldn't fall . . ."

"I don't know what you're saying."

Sweetie nudges me. "Shouldn't she call cut?"

The actors continue to walk down the corridor toward the inevitable crash.

"Pen. Call cut."

"I don't know what you're saying."

Amy whispers to Sweetie, "Mom! Tell Barry to tell that lady to call cut."

The tension is palpable.

"Pen. Call. Cut."

"I don't understand."

The three actors are about to crash into each other.

"CUT," I yell.

No one, ever, for any reason, is allowed to call cut except the director. Pen looked at me confused.

"What happened?"

"A light went out," I said.

We did another take. It went well. It's in the movie.

Greenhut, Penny, Hanks, and me on the set of Big.

The Friday night *Big* was released I was at the back lot of Universal Studios, visiting Hanks on the set of *The 'Burbs*. A couple of weeks earlier, when I showed Penny the finished product, the final color-timed answer print, she said:

"I never thought you were a good cameraman. But you picked a good film stock."

Now I was in Tom's trailer, and we were commiserating about Penny's interview in that day's *Los Angeles Times*, where she was quoted as saying she never thought Tom was a particularly good actor, so she made sure to surround him with good actors to make him seem better.

There was a knock at Tom's door.

"We're ready for you, Tom," said the production assistant.

"Are there a lot of good actors out there? I'm not coming out unless I'm surrounded by them."

At the end of the day, Penny directed a good movie in spite of having to work with a bad cinematographer and a not very good actor.

Pay or Play

In film school I was pretty sure the only way I'd find myself in the fabled Brill Building—one of two places in Manhattan where films were edited—was if I were a Federal Express delivery guy, a job I would have excelled at.

I ended up delivering packages to the Brill Building, but not for FedEx. Before Federal Express offered early morning delivery, there was Network Couriers. The company started out with a specific mission: Television shows were filmed, edited, and sound mixed on the West Coast, but the finished product had to be transported back east for broadcast. As I would eventually learn, everything in the film and television industry gets finished at the last·possible minute, so blue plastic carrying cases with 2" quad videotape were sent overnight from LAX to JFK for broadcast that night.

Network Couriers guaranteed delivery in New York City by 9:00 a.m. Soon law firms and other businesses needing early overnight deliveries caught on to the company.

The packages flew as excess baggage on a commercial flight, which was cheaper than freight. This meant every night Network Couriers needed a passenger on the red-eye to be associated with all those packages, so anyone, even us lowly delivery guys, could ask to be the LA to New York passenger on any specific date, the result being a round trip economy ticket to the land of entertainment opportunity.

My neighbor Peter Exline got wind of the need for idiots willing to work two hours a day starting at the crack of dawn. Pete and I and eventually Bill Pope would meet the company vans at 32nd Street and Park Avenue, underneath the Grand Central Station overpass. The LA to New York red-eye flight arrived at JFK around 5:30 a.m. By 6:30, we'd be waiting in the Chock Full of Nuts across the street from our meeting place at one of the U-shaped counters, drinking Heavenly Coffee and alternating between the cream cheese on nut bread sandwich and the fried whole wheat white powdered sugar doughnuts that were crunchy on the outside and warm, soft, and oily on the inside. As you reached for the doughnut, you would start to feel grease coming out your nose pores. By 7:00 drivers arrived, we'd rearrange the bags and be assigned a truck.

Several times during the three years I had this high paying two-hour-a-day job, a package took me to the Brill Building.

A decade later, during a torrential rainstorm, I found myself walking into the lobby. The Brill Building's massive entry hall floor was marble, and on rainy days the doormen put down a long brownish carpet to prevent people from falling backward and splitting their heads open on the slippery, unforgiving stone. I walked through the revolving doors and was heading for the elevators to see the Coen brothers when I passed a short guy with a trench coat buttoned up in anticipation of the wind and rain he was about to face. A couple of steps after we passed, I heard a voice, as if a question, say, "Barry?"

I turned and realized I had passed and not recognized the great director Marty Scorsese.

I was the cinematographer on the last two weeks of Scorsese's

Goodfellas, most of which consisted of filming Ray Liotta's character when he was a kid. On my first night of filming I sat behind Robert De Niro and Marty, who were watching takes on a video playback monitor. They would occasionally nudge each other, turn around, look at me, turn back around, whisper to each other, and laugh hysterically—and believe me, hysterical laughter doesn't seem like a normal night in the lives of Scorsese and De Niro.

It was Bob's last night of filming.

As dawn was breaking and I was heading to the subway, De Niro was getting into his town car. He spotted me and in an incredibly sarcastic loud voice bellowed to all of sleeping Astoria, Queens:

"See ya around, Baaaaarrrrry."

He chuckled and bent down into his sedan.

The next evening at work I asked Marty if he and De Niro had been laughing at me the entire previous night. Without hesitation he said,

"Yeah."

"Why were you guys laughing at me?"

Scorsese, in that staccato way of his, didn't hesitate:

"I mean, look at you. You're 12."

That year had been a bizarre summer and fall, thanks to Warner Bros. Sweetie and I had been in Los Angeles finishing the color timing of *When Harry Met Sally*, on which I was the cinematographer. Rob Reiner and his girlfriend, Michele Singer, were throwing a Sunday afternoon party at Rob's house.

In the middle of the party, on a weekend no less, I got a call from my talent agency offering me the job of cinematographer on *Tango and Cash*, a film directed by Andrei Konchalovsky, starring Sylvester Stallone and Kurt Russell.

The cinematographer on the show, Don Peterman, had just quit due to a "family crisis." Peterman, by the way, would later be the Director of Photography on three films I directed, *Addams Family Values*, *Get Shorty*, and *Men in Black*. Don and I were both represented by the Gersh Agency.

Years earlier David Gersh, son of legendarily grumpy but refreshingly honest Phil, called me saying he'd just seen *Blood Simple* and if I didn't have an agent, I should come to LA for a meeting. A week later, facing down my fear of flying, I Pan Am'd to Hollywood and met the family in their Beverly Hills office.

David and Bob—the Gersh sons—told me what they were going to do for my career. Better movies, bigger movies, studio movies, union movies, eventually directing gigs.

I kept looking over at Phil, the founder of the company and earlier in his career Humphrey Bogart's agent, who was growing impatient. He'd rub his face, then sigh in a "silent schmuckian" manner.

I assumed that for some unspoken reason, he hated me. I hadn't been doing much of the talking, so I wasn't sure what his problem was. Finally, with a huge political grunt, he put his hands on his knees and in a typical old Jewish guy getting up way made a scary noise to help him rise, leaned forward within inches of my face, and said:

"You can listen to my boys' bullshit all you want, but I have a lunch date, so here's the deal: we'll either get you work or we won't. And at the end of the day, you'll get just as fucked over as everyone else does in this business."

I signed immediately.

The catch was if I wanted the *Tango and Cash* gig, I had to start the following day, which meant Sweetie and I needed to find a place to live and change our summer plans for us and the girls from our home in East Hampton to Los Angeles. Jamie Lee Curtis and Chris Guest were also at the Reiner's, and Jamie Lee said, "Rent Chris' mom's apartment. They spend the summer in East Hampton." So we did.

David was on vacation, so Phil made my *Tango and Cash* deal. Films are made or broken in pre-production—the time between getting the studio's green light to hire cast and crew and when you start filming. I would have no prep on this one, since principal photography was starting in two weeks. Normally, I'd have a minimum of twelve.

My first morning with Andrei the director and Jon Peters the producer—whom I would later work with on *Wild Wild West*—made me realize that Peterman didn't have a "family crisis." He was just fleeing a sinking radioactive ship.

In our first meeting, Andrei, a Russian, explained that the Soviet Union was letting us use their biggest transport plane, in fact the biggest plane in the world, the Antonov An-225 Mriya, for an evening. The idea for the scene was that as the plane taxied down the Burbank Airport runway, the back of the plane would open, and Sly and Kurt, who were being held captive in their jeep inside the plane, would drive off the huge jet just as it lifted off.

I asked Andrei if the sequence had been storyboarded, or if there was any pre-visualization of the scene, or if I could talk to the Visual Effects supervisor and stunt coordinator. I was curious how much was going to be blue screen or was it all visual effects work, with the exception, maybe, of a two shot and close-ups of Stallone and Russell in the jeep screaming or comedy bantering—although probably even those shots would be filmed in a studio against blue screen and not on the actual plane.

Maybe second unit would film a shot of the An-225 taxiing down the runway, although probably that too would be better and cheaper as a miniature or a computer graphics model. I was more of a comedy guy, and since action films were not my forte, I was curious to hear what the plan was from the team that had been on the show for the last four months.

Andrei started screaming.

"Why are you asking about all these tricks? Why are you wasting time with questions? I just told you the scene. You read the script. Your job is to film the scene. The plane goes down the runway, the back of the plane opens, and the jeep drives out with Sly and Kurt looking cool as the plane takes off into the sky. It's in the script. You read it."

"Oh...kay...Obviously, you've thought all this out, and I'm just getting started, but here are a few, admittedly dumb, questions. The scene takes place at night, which means there's going to be a lot of lights and a lot of crew to film a plane on a more than a mile-long runway, and it's summer, so we don't have a lot of hours of darkness.

"This is my first morning, and you, Andrei, directed *Runaway Train*, so you know your way around action movies, but I still need to ask a few more, a bunch more actually, dumb, dumb............ dumb questions.

"Do we know that the Antonov can even land or take off from Burbank Airport? Do we know if the plane's systems allow the cargo door to drop down as the plane is taxiing, let alone can the plane take off with the rear door down? Do we know how long it will take, after the plane lifts off, if it even can, for it to circle the airfield, land, and come back to the starting position for take two? And, speaking of landing, do we even know if the plane can land with the rear door down? Do we really think Sly and Kurt, or their stunt guys, are going to drive a jeep off a moving plane just before it takes off? I know you've thought about all of this, I mean, for months, but it seems like I'm missing something."

I swear, Jon Peters turned to Andrei and said:

"What about a huge chase scene with one of those big dump trucks that carry coal, and a Caterpillar D9 earth mover in a quarry somewhere? Sly and Kurt could each look cool driving those really big trucks."

Andrei loved the idea. Not another word was ever mentioned about the Antonov An-225 Mriya.

"Love it! Right, Sonnenfeld?" said Peters.

On the one hand, I was thinking, a Caterpillar D-9 travels at like a tenth the speed of an old person walking, hardly lending itself to a "big chase scene," but, on the other, I said: "Love it!"

I knew I was going to be long gone from *Tango and Cash* before they got to the "big chase scene."

Andrei and I had three run-ins during my one week of filming. The last was in a police station. I suggested we film Kurt entering the office, then let him exit frame. The next shot we'd pick him up arriving at his desk.

Andrei turned red.

"Are you a pussy? Are you a girl?"

"Light the whole police station. We see Kurt come in, we follow him across the room, then we see him arrive at his desk. All in one shot."

"Well, Andrei, isn't that a lot of shoe leather? Doesn't it seem kinda boring since it will be like 45 seconds of a guy walking across a police station?"

Andrei yelled, as if obvious, "I'll tell Kurt to say some funny things to different people as he walks by. Let's go!"

Two hours later, after lighting the Grand Central of police stations, Kurt is called to the set. Andrei tells him he's going to walk from one end of the station to the other and then sit at his desk.

"Andrei. That's a lot of shoe leather. Why don't you let me walk into the police station, leave frame, and then pick me up at my desk? It's a lot of walking with nothing going on."

Uh. Yeah.

"It won't be nothing going on, because as you pass other people's desks, I want you to say funny things to them."

And here's why I'll always love Kurt Russell:

"Andrei. I'm an actor. Not a writer. If you have a writer write me funny things. I'll say them. But don't ask me to say funny things if they aren't written."

Andrei turned to me and said, "Kurt enters the police station and exits frame. Let's go."

I didn't learn much at film school from classes, since you'll remember that Ian, my directing teacher, thought *The Sound of Music* was the greatest movie ever made. The learning began once we shot our stories. We would see why we needed to change angles; film over the shoulders and singles, wide shots and close-ups; pick up the actor's pace; use the camera as a storytelling, not just a recording, device. It also taught me to have an actor enter a shot and leave frame, picking him up at the other side of a police station.

From the time I was a professional cinematographer, although there was nothing particularly professional about the making of *Blood Simple*, I never viewed myself as "the cameraman" so much as what I hoped would be considered "the friend of the director."

I would talk about the actors' energy on the first shot after lunch (always too low), how a sequence might cut together, or why filming a scene in one continuous take—Will Smith helping an alien give birth and getting thrown around the roof of the car by the creature's tentacle—might be funnier than cutting it up into different angles.

Andrei didn't appreciate my "friend of the director" approach, and didn't like my lighting, either.

The second disagreement occurred in Stallone's character's police station. The day was overcast, and the office's lighting was fluorescent. I added a little fluorescent fill light for Stallone's face and told Andrei we were ready. He looked at the stand-in for Stallone's stand-in. (Stallone was pissed I was using his buddy the stand-in too much, preventing them from hanging out, so we hired a stand-in for the stand-in.)

Anyway, Andrei looked at the stand-in's stand-in:

"You light like a girl. You light like a pussy. This is Sly, the biggest action hero in the world. Give him some guts; give him a kicker."

He jabbed his hand in an angle away from the stand-in's stand-in and toward the window, "From over there!"

A kicker is a light that you place at a three-quarter angle behind the actor that rakes their face and gives definition and contrast, in this case to an actor with not very good skin.

"Andrei. We're in a florescent lit room on an overcast day. The light I gave Stallone is flat, but directional, and he'll look good. There's no motivation for a kicker, and most of all, it will show up every scar, pore, and imperfection of Sly's skin."

"Do it. Pussy."

So I did it.

As Stallone walks onto the set, about eight feet from where he has to stand, he sees the kicker. He narrows his eyes as he turns to find me, which he unfortunately does. Pointing to the kicker, in a deep voice with too much gravel in his throat, Sly says:

"Turn off the fucking kicker."

Stallone knew lighting, and he was right.

*   *   *

Some shows watch dailies during lunch, others at the end of the day after wrap. *Tango and Cash* was a lunchtime dailies show. The room was darkened, the footage rolled...and it was beautiful. Rich and saturated and gorgeous. Which meant Andrei was screaming.

"What is this shit?"

"Sorry, Andrei?"

"This looks like shit."

"I don't know, Andrei. I think it looks pretty good."

"No one wants it to look pretty. No one wants it to look good. It should be ugly and dirty and gritty and hard to look at. This looks like a pussy lit it."

"Ya know, Andrei, I might not be your guy."

It's Friday, the end of the first week of filming, and I'm on the 110 driving east to film a night shoot when I got the call from Phil Gersh—David's still on vacation.

The film industry, by the way, is a big believer in long holidays and vacations. On the day after Memorial Day you can suggest a meeting and be told that the studio isn't booking appointments this close to the July 4 holiday.

"Hey, kid. You're fired. Tonight's your last night."

"Wait. Phil. Are you sure? Because this is incredibly great news. I'm not one to celebrate until years later when the thrill is long gone and I wished I had been happier in the moment, but if this is true..."

"I don't know what the fuck you're talking about," Phil snapped. "But you're fired. I already made Donnie Thorn's deal."

Phil was a genius at keeping work within his agency and managed to have Peterman, me, and Thorn all get hired to film the same movie.

"You promise?"

"You're fucking fired. Enjoy the summer."

*   *   *

What Phil meant when he said, "Enjoy the summer" is that some-how in Warner Bros. last-minute need to replace Don Peterman, the deal that the Gersh agency made for me as cinematographer was a "pay or play" contract for the run of the film. That meant the studio would have to pay me even if the show got shut down or, perhaps, I got fired.

I found myself making my weekly salary, living in Santa Monica a block from the Pacific, and eating twice a week at Chinois on Main, where I became acquaintances with the owner and chef, Wolfgang Puck. I also managed to film parts of two other shows for Warner Bros. that needed additional photography, including *Goodfellas*.

It was a great summer.

Addams Family

Sweetie and I were lying in bed at the Four Seasons Hotel on Doheny watching the Indianapolis 500 when our room phone rang.

"Mr. Sonnenfeld. Mr. Scott Rudin has dropped off a script for you. He's asked that you read it in the next two hours and meet him at Hugo's Restaurant."

I would soon discover this was classic Rudin. He always left messages, but never wanted to speak to you. I've been sitting in hotel rooms when suddenly my message light would glow, at which point I'd call the operator:

"Hi. I'm sitting here, and my message light suddenly went on."

"Yes, Mr. Sonnenfeld. Mr. Rudin left word."

"I'm sitting right here. Did you try my room?"

"Mr. Rudin did not wish to disturb."

Ninety-nine percent of the time, Rudin had no reason to speak to me or the other hundred people his assistants left word for that morning. Scott just wanted to remind you he was out there. After trading calls for a week, you'd realize if Rudin really wanted to speak to you, he'd find a way.

For many years, Scott and I shared the same lawyer. I once gave a speech to three thousand members of the California Bar on the occasion of our lawyer, Melanie Cook, being named Lawyer of the Year. The biggest laugh of the evening came when I said Melanie was so important to Scott Rudin, he calls her when he knows she's in.

The bellman brought up an 8.5 x 11 envelope. In it was the script for *The Addams Family*, along with a note saying I should direct it. I was in LA working on *Misery* for Rob Reiner. It was the second time I had been his cinematographer, the first being *When Harry Met Sally*.

Sweetie and I read the script and agreed it wasn't very good.

"Rudin wants me to direct this."

"I know."

"The script isn't very good, and I'm not a director."

"But you could be."

"Yeah, but the script isn't very good."

"You'll make it better."

"I don't know how to talk to actors."

"Yes, you do. You do it all the time."

"So, I should meet Rudin and say...?"

"Hear him out. Then tell him the truth about the script. Maybe he knows it's no good."

"I mean, I love Charles Addams. This would be right up my alley if I was ever going to direct, I mean, *Addams Family*? For sure. But this script..."

"Take the meeting."

There are two extreme versions of Scott, and nothing in between:

He is compassionate, sweet, lovely, warm, brilliant, a great listener, and wonderful collaborator.

He is ruthless, pathological, a liar, mean, a dictator, and a lousy collaborator.

I met Rudin at Hugo's, on Santa Monica near La Cienega. The nice Rudin showed up.

"Two Pasta Papas and two iced teas," Rudin told the waiter.

I had met Scott twice in my life and wasn't sure why I was on his radar as a director, since I had never been one.

"Thanks for sending me the script. And listen, before we talk about it, can you just explain why you think I'm the right director for this, and why you even think of me as a director?"

Years later, when Walter Parkes, Laurie McDonald, and I were having lunch with Tommy Lee Jones at his Polo Club in West Palm Beach, Tommy asked Walter, who was the producer of *Men in Black 3*, why Tommy and his character were being basically written out of the film. Walter started his response by saying, "Tommy, I'm going to err on the side of honesty."

"Well, Ba"—for some strange reason, Rudin was choosing honesty. I guess he wanted to get it out of the way.

"I sent the script to Tim Burton and Terry Gilliam, and they both passed. After those two, I had a choice—give it to some safe hack comedy director or take a chance on someone who might do a brilliant job. Someone who was a visual stylist. Don't forget I was the studio executive on *Big* and *Raising Arizona*. I know what you can do. This can't look like a typical comedy. The movie has to create a world and be amazing to look at—like Charles Addams' drawings.

"So that's why you're here. All the good directors passed."

Directors' chairs from The Addams Family *set. By the end of the show, Rudin had the props department make close to twenty fake chairs of directors he claimed turned down the job.*

I gave Rudin my notes on all the things wrong with the script. It was jokey instead of funny, the plot was a mess, and the characters were goofy. The genius of Charles Addams' cartoons are that they are dark and smart. The viewer had to work to find the humor, which is sophisticated and visual, not silly and obvious.

Since I wasn't looking for the job, I could be honest with Scott. I was a successful, nicely paid Director of Photography. Besides, no studio was going to hire me to direct.

"Everything you said about this script, and about Charles Addams, is exactly why you should direct this show."

For five hours a week, Rudin can be the most charming person on the planet. This was Sunday, the start of a new week, and since he was using up a lot of his weekly allotment he cut to the chase.

"Look. If I can get Orion to hire you as the director, will you do it? I promise we will get the script to a place where you and I will both be happy."

"Scott. If you can get a studio to hire me to direct *Addams Family*, go with God."

Then the Pasta Papas arrived. Spaghetti with garlic, parsley, parmesan cheese, bacon, turkey sausage, scallions, and scrambled eggs. I picked around the plate, basically having some breakfast eggs. Rudin never touched his.

Like my mother, he's not a public eater.

"Let's get out of here," he said, guessing the amount of the check and tip and leaving cash on the table.

Scott and I met the Orion executives: Eric Pleskow, Bill Bernstein, Mike Medavoy—who, when he left Orion and went to run TriStar years later, passed on *Get Shorty*—and Mark Platt, who would go on to become a successful producer. These four individuals were total gentlemen. Orion was known as a filmmaker friendly studio. Scott and I were offered the traditional coffee or water, then got down to business.

By the way, Academy Award winning screenwriter Bill Goldman's single piece of advice to filmmakers was take the offered beverage when having a meeting with a studio since it will probably be the only thing you'll ever get from them.

"Our first concern," said Pleskow, "is we recently did a movie, *The Hand*, with a disembodied hand in the lead, and we lost a lot of money on it. It was a disaster."

Rudin explained we were making a comedy, not a psychological horror film (directed by Oliver Stone), and that Thing, our disembodied hand, was a tangential character, not the motor for the entire movie. In addition, Rudin went on, *The Hand*'s special effects were all created by the very expensive Stan Winston (four Academy Awards) and Carlo Rambaldi (only three).

"Barry intends to use no visual effects or animatronic hands. All of his effects will be in camera, with an actor's real hand. Barry...?"

"Yeah, we'll do things like have the Thing actor below frame sticking his hand up through a hole in the table, or various tricks like that, but yes, indeed, all the shots will be in camera."

Scott did most of the talking. I sensed their takeaway was they trusted Scott—at least creatively—and I seemed like a nice boy.

They said I was hired and the movie green-lit subject to cast and budget. Eric was particularly impressed I figured out a way to get Thing "inside the camera," since he didn't think cameras were big enough to fit a hand into it—totally misunderstanding what I meant by filming Thing "in camera." Maybe that explains why Orion would go bankrupt halfway through our movie.

Now that I was hired, I started to chat with the executives about what I intended to do on their behalf, what Charles Addams meant to me...

Scott cut me off.

"Barry. Take yes for an answer. Let's go."

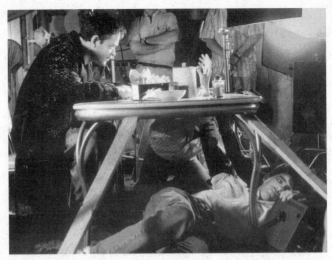

An "in camera" setup with Gomez and Thing (Chris Hart).

Rudin brought his friend Paul Rudnick on to do an uncredited page one rewrite. Paul is one of the funniest people I've ever met and really understood the tone of Addams' cartoons. We finally had a script.

Along the way, Scott and I disagreed on many aspects of the cast, sets, props, and wardrobe. Rudin, Rudnick, and I would meet in his office, and Scott would charmingly lie about everything we had opposing opinions about, or he would yell at me.

His screaming was fierce. I realized the only way to deal with it was to out-juvenile him. When he would start to bellow, I would get off the couch and remove all the bolsters and pillows. Using the back and bottom bolsters as building blocks, I would turn them into walls and build a fort on top of the couch. Crawling into the one end I had left open, I'd stuff a pillow into the gap and yell:

"I can't hear you. I'm in the fort."

"Barry. Get out of there!" Scott would roar.

"I think you may have said something, but I can't hear you because of how thick the walls are in this fort."

"I am fucking serious. Get out of the fort right now, Sonnenfeld. I am busy and this is stupid."

"Can't hear you."

Rudnick would confirm that, indeed, I was in a fort, and if Scott wanted me to hear him, he'd have to yell louder.

"Seriously, Sonnenfeld. *GET OUT OF THE FUCKING FORT.* I have work to do."

"If you say you're sorry, and promise not to yell, I'll get out of the fort."

"Ucchh. I'm sorry. Okay? Now get the fuck out of there."

Sweetie, me, and Paul Rudnick. Paramount Studios lot.

The part of this that amazed Rudnick and me was that Rudin would never invade the sanctity of my fort. He'd bend over and scream at me, but he'd never remove a pillow and say,

"Schmuck. There is no fort."

Rudin, Rudnick, and I, and a reporter for the *New York Times* were in Scott's office one afternoon when his assistant beeped his Amtel. Before the Internet or instant messaging, Hollywood had the Amtel. This super modern (for its time) two-way wired messaging system allowed Scott's assistants to type a note to Rudin and send it into his inner sanctum. He could use his keyboard to reply or hit one of the preprogrammed messages:

"Take a message."

"Come in and break up this meeting in 5/10/15 minutes."

"I need a Tab."

"I need coffee."

"I need water."

Scott read the Amtel message and announced to Rudnick, me, and the *New York Times* reporter, who was working on a *Sunday Magazine* story about Rudin,

"I'll be back in a minute."

"Tell your mother I said hello."

The *Times* writer thought this was funny, and in his eventual article wrote, "Both Rudin and Sonnenfeld have a problem with their mothers. In fact Sonnenfeld insists he wishes his mother was dead."

A few months later, a week before publication, the *New York Times'* fact-checking department gave me a call. They read me the quote. I acknowledged I said it.

The checker asked, "Would you prefer we didn't publish the quote? It's, I mean, it's pretty rough."

"I think I'm missing something. You are checking on a fact, and I'm telling you that the fact you're checking on is true."

Thursday, Sweetie convinced me to call my mother and warn

her what she was going to read in the newspaper of record, seventy-two hours from now.

"Hi, Mom. Listen. In Sunday's *New York Times*, you're probably going to read that I wished you were dead, but, um, you know me."

"Uchhh. Barry. I know you, but what are my friends going to say?"

"They know me too."

"Uchhhh. Barry. I wished you hadn't. You're nuts. You know that, of course."

"Yes, Mom. I'm nuts."

"You actually said you wished I was dead?"

"Yeah, but like I said, you know me."

"Uchhh. So are we going to see you guys this weekend?"

"Not this weekend, but soon, Mom. Gotta go."

The Sunday of publication, Sweetie once again begged me to call Kelly.

"I already called her. On Thursday."

"Barry. Call your mother."

There was an hour of busy signals before I got through.

"Hi, Dad. Is Mom there?"

"Your mother is decimated."

"I don't think you can decimate a person, Dad. It's more like an army or nation thing."

"She's very upset."

"Can I speak to her?"

"Kelly. It's Barry."

"Uchhh," I hear through the Sonny held phone. "I'm coming."

Dad hands Mom the phone, and through sobs and tears and quick breaths she says,

"I'm decimated."

"I don't think you can decimate a person, Mom. It's more of an army or nation kind of thing."

"I'm devastated. Are you happy?"

"Because of the *New York Times* thing?"

"Of course because of it."

"Yeah, but Mom, you know me. And your friends know me. It's just . . . something I said. I mean, it's kind of funny. In the context of the article. And, anyway, I warned you about it."

"It's one thing to be told it, Barry. It's another to actually read it. In print. In the *New York Times*."

Unfortunately for Kelly, the *Times* article was the first of several decimations.

Through a series of unusual events, I was invited to appear on Dave Letterman's show to promote *Men in Black*. During the pre-interview a day or two before my appearance, I gave them a lot of good stories about my mother, Will Smith, and Sweetie. In the greenroom the day of taping, the producer Katherine Pope mentioned Dave thought the mom stuff was very funny but kind of rough and wasn't sure we should go there.

"Please tell Dave to go wherever he wants, and I'll follow."

So of course, he couldn't resist the mom stuff. We talked about me being paged at Madison Square Garden, which got big laughs.

After I bumped the comedian and stayed on for an unscheduled second segment, he said,

"You have a very special relationship with your mother."

"Because of saying things like, 'Until he died, my mother could have been Vincent Gardenia's photo double?'" which got a nice laugh.

At which point, and I didn't know this was coming, Dave pulls out an 8x10 photo of the dead Vincent Gardenia, which gets Dave a huge laugh as the camera zooms in on the very masculine, bearded Vincent.

I examine the photo:

"Well. Mom has more facial hair."

Game. Set. Match.

I also told Letterman that my parents visited me on the set of *When Harry Met Sally* wearing identical brown suits and that Billy Crystal seeing them said,

"You know, Ba. Your mother's a lesbian," which elicited a call the next morning from an angry Billy.

Kelly also had a Roger Ebert thing going on.

The final public torture of Kelly came when *Newsweek* ran a cover story and review of the first *Men in Black*. Within the article the writer implies that I was neurotic and honest and was in so much pain directing the film that:

"Sonnenfeld was fond of shrieking throughout filming, 'I'll give $400,000 to anyone who does one of two things: kill my mother or get me off this movie.'"

Well, of course Kelly read this and called me on my cell phone. I remember being on lower Broadway.

She was decimated.

"Do you mean that? Do you mean it when you say those things in *Newsweek*? Do you actually wish I was dead?"

"Mom. I promise. Under no circumstances would I pay someone $400,000 to kill you."

"Thank you, Barry. I love you too," she said with no irony.

"Okay, Mom. I gotta go."

"Wait. One last thing. As a small favor. The next time you say something mean about me.... be mean to your father as well."

"I promise I will, Mom."

"I love you, Ba. You know that."

"Yes, Mom. I do."

Anyway, Sweetie and I had been summoned to Scott's Paramount office. We were sitting in his reception area and having taken Bill Goldman's advice each had a mug of coffee. Our bench faced out into a square waiting area. On the left was Scott's outer office with two assistants working the phones. His inner office, door shut, was behind them.

To our right was another office with yet one more assistant. His job in addition to rolling phone calls was to read Rudin's mind.

Suddenly, Rudin's personal inner office door opened, and he barked to no one in particular:

"Log."

He was referring to his phone log, which was the list of the people the assistants had left word for as well as the people who called while Rudin was behind his closed door. The assistants had been told by Rudin "absolutely no interruptions no matter who calls."

Rudin looked at the log and saw Sydney Pollack had phoned.

"Sydney Pollack called and you didn't put him through?"

"You said absolutely no interruptions."

"Are you a fucking moron? Sydney Pollack calls, and you say you'll take a message?"

"But..."

"Which one of you fucking morons took this call? Which one?"

"Dan."

Dan was the guy in the opposite room.

Sweetie and I watched Scott walk across our vestibule and into the little office on the right. Over Rudin's horrific, deep, booming voice of doom, as if in a Buster Keaton comedy, perfectly timed without a single cut, we watched a desk lamp, a Rolodex, a flying Macintosh SE, and finally a weeping Dan fly past us.

Rudin, as if he'd just had a particularly relaxing massage, walked out of the small office and with the charm of Fred Astaire said to Sweetie and me,

"Come on in."

Before he closed his door using a button on his desk to cut off electricity to the electromagnetic door holding device, he leaned out toward the trembling assistants and said,

"No interruptions."

Many very talented and famous cinematographers attempted to make the move from Director of Photography to film director, and most failed. Gordon Willis, my favorite cameraman—he lights for radio—having shot the *Godfather* movies, *All the President's Men*, *Pennies from Heaven*, *Klute*, and many Woody Allen films, including *Manhattan*, *Annie Hall*, *Zelig*, and *The Purple Rose of Cairo*, directed one movie, titled *Windows*.

Bill Fraker, also one of the great American cinematographers, shot fifty-five movies, including *Rosemary's Baby*, *Bullet*, *One Flew over the Cuckoo's Nest*, and *Heaven Can Wait*. He directed a couple of westerns, including *The Legend of the Lone Ranger*, but never really made it as a director.

Finally, John Alonso, whose work as a cinematographer ranges from *Fail Safe* and *The Bad News Bears* to the noir beauties *Farewell My Lovely*, *Scarface* (edited by Jerry Greenberg of "Greenberging" fame), and *Chinatown*, directed one movie: *FM*.

When Rudin hired me to direct *The Addams Family*, I felt I had one chance to succeed. I wondered why Willis, Fraker, and Alonso didn't make it as directors. They were all better cinematographers than I was. They all knew their way around a set. They probably worked with directors quite closely. What went wrong?

After some research I discovered all three brilliant cameramen moved up their camera operator to be the Director of Photography on their directing debuts.

I realized these DPs didn't want to give up being the cinematographer. And I think that's why they weren't more successful as directors. I decided the only way I had a chance as a director was to hire such a great cinematographer I would be pushed away from the camera and lighting and instead spend time with the scary people—the actors.

I went on a search to find a cameraman so good, so much better than me, that I would never go up to him or her and say, "Shouldn't the 10K go over there?" Or, "Doesn't she need a soft bounce over the camera?"

I picked Owen Roizman: *Tootsie*, *Absence of Malice*, *True Confessions*, *Network*, *The Exorcist*, *The Taking of Pelham One Two Three*, and *The French Connection*. Five Oscar nominations.

We had lunch. I promised I would totally stay out of lighting the set but there were three areas I wanted to be involved in.

"Shoot," he said.

"Well, I want to design the shots. I see things a certain wide angle lens way, and since the scene is already cut together in my mind, I need to decide where the camera goes, and with what lens."

"Sounds good. Less work for me. Next."

"I want Morticia to look beautiful and have her own lighting, as if George Hurrell was brought in just to light her. I don't care if she's standing right next to a window, with light coming in from the left side of the frame, I still want her to be lit like a 1940s movie star. As if Morticia had her own motivated light that had nothing to do with the real world."

Anjelica Huston, beautifully lit in the style of George Hurrell by Owen Roizman.

Most cinematographers base their lighting on "motivated" light. I never did.

Owen grinned—which was rare for Owen, so it might have been a grimace or indigestion—but he said, "I love it."

This was easy.

"Third?"

"The show should have rich and saturated colors. Even though it isn't particularly colorful, I want deep blacks, and crisp whites, and the movie shouldn't be grimy or muddy or brown. I hate 5254, the high-speed color film Kodak is manufacturing, and want you to use 5247."

Kodak's beautiful film stock, 5247, had a much lower ASA, which meant more lights and more time.

Owen asked me the same question I would have asked him, if the situation was reversed.

"Will I ever have to pan?"

The angle of view of a wide lens spreads out so quickly that it is hard to hide lights. It gets even harder if you pan, because the lights you have out of the frame at the beginning of the shot will come into frame as you pan. It's even harder when you are using a film stock that requires a lot of light.

I cracked up because I used 5247 as a cinematographer myself, and the one thing I begged a director not to do was pan. I loved to track, but hated to pan. Panning is a lazy way to block scenes and frame shots.

I remember being at the premiere of Scorsese's *Gangs of New York* at the Ziegfeld with Joel and Ethan. When it ended, Ethan turned to me and said, "Why was that so bad?"

"Too much panning," I replied.

"No panning," I promised Owen.

He reached out to shake my hand: "You've got yourself a cinematographer."

Scott convinced Dede Allen to be our film editor. He felt that having someone with Dede's history and ability would be an asset to the movie, but mainly to Scott. He was sure Dede would police the footage we needed from both performance and coverage and, if necessary, would be another person besides himself who could push me around.

Dede was the most legendary film editor on the East Coast. She was also a lovely woman who wore a single strand of pearls around her neck that always captured errant snippets of film, called trims.

Some of the films she edited: *Breakfast Club, Reds, Slap Shot, Dog Day Afternoon, Serpico, Little Big Man, Bonnie and Clyde,* and *The Hustler.*

West Coast editors didn't like Dede because she cut more like a European: jump cuts and a purposeful mismatching of takes to add a sense of energy was her style. Dede once looked at a scene cut by her associate editor on *Addams Family*, twenty years her junior, and said,

"Get out of the way, Jim. You cut like an old lady."

She took the same footage and by trimming the beginning and ends of shots—often creating mismatched action—suddenly the scene with the same exact footage had energy and pace.

Dede and I had lunch at the Russian Tea Room. At the time, she was 67. She told me Scott had offered her the job, she was thrilled to do it, but she wouldn't take it until we had lunch and I hired her. She worked for the director, not the producer.

She often talked about the dialectics of film editing and taught me that sometimes if the ending isn't working, the problem is in the second act, not the third. She made scenes better by changing the previous one.

By the end of *Addams Family* Dede had taught me more about film, more about the fluid dynamics of how movies are edited, how stories are told, than my three years at film school and the nine feature films I had photographed (not including the pornos).

I had never directed actors, so at our first rehearsal, which included Raul Julia, Anjelica Huston, Rudin, and Paul Rudnick, I thought I'd break the ice by telling Raul and Anjelica about my career in porn.

In great detail.

It didn't go well.

I will say in my defense Raul loved the story.

*　　*　　*

A few weeks from the start of photography we had our table read. This two-hour event is where the actors sit around a table and read the script out loud.

Our story revolved around the disappearance of Fester Addams and how twenty years later Gomez still pined for his missing brother. After an Addams family séance, an impostor who looks just like Fester appears at their door. Wednesday is suspicious, but Gomez and Morticia, desperate for Gomez to regain his joie de vivre, believe this Fester is really Gomez's brother. The fake Fester and his mother kick the Addams family out of their mansion and steal their fortune.

The script ends with the impostor feeling terrible about what he and his mother have done. Grabbing a book from Gomez's library called *Hurricane Irene, Nightmare from Above*—Irene is my mother's given name—he unleashes a huge cyclone from the pages of the book, killing the villain (his mother) and saving the day.

Fester's last line to his mother, right before he sends her to her demise, is,

"You were a terrible mother. There. I said it."

"There, I said it," I thought.

Gomez tells the impostor he has out-Festered Fester and that family is a state of mind, not necessarily biological, and invites the impostor to join the family.

Rudin, Rudnick, and I thought the table read went well.

The cast was outraged.

They huddled in a corner of the large room, clasped hands in unity, and then approached the long table where the director, writer, and producer were sitting in suspense.

Anjelica spoke:

"We are very upset about the ending of this script, and we have appointed a spokesperson to explain our concerns."

And then, pointing to a 10-year-old girl:

"Christina."

"Thank you, Anjelica," said Christina Ricci, who was playing Wednesday, as the cast sat down in a row facing us.

"Here are the reasons why Fester has to be Gomez's real brother. The entire script is building to this conclusion. We are in suspense about where his brother has been these last twenty years, and how the filmmakers will give us a satisfying answer to that question. The solution you have come up with is neither intellectually nor emotionally satisfying."

Her fellow actors nodded in agreement.

"The audience will feel cheated, and have mixed feelings trying to celebrate your ending, knowing that the Addams family is letting an impostor live with them. Plus, in your version, shouldn't Gomez still be upset about his missing brother?"

Again, the cast nodded in agreement.

All the cast, except Christopher Lloyd, who was playing Fester.

"Finally, we think the movie's ending will be very hard for Chris to play if he isn't the real Fester."

The cast patted Christina on the back and gave her a round of smattered applause.

Everyone except Chris, who was concentrating on peeling garlic cloves.

"Hey, Chris. Which version would you rather play?" I asked. "Real brother or fake?"

Chris, who was in an eating raw garlic stage of his life, stopped chewing and said,

"I don't care."

"Since Chris doesn't care, why do..."

I was staring at a murderous Anjelica, Raul, and Christina. "Give me a second."

Christina Ricci thinks she's found a better angle than the one I am lining up.

Hmmmmmm.

Rudin, Rudnick, and I huddled in the corner and agreed that Christina's arguments were pretty damn convincing and we were going to have a very rebellious cast if we didn't make the change.

After the Addams family are kicked out of their home by Fester and his mother, they are penniless. The family moves into a crappy motel with a motor court. Gomez is a shiftless layabout receiving cranial massages from Thing.

Morticia has gotten a job as a kindergarten teacher and reads the class of 5-year-olds *Hansel and Gretel*, from the poor witch's point of view. The evening we filmed this scene, both versions of Rudin reared their ugly heads.

Comforted by Anjelica.

It was an incredibly tough day for me personally. Sweetie was home in New York City, in the hospital. Several times while filming, I feared Sweetie was dying, and this was one of them. The doctors were going to operate the next morning to see if she had cancer or was totally fine. I was booked on the red-eye that night, scheduled to get to NYC the next morning during her surgery. The good Rudin had somehow convinced the studio we needed to shut down on Friday so I could be in New York for my wife's surgery. The bad Rudin almost made me miss the plane.

Anjelica did a great job reading the story to the kindergarteners. I needed to make the plane, and due to the child labor laws in the state of California I had only a limited amount of time with the kids anyway. We had two cameras, so we could shoot various angles of kids at once. I had the 5-year-olds stare in rapt silence as they listened to the story.

Morticia tells the children that Hansel and Gretel threw the wicked witch into the oven and asks, "How do you think *that* would feel?"

Obviously, the kids should be freaked out. We rolled cameras, and I said to the kindergarteners, "Look sad. Look worried. Look surprised. Look shocked."

I looked at my watch and thought, "Time to go."

"Okay. I think we got it. Thanks, guys."

Rudin, sitting in his chair watching the video monitor, frantically motioned me over.

"You don't have this."

"It's fine. We don't need a lot of stuff. We can go out on Morticia," I lied.

"You don't have this. Those kids have to cry."

"Scott. Come on, man. How am I going to make a bunch of 5-year-olds cry?"

"You're the director. Figure it out."

"Scott. I don't have a lot of time…I mean, Sweetie. She might be dying."

Rudin countered, "The teamster has the car running and is at the exit right down that corridor. It takes fifteen minutes this time of night to get to the airport [lie]. Right now, your job is to make those kids cry."

"On cue. Just like that. Tell them to cry?"

"Whatever it takes, Barry. Those kids have to cry. You're the director. Go direct."

I went back and told the camera crews to put zoom lenses on their cameras and to start filming once the kids start to cry, finding different sized close-ups of each wailing child.

"You're going to make them cry?" asked one of the camera operators.

"Good luck," he silently schmucked.

Just roll the fucking camera, I thought.

"Okay, kids. You guys did great. We're done filming, and all we have to do now, so stay where you're sitting, is to give you your measles vaccination."

A smart ass, adorable blond curly haired boy said, "He's just kidding."

Damn.

"No. No. Didn't your parents tell you? It's a rule. Whenever you work on a movie set, you have to get a measles shot. It's a rule. I'm surprised your parents didn't mention it."

Man, this was a horrible, horrible thing I was doing.

Silence.

Silence.

And then, the adorable, smart ass curly blond haired kid crumples up his face, and then...wait for it...starts to cry. To bawl. Which makes all the other adorable blond haired kids start to cry, since he was their de facto leader. Every child in the classroom is sobbing. I see the camera teams panning from one kid to the next. I know we have the shot.

"Cut!" I yell.

Out of the corner of my eye I see a burly, red-faced, red-necked dad barreling toward me. Luckily, the classroom has two exits. I race out the back one and run down the long corridor, where I see my station wagon through the glass door at the end of the hallway.

The dad is now also in the corridor, moving in a singular deadly daddy stampede, furiously chasing me—and really, who can blame him?

"Come back here, you fucker. I'm going to fucking kill you."

My driver, who had been leaning against the car smoking a cigarette, sees what's happening, flicks the cigarette to the ground, opens the rear driver's side door, and races to the school door to open it. I run past him and dive into the car. He pulls the school door shut, shoves my door closed (I'm laying across the back bench), and jumps into the driver's seat.

As we pull away, the out of control—and again, who can blame him?—dad is banging on the back window of the Ford wagon like Dustin Hoffman at the end of *The Graduate*, although instead of yelling, "Elaine!" the ruby-faced father is screaming, "You shithead!"

I made my flight and spent the five hours of red-eyeing deeply worried about Sweetie. There was no other explanation for her blood levels than cancer. She was going to die.

I arrived at the hospital the next morning as Sweetie was being wheeled back into her room having had her exploratory surgery. The doctor came in and explained what had happened, why they thought she might have had cancer, and why, in fact, she was totally fine and cancer free. I asked Sweetie how she was feeling.

"A little groggy, but fine."

"Well, I feel pretty horrible. If you're okay, can you sit in the chair and let me lie down?"

The nurse came in to give Sweetie some painkillers.

Lying in the hospital bed with the worst headache of his life, a towel over his face, was me.

"I think he needs those more than I do," Sweetie said.

The Addams Family *dynamic between Rudin and me.*

CHAPTER 29

Sophie's Choice

In one sentence, here is my feeling about Scott Rudin: I love him dearly and wish he were dead.

One night while in post-production on *Addams Family Values* I spotted Bob Benton and his wife, Sally, having dinner at Nick and Toni's, our tony restaurant in East Hampton where we lived for thirty years.

After we paid our check I said, "Sweetie. I need to talk to Benton. He's working with Rudin on *Nobody's Fool*. He's flying with Scott to London tomorrow. I have to tell him something."

Sweetie deflated.

"Please don't. Let them eat dinner in peace. They look like nice people. Please don't be your father."

"I'm sorry. I have to."

"Mr. Benton. Hello. You don't know me, but my name is Barry Sonnenfeld, and this is my wife, Sweetie."

Wanting to be anywhere but where she was, Sweetie gave a beautiful Miss Flame smile to fellow Texan Bob.

"Anyway. Mr. Benton. I too am working with Scott Rudin. I know you're flying with him to London tomorrow, and although I so love your work, I mean, *Places in the Heart* made me weep uncontrollably. It was so brilliant, and that ending...? Um, *Kramer vs. Kramer*? Wow."

Sweetie gave me a wife nudge.

"But in any case, I want you to know that, artistic genius though you are, I hope your plane to London goes down in a horrible flaming crash that kills Scott Rudin, but leaves you and the other passengers unscathed."

There was a momentary silence. And then Benton said, "Please. Have a seat young man. Sweetie, is it?"

We joined Bob and Sally and became East Hampton friends for decades.

Although *The Addams Family* started at Orion, the studio had recently had a series of flops and needed money. Our film was the most commercial project they owned, and though we were halfway through filming, Orion felt they could sell it to another studio and get some cash for it.

Dede cut together a fifteen-minute highlight reel, and Orion and Rudin took it around to studios. Tom Pollock, who ran Universal Studios and looked like Ben Turpin, was close to buying it but wasn't offering enough. At the last minute, Frank Mancuso Sr., who at the time ran Paramount, saw and loved the footage and bought it on a Friday morning. That afternoon, having nothing to do with our purchase, Frank was fired. He was replaced by Stanley Jaffe, one of the most humorless people I have ever met. He looked like a meaner version of Mussolini meets Dick Cheney but with a less happy demeanor than either of those guys. Monday Stanley looked at the same footage Frank had watched and declared the movie un-cuttable and un-releasable.

The second half of directing *Addams Family*, now for Paramount, was even more of a nightmare since I was now making a movie that the chairman hated. They cut back our budget including bottled water. We had to go to the bathroom, or a rare studio water fountain, to fill up personal water containers. This was not due to environmental concerns. We were just hated and unworthy of such luxuries.

The executives assigned to *Addams Family* would call Dede every day after seeing dailies, telling her they couldn't imagine how the scene could cut together. Dede assured them it was cutting together fine. Scott, of course, continued to badger for more takes, more coverage, more options, and totally ignored the studio's mandate to cut costs. Scott's insistence to put the film first is what makes him such a great producer. Somehow, we completed principal photography.

On a feature film, the director, by contract between the studios and the Director's Guild of America, has a ten-week director's cut. After the editor assembles all the footage into a version of the movie as scripted, the director and editor then have ten weeks without any interference to create their version of the movie. At ten weeks the film is shown to the studio. This DGA director's cut is sacrosanct.

The day I wrapped principal photography I received a call from Gary Lucchesi's office. Gary was the President of Production at Paramount, a position two below that of the dour Stanley Jaffe. Gary asked if I would have lunch with him and Bill Horberg, the creative executive assigned to *Addams Family*, in the executive dining room.

As an aside, on the sequel, *Addams Family Values*, Sweetie and I were eating in the executive dining room at the table next to most of the in-costume officers of the Starship Enterprise—Klingons were not allowed in the executive dining room by the way. As Bill Shatner was being led to his special two-top, he stopped at his crew's table:

"Why, hello, Lieutenant Uhura," Shatner said in a somewhat creepy way.

"Fuck you, Captain Kirk," responded Nichelle Nichols, the actress playing Uhura.

The purpose of my lunch, as it turns out, was for Lucchesi and Horburg to convince me not to use my contractual ten week cut and instead show Paramount my movie right away. Obviously, Stanley had convinced them the film was a disaster.

I politely told them no. I had a contract protecting me and I intended to use the time to make the movie as good as possible before they saw it.

"Barry," said Lucchesi:

"When you say the DGA contract 'protects you,' it makes it seem like you think we're the enemy."

"You *are* the enemy."

"Enemy? We're your friends."

"No, you're not."

"You're acting like we have a say in how the film gets finished. As if we have final cut."

"Well, I don't have final cut. Rudin doesn't have final cut. If the studio doesn't have final cut, who does?"

"The audience!" Lucchesi beamed.

"I'm really sorry, but I'm not going to show you guys the movie, nice as you are, until my ten-week cut. I do, however, thank you for the Cobb salad."

I started to leave.

"Wait," Lucchesi pleaded, slightly rising from his chair. "If you won't show us the movie, will you at least tell us what it's like?"

I thought for a moment and then heard myself say:

"I really shouldn't do this."

I took a breath.

"*Addams Family* is like a much sadder version of *Sophie's Choice*."

I turned and left the executive dining room.

Hearing the phone ringing in my office at the Dressing Room Building on the Paramount lot, I ran down the long corridor to see if I could grab it before it went to voice mail. I picked up the phone, and it was, of course, Rudin.

"Did you just tell Lucchesi and Horberg that *Addams Family* is a sadder version of *Sophie's Choice*?"

"No."

"What did you tell them?"

"I told them it was a *much* sadder version of *Sophie's Choice*."

"They believe you!" screamed Rudin. "Call Lucchesi back and tell him it's good."

"Oh, come on, Scott. They've seen the dailies. Do they really believe I could turn our movie into a *much* sadder version of *Sophie's Choice*?"

"Studio executives don't know how to look at dailies. And they're scared. Their boss told them our movie sucks."

"Yeah, but Scooter. Those words were uttered by a fascist who doesn't have a funny bone in his body."

"Call Lucchesi!" Scott bellowed. "Now!"

Cut to:

"Hello. Gary Lucchesi, please. Barry Sonnenfeld calling."

In a very dull, flat, emotionless voice, Gary said,

"Hello, Barry."

"Hey, Gar. Listen. You know when I told you and Horburg that *Addams Family* was like a much sadder version of *Sophie's Choice*?"

"Yes, Barry. I do."

"Well Gar...that was kinda...like a joke. It was meant to be a joke."

"Well, then," he sourly asked, "what's it really like?"

"Well, Gar. In truth, it's actually incredibly funny."

Gary reacted as if I had told him his brain tumor was just a bad headache and to take two aspirin. He practically leapt through the phone to hug me.

"Really?! That is so fantastic! Just great. Fantastic. I love you, kid. Thank you, sir."

Not exactly the set of Sophie's Choice.

My ten week edit finished, Rudin and I screened *Addams Family* in the Paramount Theater. Attendees included the aforementioned stiff, chairman Stanley Jaffe; president Brandon Tartikoff, who until recently had run NBC; Barry London, head of distribution; and Arthur Cohen, head of marketing; along with Gary Lucchesi and Bill Horberg. Rudin and I sat in the back to gauge body language and reactions.

During the 88 minutes of screen time, the three-hundred-seat theater was as silent as a morgue.

Not a laugh.

An occasional nervous cough, where a laugh should have been.

The show ended, the lights came up, and Scott and I stood in the aisle so that as the assembled viewers exited, they could hand out a little encouragement. A head nod, a subtle grin, a hearty handshake...

Not a fake smile. Nor a nod. Just a line of men walking past us staring at their shoes. Stanley was the only one who spoke.

Not making eye contact, he said,

"Thank you."

We had been told to wait in our offices until called. As I sat deeply depressed, wondering how I could have spent the last ten months of my life for this result, the phone rang.

"Let's go," said Rudin.

As Rudin and I walked into Brandon's inner office, the entire group, minus Mussolini, was standing on the other side of the threshold—a corridor of bodies as if Rudin and I were in a hazing and were going to have to run the gauntlet and get punched in the face by each executive.

Rudin and I did run the gauntlet, but it was one of hugs and back slaps. They were cheering.

"Wait," I said. "What's going on here? You hate the movie. Not one of you laughed the entire time."

"We couldn't," giggled Tartikoff.

"Stanley wasn't laughing, so we couldn't," said Barry London, head of distribution.

"It's huge," said Cohen, who was going to market it.

Lucchesi looked at me with tears in his beautiful blue eyes.

As much as Rudin and I spent a year disagreeing, as much as he made my life a living hell, we were together in the control room as the last music cue for our movie was being recorded. Marc Shaiman had written a wonderful score.

The eighty-piece orchestra played a romantic version of *The Addams Family* theme as Morticia shows Gomez that she's been knitting a three-legged stocking for their new baby. It is how she tells Gomez she's pregnant.

"Cara mia."

"Mi amor."

Raul Julia bends Anjelica Huston into a romantic embrace.

The camera pulls back.

And back.

The music swells.

And Scott Rudin, his eyes moist with emotion, turns to me and says:

"If I were not a part of this movie, I would be very, very jealous. I love it."

When *Addams Family* opened, Hollywood was in a slump. Nothing was doing well at the box office. The industry rumor about our film was that it was good and might make money. I guess no one asked Stanley Jaffe. It was opening on Thanksgiving, and some pundits were even predicting $12 million for the weekend, which, at the time, was huge.

Addams Family opened to twice that amount.

The entire weekend I was sitting around our home in East Hampton, taking phone calls from famous people I had never met. Most congratulated me on the box office. Jeffrey Katzenberg actually went on about how good the film was. I hadn't heard from Rudin until Sunday night.

"Helllllooooo," he basso profundo'd.

"Hey, Scott."

"Congratulations."

"Well, ya know, Scott. I'm not the one who should be congratulated. I mean, the marketing and distribution people did an amazing job opening the movie. And even if it hadn't done well at the box office, I would still love the movie—it's like a child to me, so I'm not sure I'm deserving of congratulations."

"Barry," Scott sagely offered.

"If you can't be happy today, your mother won."

CHAPTER 30

Kids

When Sweetie and Elliott split up, Sasha was seven and Amy three and a half. Sweetie moved out of their apartment and into their weekend home in East Hampton. I had my "starter house" down the road in Springs. Whenever I wasn't working, which was often, I was in the Hamptons hanging out with Sweetie.

Elliott hated me for choosing Susan over him and for becoming a successful cinematographer. If my name came up when talking to Susan or others, he referred to me as "Susan's Hairdresser," his implication being I was gay.

To his young children, he called me "the Scumbag." I preferred "Hairdresser."

As Sweetie and I grew closer, getting married five years after Susan and Elliott separated, it was hard for me to figure out what my role in Sasha and Amy's life should be. I was not their dad. Nor did I feel right calling myself their stepdad. I settled on being their younger brother (older brother would be too mature). I was their defender when I disagreed with Sweetie about their welfare. I was often their chauffeur, teaching Amy and her friends the words and music to "Diarrhea," sung in the opening scene of Ron Howard's *Parenthood*. "When you're slindin' into first and you're feelin' something burst..." as we drove to and from school.

I was never their disciplinarian and never wanted Elliott to have a reason to be angry about my relationship with his children.

Perhaps my biggest contribution to their young lives was teaching them both how to hock like an old Jewish man. Years later, when the four of us took a road trip through Ireland, I hocked them a goodnight hock and they responded similarly from their room next door, through our common wall, as if we were the Waltons.

I remember how embarrassed Sasha was when returning to New York from boarding school on the Boston shuttle she started up her laptop and forgot she had recorded me hocking as her start-up sound.

The first time I mentioned the possibility of marriage to Sweetie, she was visiting me in Scottsdale near the end of filming *Raising Arizona*. This was a couple of years after Susan and Elliott went their separate ways, but three years before their divorce was final.

"Hey, Sweetie. When you and Elliott eventually get divorced, do you think we should get married?"

"Excuse me," said Sweetie, as she ran to the all-fiberglass bathroom to throw up. Sweetie is an adorably quiet vomiter, almost like a dove cooing. There was no sympathetic vomiting at my end.

She came back quite pale and explained she didn't ever want to get married again. Marrying Elliott was never her goal, but she had wanted kids. After she got pregnant, she married Elliott for the sake of her southern parents. Her first marriage (Elliott was her second) was right out of college and, although she loved John, wasn't sure why she married him. They divorced amicably a couple of years later while living in the Bay Area.

I was sad but understood. I wanted a kid with Susan, who was a great mother and a wonderful, smart, funny, sassy, sporty friend, but I wasn't going to push it. All through *Throw Momma from the*

Train, Big, When Harry Met Sally, and *Miller's Crossing,* Sweetie was still technically married to Elliott.

New York was not a no-fault divorce state, and although Sweetie was taking the "fault" for the divorce (abandonment) and was asking for no alimony, Elliott stalled the proceedings for as long as he could. He insisted Sweetie see a psychiatrist, saying she must be crazy. No one had ever left him before.

Whenever their trial date approached, Elliott would find a job out of the country. The next availability in the busy New York court system would be at least five months down the road.

Over the years Sweetie warmed to the idea of marrying me. In 1989, I was in New Orleans filming *Miller's Crossing.* We got married at the movie's wrap party, eleven days after Sweetie's official divorce. The Coens hired a riverboat for the party. Sweetie and I took care of the band and catering. Two people wore white to the ceremony: Sweetie and my mother.

The riverboat captain officiated our wedding, surrounded by grips, gaffers, the camera department, and actors from the show. A few friends and relatives came from out of town, including our parents. Rob Reiner and Michele Singer, whom Sweetie and I introduced on the set of *When Harry Met Sally,* were also there. They married a month later in Hawaii.

When the captain turned in my direction and said, "Repeat after me," I began to sob. I couldn't get the words out. For literally two minutes, I wept. I was just so happy. The captain looked annoyed. Sweetie looked very, very worried. Behind the captain I was staring at a group of the manliest grips and electricians you'd ever want to work with. Their mouths were open in confusion, disbelief, and awe. "How could one man cry for so long without stopping?" they wondered.

After the ceremony, one of the makeup women came up to me

and said, "You could have any woman you want. Right now. That was amazing."

As dusk descended on the wedding, champagne glasses were handed out, and Albert Finney, one of the stars of *Miller's Crossing*, made a speech full of metaphors.

"Barry. Sweetie. As you drift through the river of life, you must avoid the rocks and driftwood..." He finished his moving speech and asked us all to raise our glasses in a toast, at which point the entire Mississippi River lit up in a huge display of fireworks. Finney loved a party and had spent an exorbitant sum to buy a barge's worth of aerial display. For several decades, when I ran into Albert at some LA restaurant, he'd poke a finger in my chest and bark,

"You still married to Sweetie?"

April 22, 1989. New Orleans. Sweetie wondering what she just agreed to.

Albert Finney wondering if the marriage will last.

"Yes, sir," I'd reply.

"You better be. Those fireworks cost me a fortune."

In the words of Nic Cage in *Raising Arizona*, Sweetie's "insides were a rocky place where my seed could find no purchase."

Or in Sweetie's case, my seed would find a purchase, but not long enough to reach full term. Over the next few years, Sweetie had seven miscarriages. When I was directing *Addams Family* in Los Angeles, because Elliott had gotten a court order preventing Sweetie from taking the kids more than one hundred miles from New York City, Susan was pregnant, alone, and confined to bed. We lost that one too.

These pregnancies were becoming dangerous for Sweetie. The morning after I raced from LA back to New York from the *Addams Family* set, having traumatized those kindergarteners, when the doctors thought she had a cancerous molar pregnancy, Sweetie suggested adoption.

I was concerned.

"What if we just don't like the kid? Would we have regrets?"

"We'll have no regrets."

Sometime after this discussion Sweetie and I were having dinner at The Laundry Restaurant in East Hampton with an agent and his wife. The agent came to dinner with his right hand bandaged and his arm in a weird upright sling. I asked him what happened to his hand.

"Andy," his wife said.

Andy was their 10-year-old son, who was adopted.

"Andy?" I asked.

"Andy slammed the window down on Robert's hand. Lots of blood, lots of stitches."

"Can I ask you a question? Are there any times, ever, even once a year, or once every five years, where you think, 'I wish we hadn't adopted Andy'?"

"How about every single day?" the wife jokingly answered.

I sat through the rest of the dinner in silence.

The next morning, I got a call from the agent, promising they both loved their kid and since Sweetie and I were about to be in LA filming *Addams Family Values*, I should hire their adoption lawyer.

In December 1992 we met the lovely David Radis. He told us all the reasons we might have a challenge adopting. We were relatively old, of mixed religions, and Susan already had two birth children. But he would see what he could do. His MO was to take out ads in various local newspapers in the Carolinas and other states with a high rate of unwed pregnancies and an anti-abortion bent.

Since I was a "public figure," we told David we preferred a "closed adoption"—one where the birth mother never learned our identity.

"I can do that," he said, "but by meeting the birth mother you'll know if you feel a connection. She's carrying your baby."

We had to agree.

In mid-January, Sweetie and I were in our rental house in Santa Monica fast asleep when we received a call from Candy. We talked to her a long time. She was five months pregnant and agreed to let us fly her out to LA and meet over President's Day weekend, 1993.

Candy was 18 at the time. We liked her and she liked us. She agreed to let us adopt her baby.

As per David's suggestion, we moved Candy out to LA and put her up at the Oakwood apartments in Burbank. Sweetie and

11-year-old Amy, who had a small role in *Addams Family Values*, would visit Candy every day while I directed. Sweetie's older daughter, Sasha, was in boarding school back east.

Our adoption audition photo.

After two ultrasounds that circled the fetus' penis, we knew we were having a boy. Sweetie and I had previously agreed on the name Skyler, although we were having disagreements on how to spell Skylar's Skyler's Schuyler's name.

I was directing Christine Baranski and Peter MacNicol, playing two hideous camp counselors at Camp Chippewa, when Sweetie called.

"Come to the hospital. It's happening."

"Hey, Ames. It's time," I said to Amy, who was in the scene playing a camper.

It was the last shot of the day. I went to Christine and Peter and told them I had to leave. That our son was about to be born at Van Nuys Hospital. I told them to do one take fake saccharine, one very sarcastic, and one fast and flat, suspecting I'd use the fast/flat version, but it's always good to have choices. I got in the studio station wagon with Amy and raced to Van Nuys Hospital.

May 19, 1993: telling Peter and Christine they're on their own.

Candy allowed Sweetie in the delivery room. I was stationed in the doorway.

Amy was down the hallway on the other side of a set of double doors with a window, so we could see each other.

When our baby came out, I truly had never seen anything so purple. The doctor let Sweetie cut the umbilical cord in what felt like a symbolic move. For some reason Candy demanded they check the baby's feet. The doctor announced it was a girl with fine feet.

What?

"It's a girl," I mouthed to Amy, on the other side of the hospital double doors.

"What?" she mouthed back in amazement.

Sweetie had been blessed with her third daughter. Chloe had been blessed with a fantastic mother and, although not fantastic, at least a very loving father.

Chloe was born two weeks premature. She weighed five pounds and seven ounces. I loved her instantly. If a madman with a knife had attacked her I would have in that moment and from then on thrown myself in front of the villain to protect her. As Joel Coen says:

"It's like joining a cult."

The next morning, I got to the set, where an overly enthusiastic crew had bought a truck load of blue balloons, "It's a Boy" banners, and boxes of cigars with "It's a Boy" bands wrapped around each stogie.

"Actually, team, it's a girl."

And she is perfect.

"I'm glad we picked a name that works for a boy, or a girl, don't ya think, Sweetie?"

"We're naming her Chloe Elizabeth."

"How did that happen?"

"You know I feel uneasy naming kids. Chloe Elizabeth gives her a lot of nicknames to choose from. It's a big responsibility to stick a child with a bad name."

"Believe me. I know. I got stuck with Barry. The only thing that could have been worse is that if I had been a girl, they were going to name me Bertha, after my mother's mother."

Bertha Kellerman

Sweetie didn't want to make this moment about me, so she plowed through.

"The hospital couldn't fill out the birth certificate without a name. She's so tiny and girly, she needed a more feminine name. So I picked Chloe."

"Chloe."

"I looked it up. French. Small green shoot. Also, David Radis said we could change it in six months at her adoption hearing.

"Chloe it is."

And Chloe she is. I'm a slow learner, so for a while I called her Cleo. A few years later when we got a dog, I'd call her Lucky, the name of our 110-pound Rhodesian Ridgeback.

The problem is, over the years, like many well-meaning moms and dads—and perhaps this is why I have so much self-loathing—I became my parents. I have my dad's salesman shtick, slapping strangers on the shoulder and telling them why they should hire me. I'm friendly and self-involved. I have my mother's traits of a frightened, nervous, overprotective, self-centered mess. I hover over Chloe and worry about her constantly. When she's flying, I track her flight from takeoff to landing, which is a real problem when she's on an overnight flight to Asia. I didn't want to become my parents any more than I wanted Chloe to become Barry.

I will say, unlike me, and this is thanks to Sweetie, Chloe had many sleepovers and at 14 headed off for "sleepaway school" in Pennsylvania before college in Boston and LA.

Chloe is a combination of Sweetie and me, although the me part of her embodies many of my worst personality traits. She worries. She is a tad pushy and is very, very opinionated. We both arrive at airports many hours too early in anticipation of what could have been four flat tires and a traffic jam. She has the skills and personality to make a great director. Luckily, she also has some of Sweetie's traits, so she is compassionate and generous and kind.

Shortly after Chloe's birth, Sweetie brought her up to Fresno, California, to visit Amy and me on the *Addams Family Values* set. We were filming the exterior of Camp Chippewa. Sweetie had told me that babies are comforted by the touch of skin. Every time I had a break from filming, I'd rush into the camper, rip off my cowboy snap-button shirt, put Chloe next to my chest, and feed her a bottle.

Chloe Elizabeth Ringo Sonnenfeld. Santa Monica, California, 1993.

CHAPTER 31

Get Shorty

Christmas 1989, Sweetie and I had been married eight months. Sasha and Amy were scheduled to be with Elliott. This would be the first Christmas Sweetie spent without her girls. We needed a distraction.

Neither of us had been to the Caribbean, been on a cruise, or vacationed at a Club Med, which had recently launched their first sailing ship, *Club Med One*.

Three birds, one stone.

It was offering "A unique experience combining the elegance of a sail cruise ship with the luxury of an all-inclusive holiday."

Hmmmmmmmm.

After checking in hours too early for our flight to St. Maarten, where we were meeting our ship, we were wandering around JFK's various magazine shops when I realized I was about to get on a boat for many days with only one book, John Clancy's *Clear and Present Danger*. I panicked. Having read *Hunt for Red October*, I knew I was going to be on page 1,100 before I could tell if it was any good.

I spotted a rack of paperbacks. I had heard of Elmore Leonard but had never read his books. *Get Shorty* looked interesting. It was about Hollywood, so at the least I'd learn a thing or two.

Sweetie and I came away from that vacation with a clear

understanding we're not Caribbean, cruise, or Club Med people. The first night at dinner, we discovered we were expected to sit at large tables and make friends. We spotted two two-top tables and raced for one of them.

"Okay. I'll hold the table. You get some food."

Each night we stood in front of the restaurant's doors a half hour early to be first in line to get one of those precious tables for two. We never met another soul on the ship, thank God. The all-inclusive, all-you-can-eat buffet was decent enough, especially if you stuck exclusively to shrimp cocktails. Typically, Sweetie was more adventurous and would soon pay the price.

I decided to read *Get Shorty* first. It was about 250 pages, and I'm a slow reader.

I loved it. Loved the writing style and dialogue. I also felt it would make a great movie and knew who the lead should be.

"Sweetie. Read this book and tell me who the lead is."

Sweetie was desperately ill, having, like most people on the boat, come down with some sort of Norovirus, or food poisoning.

"I'm just a little nauseous at the moment."

"Okay. Just read it before we get off the boat."

"Yes. I will. Just not at the moment, please."

"Sure. I'm just saying that I know you don't like giving in to your illnesses, you know, when you're feeling sick, so maybe reading this will take..."

"Excuse me," Sweetie said, as she raced to the bathroom to puke.

"Should have stuck to the shrimp cocktails," I yelled toward the cabin's tiny bathroom.

Despite Sweetie's sad stomach issues and the rocking of the ship, she knew not reading the book was not an option. She finished *Get Shorty* before we got off the ship.

"Okay. Who's the lead? Who is Chili Palmer?"

"Danny DeVito."

"Exactly!"

Danny and I became close friends on *Throw Momma from the Train*. In late 1986, although I had been hired as the cinematographer and was in pre-production on *Big*, Sol Lomita, the head of post-production for Orion Pictures called, asking me to meet Danny that night in hopes I would be the cinematographer on *Throw Momma*. I told him I wasn't available. I was in prep on *Big*, and it was going to start filming in six weeks. Sol told me it wasn't going to happen. That Barry Diller, the president of Fox, hated the idea of doing *Big* with Robert De Niro and he was going to suspend filming until Tom Hanks was available.

I told Sol he was nuts, that I hadn't heard anything about shutting down, but I was happy to meet Danny if he didn't think I'd be wasting his time. "Trust me, Ba. *Big* is shutting down," Sol said.

One of the secrets in the film business is that teamsters know what's going on way before the rest of the crew. I went to the teamster captain and said, "I know this sounds stupid, but have you heard any rumors about us shutting down to wait for Tom Hanks?"

"Sure, Ba. It's happening. Greenhut's going to let everyone know in a coupla days."

That night I met Danny at Lenge, a Japanese restaurant at Columbus and 69th. We chatted for a couple of hours and then he asked,

"So if we worked together on this, could we use those lenses with 'lots of millimeters'?"

"Lots of millimeters?"

"Yeah. You know, the ones with a lot of 'em?"

"You mean a telephoto lens?"

"Yeah."

"Sure."

"Okay. So you're hired. Only thing, I have to let Fred Elmes know he's fired. But since I just hired him today, it's not gonna be a big deal."

Danny and I never used those lots of millimeter lenses. I turned him into a wide angle guy, which has very few millimeters.

On the set having just finished my grilled cheese, tomato, and extra crispy bacon sandwich. Throw Momma from the Train. *Point Dume, California.*

Danny's wife at the time, Rhea Perlman, was filming out of town, so Danny and I pretty much spent every waking minute of pre-production together seven days a week. We were either shot listing and storyboarding the film, going to movies, drinking espressos, or napping in his bungalow at Hollywood Center Studios. Danny would nap on the couch, and I'd be on the floor.

At some point in the afternoon, Danny would kick me awake and say, "Ba. Ya wanna espresso?"

We'd have a short shot and get back to work.

So that's how I came to know Danny and knew how perfect he would be for the lead in *Get Shorty*. Like Chili Palmer, *Get Shorty*'s main character, Danny is the single most self-confident person I have ever met.

After our cruise adventure, I called Danny and told him I read a book I'd love to do with him.

"Okay. I'll buy it. You direct. I star and produce."

The next day Danny called me.

"Ba. Joe Pesci is trying to buy the book, but I'm a bigger star. We're good."

About a week after my first conversation with Danny, he called to tell me Elmore "Dutch" Leonard wanted to talk to me before Danny could option the book. It seemed like the combination of the guy who directed *Addams Family* and Danny DeVito playing Chili Palmer made Dutch a little worried. I suspect he feared I'd make his book into a wacky comedy with a "K."

Until *Get Shorty*, Elmore's novels that were made into movies were critical and financial failures, which was why the rights to the novel were still available. Many books by successful authors are optioned before they're even published, which I hope is the case with *Barry Sonnenfeld, Call Your Mother*.

I gave Elmore and his agent, Michael Siegel, my thoughts about comedy, which is that no one on the show should think they're working on one. The formula for a successful comedy is to have an absurd situation, or an absurd character, played for reality.

If the situation is funny, the scene will be funny, but only if it's played totally real. If the cinematographer knows it's a comedy, it will be too bright. If the film lab knows, it will be even brighter. If the wardrobe department knows, it will be colorful. If the composer thinks it's a comedy, there'll be slide whistles and triangles. The worst, of course, is if the actors or director decide they're making a comedy. I promised Elmore our show would be funny, because it would be real.

Six weeks later Danny called.

"Ba. We're in. I bought the book."

"That's fantastic, Danny. Do you like it?"

"Haven't read it. I'll get around to it."

Scott Frank was hired to write the screenplay. His script was 136 pages, which was about 15% fatter than a typical script, but given my "faster/flatter" style of directing, the movie would still have a finished length of a typical comedy. Scott gave the story a structure, an ending, and a comedic touch. Although the book had brilliant characters and dialogue, the last line in the book is, "Fucking endings, man, they weren't as easy as they looked."

Which is to say the book had no ending. Fine for a novel, deadly for a movie.

Danny had an overall deal at TriStar, whose chairman was Mike Medavoy, one of the execs who had hired me to direct *Addams Family* when he was an executive at Orion. "This will be a breeze," I thought.

Here's what we discovered: no studio wanted to make an Elmore Leonard movie since none of the films based on his novels had made money.

In addition, no one wanted to make "an insider" movie about Hollywood because none of those made money, either. We went to every studio with our script. Not one was interested. Over a couple of years, still not able to get it set up, TriStar's CEO was replaced. We went back to the studio a second time since Danny still had his overall deal there.

They declined.

Although I was intent on directing *Get Shorty*, I was sent the script for *Men in Black*.

I continued to push for *Get Shorty* but agreed to develop *MIB*. The two producers who worked at Columbia Pictures at the time were Walter Parkes and his wife, Laurie McDonald. Over the twenty-five years of developing and filming the first three *MIBs* we have had huge fights and big laughs. If I never worked with Walter and Laurie, we might even be friends.

Laurie is smart, blonde, and perfectly put together. Walter went to Yale, plays the guitar, and has a full head of perfect silver hair. He also has an excellent vocabulary that put me at a disadvantage when we were on opposite sides of an idea, which happened often.

The original Ed Solomon script that Sweetie and I read, good as it was, needed some work, but it mirrored my philosophy of the universe, which is we don't have a clue.

Walter and Laurie flew me out to LA to meet Lisa Henson, the president of production at Columbia. Over the next eighteen months I traveled to LA, risking my life on too many planes for too many meetings.

There were several script issues I was trying to solve. For one, I wanted the story to take place in New York. Walter wanted Kansas. My theory was if aliens did exist, the hub for all their activity would be New York, where they could fit in without wearing disguises.

Wonder why that person talking to themselves on the corner of 42nd Street and Broadway is wearing four down jackets even though it's mid-August with the temperature hovering at 95 degrees with 90 percent humidity? It's because on his planet, that's Antarctic weather.

Walter was particularly stubborn about the theme of the show. His version was about pheromones and how they are released when humans are fearful, attracting alien bugs. Agents J and K realize that if they could convince all of humanity to laugh in the face of danger, we'd be saved.

Because he had a better vocabulary, I was stymied.

But back in the world of *Get Shorty*, something I never believed in happened: a Christmas miracle.

CHAPTER 32

A Christmas Miracle

Over the 1993 holidays, Fred Specktor, Danny's CAA agent, found himself on the ski lift in Deer Valley with Mike Marcus, until recently a former colleague at CAA, now chairman of a reimagined, rebuilt, MGM Studios.

Mike needed content and wanted to quickly make an announcement of a film acquisition showing that MGM "was in business." Mike was either very smart or he didn't know the double curse of Elmore Leonard and movies about movies.

"Ba," Danny said, "MGM wants to make the movie. All they need is a star and a budget."

In the two years since we started this project, Danny had gotten the financing he needed and the actor he wanted for *Matilda*, a movie he'd been trying to direct for years. He wasn't sure he'd be able to star in *Get Shorty*.

We needed a reality check. Was this film worth making? Maybe every studio with the exception of MGM knew something we didn't. Maybe *Get Shorty* was not going to work as a movie.

Danny had two partners in Jersey Films, his production company—Stacey Sher and Michael Shamberg. The fact that Stacey at one time dated Quentin Tarantino would be very helpful before the end of this chapter.

Jersey's offices were located on the lot at Columbia Studios (now SONY) on Stage 6, a soundstage with the tallest ceiling in North America. Jersey had no walls or offices, just a few tables in the middle of an enormous soundstage.

Stacey, Danny, Fred Specktor, and David Rubin, the casting

director, called in favors, and one Sunday afternoon we gathered on Stage 6 and had a table read of *Get Shorty*. Danny played Chili, Gene Hackman (who was a client of Fred Specktor's) was Harry Zimm, Dennis Farina was Bones, we had Samuel L. Jackson as Bo Catlette, and Lesley Ann Warren as Karen Flores.

The table read was fantastic. Sweetie came up to me, tears in her eyes, and said, "Even if Danny doesn't do it, as long as you have Gene Hackman and Dennis Farina, it's a slam dunk."

"Yeah, Sweetie, but..."

"I know. I know. Can you please be happy today?"

I told Hackman how great he was. How funny he was. Gene said, "I'm not a comedian."

"I know. That's why you're so funny."

"I don't have a fucking clue what you're talking about," Gene snapped as he walked off.

Here's birthday boy Gene Hackman on the set of Get Shorty. *My expression was due to the fear that Gene was going to spin around and plunge that knife into my chest.*

Danny was thrilled by how it went and told me no matter what, if he couldn't play Chili Palmer, he'd play Martin Weir, the "Shorty," of *Get Shorty*.

A week later it was official. Although still producing and acting in a smaller role, Danny would not be the lead.

We needed a new Chili.

The studio sent us their list of bankable actors they would make the movie with, which included Harrison Ford, Clint Eastwood, Michael Douglas, Dustin Hoffman (rumors were that Hoffman was the actual "Shorty" of *Get Shorty*, as in the real-life person the character is based on), and Warren Beatty.

Many of the actors on the list passed without a meeting. However, Hoffman was willing to have an in-person discussion. I risked my life and flew out to LAX on TWA's Lockheed L1011 wide-body to meet Dustin in a small dark luncheonette near the Brentwood Market.

I was early. Hoffman was late.

Dustin was one of those guys who had a power whisper.

With the constant clinking of silverware and buffalo china, my leaning forward served the double purpose of getting my ears closer to Dustin's mouth to hear the words and my eyes closer to try to lip read. After a few whispered pleasantries he asked the question that made me realize he wasn't here to talk about doing the movie so much as to investigate.

"So, Barry. Am I the 'Shorty' of *Get Shorty*?"

In the '80s Hoffman wanted to make a film of Elmore's book, *LaBrava*. It famously became such an endless headache that although the movie never got made, Elmore's experience with Hoffman lead to the writing, some say, of *Get Shorty*.

"You know, Dustin. I have no idea. Dutch has never mentioned you, so I'm going to guess you're not unless you want me to say you are."

"Well, I was just curious. Look. I'm not going to do your movie. Okay?"

"You bet. Thanks for meeting me." (And thanks for making me fly out to LA.) I think Hoffman wanted me to stick around and waste my time trying to convince him why he'd be great in the lead role, but I knew he was on an ego fishing expedition and would never be in the film.

Before there were Google Maps and Waze, there was Barry Being Lost. A drive to the Hotel Bel-Air that should have taken fifteen minutes took several hours. I arrived in the early evening, said hello to Dawn the concierge and Roger the bellman, got to my room, and ordered an iced tea, brutally shaken Belvedere vodka in a martini glass, and a medium rare New York strip. I prepared for a sleepless night, worrying about tomorrow's flight back to New York.

A couple of weeks later Danny called.

"Beatty wants to do it. You need to fly out to LA. He'll meet you at some point between Thursday and Sunday. He's staying at the Bel-Air."

"Danny. Please don't make me do this. Warren's not going to do *Get Shorty*. We both know that."

"No, Ba. He's into it."

"No, he isn't. He's just saying that so I risk my life flying to LA."

"Ba. He's into it. Get on the plane."

"Danny. Let me ask you this. An airplane that weighs hundreds of tons can fly six miles above earth because the air flowing over the wing is moving slower than the air flowing under the wing? It makes no sense. Think about it for just a second."

"Get on the fucking plane."

"Ugh. Okay. I'll go. But can Beatty narrow it down just a bit? Normally when you have a meeting, it's like three o'clock on Tuesday. Does it have to be 'some time' between Thursday and Sunday? That's kinda inconsiderate."

"Ba. Get on the plane."

So I did.

It was a Pan Am Boeing 747, which weighs 404,000 pounds, but somehow flies. Pan Am's first class was upstairs in the hump of the 747 right behind the cockpit, and I was the only one in the small upper cabin that day. As soon as we took off, I knew something was horribly wrong.

From the ceiling came a squealing sound unlike anything that should be heard on an airplane, or any other vehicle, or non-vehicle. Within a minute, I was racing down the stairs to find a flight attendant, who admonished me that the seatbelt sign was on.

"You've got to hear this sound. Something is very wrong with this plane."

We ran up the circular staircase. The stewardess screamed in my ear:

"What is that sound?"

"Exactly!" I shrieked.

The stewardess knocked on the cockpit door (this is a decade before 9/11) and screamed for assistance. By this time I had taken my seat and buckled in for what would surely be a catastrophic crash. The copilot came out, looked up, and pushed a ceiling tile out of the way, which increased the decibels of the screech. The pilot screamed something into the flight attendant's ear. She raced down and then back up the stairs, carrying a dinner plate, salad plate, and a saucer.

My head was turned around into a nauseating position to get a look at the false ceiling, and I'm crapping you negatory, the sky above. As the copilot moved his salad-plated hand toward the hole in the fucking airplane, the dish shot out of his hand and whooshed into the wild blue yonder.

He reached up with the dinner plate, which floated off his hand and adhered to the gaping hole. Not only was it a perfect fit, it sealed the hole with such perfection the cabin went silent.

The copilot looked down at my ashen face, gave me a thumbs-up, a reassuring Tom Cruise smile, and said,

"I guess we're going to have to get that fixed in Los Angeles."

"Wait. What?"

"Not a big deal. We lost our beacon. But it's a daylight flight. We're good."

"Mr. Sonnenfeld. Back so soon?" Roger the bellman smiled.

On January 14, 1994, at 4:31 a.m., the Northridge earthquake hit Los Angeles. Later that day Warren Beatty, Annette Bening, and their 2ish-year-old Kathlyn (now Stephen) checked into the Hotel Bel-Air. Months later when I arrived, Thursday late lunch, they were still ensconced at the Bel-Air, waiting for their home to be repaired. After Roger got me situated in suite 199, a large open room with a view of the pool, I called the operator, announced myself, and asked to be put through to Warren Beatty's room. I left a message.

"Yes. This is Barry Sonnenfeld. I am here in room 199. If you would like to get together today, Thursday, at any time, please let me know—or let me know what time on Friday you'd like to meet."

Thursday evening, I ordered the New York strip, an iced tea, and brutally shaken Belvedere vodka in a martini glass from room service.

These days when I can't sleep I scroll through the endless options on Amazon until I buy something I don't need, as long as it's Amazon Prime.

But 1994 was a long time before Amazon, which meant staying up all night watching infomercials. There was a compelling one on how to train your dog as taught by the Monks of New Skete, a monastery in upstate New York known for training German shepherds. If I acted now, in addition to the VHS training tape, I'd get a forty-foot webbed nylon leash in four to six weeks. I ordered it that night.

Friday, I waited until 10:00 a.m., figuring it was late enough I wouldn't wake anyone up, but early enough we might still be able to have some form of breakfast.

I left a message:

"Hi, Warren. This is Barry Sonnenfeld. It's Friday at 10:00 a.m. I'm in room 199. I'll hang around my room waiting for your call. I'm available at any time, or, if you're not available, please call me and let me know a specific time when you will be. Thanks."

I had breakfast, lunch, and the New York strip dinner with an iced tea and brutally shaken Belvedere vodka in a martini glass in my room. I called Danny. I called Fred Specktor. Fred got back to me:

"Barry. How are ya?"

"I'm really bored, Fred."

"I know. I know. Look, Warren's covering agent tells me Warren is incredibly busy, but he knows you're at the hotel, he's gotten your messages and he'll definitely be seeing you this weekend."

"Hey, Fred. If Warren could give that message to his agent, couldn't he have given it to me? Room service is running out of New York strips."

"Barry, this is all going to work out."

"I doubt it, Fred. But thanks."

Late in the day on Friday I noticed the pool had a house phone. Saturday morning, I asked the operator to forward my calls to the pool.

"Of course, Mr. Sonnenfeld. I'll make sure Mr. Beatty reaches you at the pool."

As I left the room to head to the pool, Roger was placing the morning papers on my doormat.

"I bet Mr. Beatty calls you today, sir."

I spent the day at the pool. No calls, no sightings. I had had enough. At sunset, a tortilla soup, Cobb salad, and many iced teas later, I left the pool, walked the thirty feet back to my room, ordered my New York strip and Belvedere, and called Warren's room, which was kicked back to the message system.

"Hi, Warren. This is Barry Sonnenfeld in room 199. I'm leaving tomorrow and heading home. My plane is at 2:00 p.m., and I like to get to the airport very, very early, so please call me tonight or first thing in the morning so we can possibly meet before I head to the airport. If, which I suspect will be the case, we don't speak, I've enjoyed my time at the Hotel Bel-Air."

About thirty seconds later my phone rang.

"Hello?"

"Um...yes...This is Warren Beatty?"

"Hi, Warren."

"Um...yeah...listen, could we meet tomorrow? I'd love to talk about...um...your project."

"Sure. What time? My plane is at 2:00. I'd like to leave here by 10:00."

"Um...Let's speak in the morning, and we'll set something up."

"Wait. Warren. That won't work. I need to arrange for a car. My plane is at 2:00, so I'll be leaving by 10:00."

"Um....hmmmm...Okay. 2:00."

Since my plane was actually the 10:00 p.m. red-eye, I decided to let this surreal moment pass and agreed to meet him at the Hotel Bel-Air restaurant at 2:00.

It was a one-minute walk from my room to the restaurant, so I managed to get there fifteen minutes early. When Warren and Kathlyn showed up at 2:35, I was on my sixth cup of coffee. Two-year-old Kathlyn needed a lot of attention, and it took a long time for her to "settle down" so Warren and I could discuss *Get Shorty*.

"So...um...hello. Nice to finally meet you," he ummmmed.

"Yes. You too. We have a love of Dede Allen in common."

Warren and I chatted about Dede for a little too long, and I was starting to panic about making the red-eye.

"So, Warren. What about *Get Shorty*?"

"Um...here is what I am thinking. I, ummm....loved your script. I want to make the movie with you. I want to be Chili Palmer."

"Well, that's pretty great."

"Um...Sure. Yes. Ummm...I just have one question, and if you can answer it, I'm in."

"Shoot."

"Wellll, correct me if I'm wrong, but Chili is a numbers runner at the start of the film. He's on a pretty low rung of the mob hierarchy. Am I right?"

Uh-oh.

"Yes, Warren. He's a numbers runner. But by the end of the film he's a big time movie producer."

"Yes. Right. So here's my question. Why would someone who looks like me be so far down the mob pecking order at the beginning of the movie?"

"*Riiiiight*. I see where you're going with this, and I have an answer."

"Really?" He silently schmucked me.

"Warren. I live in East Hampton, Long Island. We have a

plumber whose name is John Ward. He's gorgeous. Yet a plumber. Sometimes it just works out that way. But...um...[I was starting to sound like Warren] sometimes it just happens. And besides, as we discussed, by the end Chili is a huge Hollywood producer."

"Yeah. I get all that. But I look like Warren Beatty. Warren Beatty wouldn't be a numbers runner."

"You know, Warren. I never thought of it that way, and you are absolutely, totally right. You are too good looking to play a numbers runner, and I'm sorry I wasted your time. I really have to make this plane, so I'm going to head out. Please ask the waiter to charge the meal to room 199. What a pleasure it was to meet you."

I raced to the airport, where I spent many hours in the Pan Am lounge waiting to risk my life yet again on the 10:00 p.m. red-eye, regretting that I hadn't checked out the tail number on the westbound flight. I didn't want to get on that salad-plated, beacon-free plane again. I debated about rebooking on TWA.

As an aside, after eventually making *Get Shorty*, without Warren, I was at Steven Spielberg's vacation home in East Hampton taking a meeting on *Men in Black*, which was once again back on track with me as the director. Steven's East Coast assistant was a woman named Mary Squillante—now Mary Couch. Mary had been Sweetie and my favorite waitress at The Laundry, one of only two good restaurants in East Hampton in the early '90s. Steven hired Mary and her bartender husband away from the restaurant to become caretakers for his Hamptons house.

So there's Mary, working for the Spielbergs. I told her how much Sweetie and I missed her at The Laundry and said if she ever got tired of working for Spielie to call me. The next day she was my employee and is to this day.

The first assignment I gave Mary was to track down the VHS

dog-training tape and forty-foot dog leash that never arrived from the Monks of New Skete. Mary asked what the promised delivery date was, and I told her that it was a couple of years ago. She got right on it, though a bit confused.

I asked her about the VHS tape and leash every day. About three weeks into my nagging, she finally asked the question that had been on her mind from the beginning of her employment.

"You're really worrying about this VHS tape and leash."

"Well, yeah. It's been years, and I forgot about it, but now that I remember, I'm really angry I never got it."

"Yes. No. I can see that. You ask about it every day. It's just...I just...have a question about the urgency."

"Yeah?"

"You do know that you have no dog. Right?"

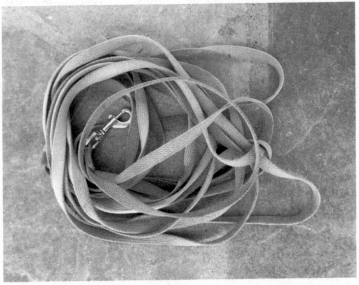

Mary tracked it down. Two decades and two dogs later, it's still with me.

*   *   *

We were out of names. We were running out of time. Studio execs have a short life span. It was only a matter of time before Mike Marcus would be fired and the only studio executive in all of Hollywood who wanted to make *Get Shorty* would be yesterday's news.

Sweetie and I were in LA for more *Men in Black* meetings when Stacey Sher, one of the three principals of Danny's company, had an idea.

"What about Travolta?" she said.

Sweetie instantly thought it was a great idea. I wasn't so sure. He had been in a litany of bad films in recent years, and I didn't think MGM would make the movie with John as the lead. On the other hand, *Pulp Fiction* was about to come out, and rumor was it was great. Maybe Travolta was back. Jersey Films had produced the film, and Stacey discovered there was going to be a technical playback of the sound mix at Disney Studios later that night. Stacey called Tarantino, and he agreed to let Sweetie and me sit in on the session.

The movie was fantastic. Travolta was perfect for the part of Chili Palmer.

Everyone, including MGM, agreed.

Everyone except Travolta.

He passed.

Stacey arranged for John to have dinner with Danny, Scott Frank (the screenwriter), and myself to see if we could convince him to change his mind. John suggested dinner at the Celebrity Center in Hollywood.

The Celebrity Center is the headquarters of the Church of Scientology.

Danny, Scott, and I were led into a huge ballroom—Fontainebleau Hotel sized. There were like three hundred twelve-tops in the room, all of them empty except for one table, about half a football field away, where two people were sitting with Luciano Pavarotti. The room was ringed with men in crisp sea captain outfits.

Travolta arrived late and told us he didn't get the script. Didn't understand it, didn't get the tone. The good news was at the time Scott Frank had long curly hair down to the middle of his back, and John was fascinated by it. A poodle wished it had the curls Scott Frank's hair had. It was hypnotic to John, and he agreed to think about it overnight. Danny drove me back to my hotel. We rode in sullen silence until Danny said:

"Boy, you wouldn't think Pavarotti was a Scientologist."

"He's thinking the same thing about you, Danny."

Later that night, after we reported back to Stacey that John was pretty definitely not going to do our film, Stacey called Quentin and asked for his help. Tarantino had read and loved the script for *Get Shorty* and was a huge Elmore Leonard fan. He called John.

"This is not the movie you pass on."

John protested.

Quentin repeated,

"John. This is not the movie you pass on."

Travolta agreed to do the movie, and MGM made his deal, with bonuses based on the performance of *Pulp Fiction*. All we needed was an approved budget and we had a green-lit movie.

Our budget was $30,250,000. MGM insisted we get it down to $30 million before they gave us a green light. I went to their offices in Santa Monica with Danny and the line producer, my good friend Graham Place. I had worked with Graham since I was filming ABC After-School Specials. Our budget was lean, with no hidden money for running into trouble once we started filming. Danny came along to listen and show face.

On the studio side, in addition to Mike Marcus, was David Ladd, who was the president of production and would be our day-to-day guy, and Bob Relyea, the head of MGM's physical production.

"Look, Barry. We love this movie and want to make it, but you're going to have to lose $250,000," said Mike.

"Absolutely. So how should we find this two-fifty?" I asked.

David jumped in. MGM was prepared.

"We've looked this budget over closely, and I admit it's pretty tight, but on day five, you have $2,000 for crew parking. Let's lose that."

"Can't," said Graham. "It's a union thing. We have to provide parking."

"Okay. But isn't $2,000 kind of steep? Can you make it $1,500?"

"Not really," said Graham. "It's a downtown location. Two grand."

"Got it," David cheerfully said. "On page 7, we were thinking of losing the first two lines of dialogue."

I saw where this was going. Death by a thousand cuts, and we still wouldn't find $250K. I jumped in.

"Ya know, you guys are busy, and I really want to make the movie, so here's how we lose a quarter of a million in one move."

Not only did David and Mike lean forward, so did Danny and especially Graham, since he knew there was no way to trim that much out of the budget.

"I'd rather do eighty scenes the right way, than eighty-one where every scene suffers either because I didn't have the right equipment or enough time to shoot it correctly. So, what I propose is losing the scene where Travolta visits Hackman on the set of one of Hackman's horror films. We were going to film it over two nights, and each night is a hundred and twenty-five thousand. We cut the scene, we lose two days of shooting, we save two-fifty, and we can leave the room with a green-lit picture. Deal?"

"No deal. I love the scene. Find another way," Mike said.

"Mike, I love the scene, too. It's great for so many reasons, including one you don't even know. Ben Stiller has agreed to play the recent film school graduate/director. It's also great because Chili loves movies, and it's the only time in our film he gets to see a movie being made. We also see that Hackman, for all of his neuroses, is actually a good film producer. I love the scene, but it doesn't move the plot along."

"Absolutely not."

"Mike. It saves two hundred and fifty thousand dollars."

"Find another way."

David, who had been riffling through our budget, happily chimed in. "Do you really need a chapman crane? That's $2,000, not including the driver."

"Actually, David, good call. We don't need the crane, because it was for the very scene we're taking out of the movie."

"You're not taking it out of the movie."

"Mike. We have to. We have to lose the scene. End of story."

"Don't tell me end of story. I want the scene in the movie."

"You can't have it."

"What would it cost to put it back in?"

Graham and Danny were amazed I might pull it off.

"To put the Hackman/Travolta scene back in the movie will cost you two hundred and fifty grand."

"You got it."

"Okay. You're saying that you want the scene and you'll give us two fifty to film it."

"Yes."

"So our budget is $30,250,000. And we have a green light."

"That's what I just said, asshole."

"Just checking."

Danny, Graham, and I walked down the hallway toward the elevator, stifling our giggles.

Danny said, "Hold up. I gotta piss."

I never pass up a chance to pee, so we stopped off at the men's room. As we opened the door, I discovered I was lined up for the short urinal, and Danny was in line for the taller one. Quite a dilemma. I didn't know if I should cross over in front of him, acknowledging he was really short, or keep walking straight ahead, putting Danny at a possibly uncomfortable position.

Both of us continued to walk parallel to each other, toward the asymmetrical urinals.

I kept to my line.

Straight and narrow.

We were getting pretty close.

Zipper pull down close.

I kept walking straight ahead toward the short urinal.

About a step away from full commitment, I heard Danny say:

"What are you? A fucking moron?"

In the last ten minutes I had been called an asshole and a moron, and it wasn't even 10:00 a.m., but it was turning out to be a great day.

On October 20, 1995, *Get Shorty* was released, almost six years after I read the book.

CHAPTER 33

A Final Promise of Suicide

Eight days after my mother died, about fifty-three years into the long, sad Sonnenfeld marriage, my father—who was married to Kelly at the time of her death—wed one of the women he had been having an affair with.

Honey Rose had been a "Vegas showgirl" in her prime. Dad bragged that she slept with Frank Sinatra.

Honey Rose and Sonny on their way to get married.

The affair with Honey Rose wasn't a surprise. Several years before Kelly's death Sonny announced he was leaving Mom and moving to Vegas to live with Honey Rose. My mother once again using weakness as her strength pulled the old suicide card out of her emotional deck. Sonny was about to call her bluff when Mom realized she had overplayed her hand. She offered an alternative: What if Dad spent weekends and one night a week with Honey Rose and Kelly wouldn't commit suicide? Sonny agreed, and Honey Rose moved to New York.

For two years my mother would call on the nights when Sonny was with his paramour.

"Barry. I'm decimated."

"I don't think people are decimated, Mom. I think like armies and nations and cities..."

"Uccch. Barry. You know what I mean."

"Devastated?"

"Fine. I'm devastated. Is that better?"

"I don't know. Why are you devastated?"

"Take a guess."

"Because of Dad?"

"Of course because of Dad. Why else would I be decimated?"

"Devastated."

"Uchhh. Barry. Will you listen to yourself."

"Well, you could have lots of reasons. I mean, have you been reading the *Times*?"

"Barry. Get serious. I am truly decimated."

"Um...OK."

"Are you nuts? Do you condone this?"

"If condone means accept, sure."

"Uchhhh."

"Imagine how Honey Rose feels. She thought Dad was divorcing you and marrying her. Now she's stuck in New York, and Sonny is with you half the nights. Do you think she's devastated?"

"Thank you, Barry. Thank you very much. That's your actual attitude?"

"Mom. I'm not your husband. Leave me out of it. Please. Work this out with Dad."

"Good night, Barry."

"Night, Mom."

"Wait. Barry?"

"Yup."

"I love you very much. You know that."

"Yes, Mom. I do."

After a couple of years Honey Rose told Sonny she was heading back to Vegas. Dad moved back in with Mom, although he kept the Honey Rose affair going via Southwest Airlines, along with, I assume, his other affairs. Sonny was in his late 70s at this point, but still a playa.

I suspect the reason he didn't leave Kelly was money. Mom retired from teaching with a decent pension, and although Dad had a few financial years above water, his income was less reliable than that of a UFT pensioner.

Now that Kelly had passed away, he had Mom's retirement savings and lived in Vegas with a retired showgirl.

CHAPTER 34

Reenactors

A very public display of my overwhelming fear of Sweetie's death happened on the set of *Wild Wild West*, and it involved Will Smith. Sweetie had been feeling occasionally dizzy for a few days, and I finally nagged her into going to Dr. Koblin, our LA doctor—and somehow this makes sense in Hollywood—a former business partner with Wolfgang Puck in the frozen food industry.

That night we were filming at Lake Piru, about an hour and a half north of Los Angeles. The scene included four hundred Civil War reenactors—all on the Confederate side. These reenactors are the real deal. I got a sense that if we told them we needed to bring back slavery to make the scene more realistic, they would have whooped and hollered.

Sweetie had just gotten back from Koblin as I was leaving our rental house for the set.

"How did it go?"

"Well, you know Koblin. He couldn't find anything wrong, so he's sending me to get a brain scan tomorrow just to make sure."

"What?"

"Barry. I'm fine. Go do your job. Have fun. I'll see you in the morning."

Filming a scene with Civil War reenactors is always hard because they're sticklers for reality.

"We wouldn't stand like that."

"We wouldn't run; we'd march."

"I should say that line, not him. I'm a lieutenant."

The reenactors were driving me crazy with their regulations and negativity and, um, fellas, just in case you didn't know ... *Wild Wild West* is a movie with a made-up story that has an eighty-foot mechanical spider in it. Relax.

The areas surrounding LA are always cold at night. Often frigid. This was one of those nights. We had a Civil War tank that had to start submerged in the lake and drive out onto the land. The mechanical effects kept breaking down. The lighting was taking too long. I'm frustrated and cold. I'm worried we're not going to get our work done and we're scheduled at the Lake Piru location for only one night.

At around midnight, which means we're close to our lunch break, I start to think about Sweetie and her brain scan, and I realize she is going to die.

No one gets dizzy for no reason. I collapse on the ground and start to weep. I'm howling and shivering like an injured animal.

Will rushes up to me,

"Baz. What's wrong?"

"Sweetie's dying."

"What?!"

"Sweetie's dying."

"What are you talking about?"

"She has brain cancer."

Will looks at my sobbing face and collapses on the ground next to me. He grabs me and hugs me like Sweetie's life depended on it.

"If anything were to ever happen to Jada. Oh, poor Baz. Poor Sweetie. I am so sorry, Baz," Will wailed.

The producers Jon Peters and Graham Place signal for a John Deere ATV with a flatbed. They load Will and me onto the back of the vehicle as we're holding onto each other in a death grip, yowling like dying beasts.

We are, of course, John Deere'd past 400 Confederate reenactors, each and every one staring at the sobbing, hugging Jew and Negro.

It took about five minutes to get to base camp—Will and me blubbering our way up the dirt road where the caterer, trailers for makeup, grip, electric, and all the personal campers are set up in a circle. We pull to a stop. Will looks at me, his eyes red from crying. Both of our shirts are soaked from each other's tears. I see the pain he's feeling for me and Sweetie.

And I say:

"Maybe I'm just hungry."

"What, Baz?" Will says gently.

"Maybe I'm just hungry. Sometimes that makes me emotional. Or dizzy."

Less gently: "What, Baz?"

"Maybe Sweetie is okay."

"She has a brain tumor. How is that okay?"

"Well, we don't know that for a fact. At the moment it's just that she's a bit dizzy."

Will looks at me and realizes that he should have known better. Suspiciously, he says,

"So, what's with the brain cancer?"

"Well, the doctor couldn't find anything wrong with Sweetie, so he's doing a brain scan tomorrow. She's probably fine. I'm going to get some food. You want anything?" I say as I walk toward the catering truck.

"Baz. I was just bawling like a baby in front of four hundred Confederate troops because you were hungry?"

"I guess."

Five minutes later I'm pounding on Will's door.

"Will. Come quick. Graham's dying!"

"I'm not fallin' for that, Baz."

"No, seriously. He's got a piece of cauliflower stuck in his throat. He's making horrible sounds and he's blue. Ya gotta come."

"He better be dying, Baz," Will says as he opens his camper door.

We race across base camp to my trailer, where Graham is bent over, looking very blue.

"Will," I scream, "do you know the Heimlich maneuver?"

Will shakes his head. But he knows he needs to do something fast. He grabs Graham by the legs and holds him upside down, newborn baby style. He then starts to swing Graham like a pendulum, each time on the down swing crashing Graham's back against the camper's fridge. After five brutal swings, Graham, as if in a Warner Bros. cartoon, coughs out a rosette of cauliflower.

Will places Graham on the floor.

"White folk."

Then he walks out of my camper.

CHAPTER 35

Calabasas

We were filming a night exterior on *Men in Black II* when Will came bounding out of his camper, Great Dane puppy style:

"Baz. I know the plot of *Men in Black 3*."

"Okay. Let's hear it."

"I arrive back at MIB Headquarters, and it's destroyed. Just smoking rubble. I can't find Tommy, and nobody at MIB knows who I am. I realize a villain that Tommy had put away a long time ago has escaped prison, time traveled back twenty or thirty years, and killed Tommy in the past. Now that Tommy is dead, everything in modern times has changed, which is why the villain was able to destroy MIB headquarters and the reason that no one knows who I am, since Tommy never recruited me.

"I have to travel back in time to protect Tommy.

"I arrive slightly late. I see my father killed while saving Tommy. Tommy shoots the time traveling villain, rescues young me, who is like 5 at the time, and then neuralizes me. The audience realizes that Tommy raised me and has probably erased my memory many times over the years. It was no accident he recruited me."

"Wow. That's a pretty great story. Although do either of us ever want to make another *MIB*? Especially with time travel?"

"Good point, Baz."

Ten years later, the producers along with the writer Etan Cohen (the guy with the "h" in a different place than Ethan Coen) teamed up to make Will's idea a reality.

Time travel scripts are difficult. When SONY hired me there was a detailed outline of the script and a lot of disagreements. Only the first act was ready to be filmed. Will and I lobbied to have a finished script before we started, but SONY wanted to get going. This meant only shooting the first third, then shutting down for several months to finish the rest of the script.

Before filming started, Will and I spent time at his home in Calabasas, trying to figure out the structure of our story. In addition to his very large mansion on many acres, the Smiths had several outbuildings. Since I was going to spend a few days with them, Will showed me around and gave me options of where to sleep.

"This is Jada's mother's favorite guest room."

"Uh-huh."

"Over here is a bedroom with a great tub and shower."

"Uh-huh."

We walked out of the main house toward one of the other buildings.

"This is Jada's yoga studio but is also a great guest room with a wonderful bed. So whaddaya think, Baz?"

"Well. I kinda like the privacy of the yoga studio, but, to be honest..."

"You'd be afraid. I know you, Baz. There's nothing to be worried about. We have twenty-four-hour security."

"That's not what I'm afraid of."

"Ah. Aliens," Will sagely remarked.

"And ghosts."

"You'll be fine. If you hear anything not of this planet, grab that phone, press 7, and I'll be over here in seconds with a Series 4 De-Atomizer."

"And, would it be okay with Jada if I turn all the Buddhas to face the other way? They scare me."

"Not a problem."

The next morning I met Will, Jada, Jada's brother Caleeb, and Darrell, Will's trainer, in the gym at 4:30 a.m. for the first of our twice-a-day workouts.

"Okay. Chin-ups," said Darrell, previously Sugar Ray Leonard's trainer and now my drill sergeant.

"Let's go, Sonnenfeld."

I jump up and hold onto the bar, my body hanging in space.

"Hey, Darrell. This isn't going to work. I've got no stomach for chin-ups."

"You will do ten chin-ups."

"Yeah, but…"

"Now."

At this point, I'm just hanging there, incapable of pulling myself up, but afraid to drop to the ground.

"Hey. Darrell. This is stupid. I can't do it, and I'm holding up the line."

"You will do ten chin-ups or get out of my gym. And if you leave, you will never come back. Your choice."

"Hey, guys. I mean, we're not really in the army…"

"You can do it, Baz," pleaded Will.

"Yeah, Baz. You can do it," cheered Jada.

"Seriously, guys. Look at me. I ca…"

"Get out of my gym," drill sergeanted Darrell.

"Seriously?"

"Out! Now!"

Will grabbed my knees. With me holding onto the bar panto-miming a man doing chin-ups, Will did ten 175-pound lifts, each one a couple of feet in height. After ten lifts, Will dropped me to the ground, and it was high fives and hugs.

The problem with living in the semi-arid wilderness of Calabasas is there are snakes. This particular reptile was in Will's living room.

Jada had run out of the house, and Will and Caleeb were stand-ing on the couch screaming. Someone needed to take charge. Not unlike my plane crash in Van Nuys or my mugging on 14th Street, when events get scary, I get calm.

I tiptoed across the stone floor past the snake and Will's jumping up and down on the couch, yelling, "Be careful, Baz!"

I entered his huge kitchen, grabbed a dish towel, and snuck back to the living room. I carefully leaned down, dropped the towel on the snake, grabbed the outline of the reptile's body near its head, and then, screaming as loud as I could, ran to the outside door and flung the squirming thing and towel as far as I was able.

From the darkness of the Calabasas night came the truly fright-ening high-pitched trill of Jada Pinkett Smith's scream. As it hap-pens I had flung the snake into the darkness and directly at Mrs. Smith, who had earlier fled the scene.

Luckily, the snake flew past her head and into the cool, dark night.

Jada raced in, just clearing my forceful slamming of the kitchen door.

We were safe.

I received a hearty round of hugs.

Truth be known, it was not a very large snake.

Years earlier, during the filming of *Wild Wild West*, I introduced Will to Tucks Medicated Comfort pads. Sweetie had gifted Tucks to me. I guess it's a product that women learn about after giving birth, for some female reason.

I don't want to know.

Anyway, they are pads of moistened toilet paper–like material. They changed my life and they changed Will's.

Will became a Tucks zealot.

He loved Tucks so much he asked four thousand film exhibitors at the annual Las Vegas Movie Exhibitor's Show,

"If a madman came up to you and put shit on your arm, would you wipe it off with a dry paper towel, or, instead, reach for something wet? Same thing with your ass."

Every bathroom in his house, including the guest powder room, had a jar of Tucks tucked inside an artfully macraméd holder. He always had plenty on hand, since my birthday present to him each year was a case of the pads from Costco.

I was leaving Will's place for a couple of days, returning later in the week. In anticipation of a long drive back to Santa Monica I used his powder room for a precautionary pee. Spotting the macraméd object, I opened the Tucks jar, took out a moistened towelette, removed a pen from my shirt pocket, and wrote:

"Dear Will. I'm your biggest fan."

I didn't sign it.

I put the single pad of Tucks back in the jar with its teammates, closed the lid, and left.

When I returned four days later, Will asked me to wait outside his dining room, where he was having a tense meeting with his head of security. I overheard enough of the conversation, especially the mentioning of the FBI, to know I'd better intervene.

"Hey, Will."

"Hold up, Baz. Let me finish this."

"I think I can help, depending on what you're talking about."

"Jada is pretty upset about something, Baz. Not sure you can."

"Um. Does it have anything to do with a note left in a jar of Tucks?"

Will shook his head in disbelief.

"I should have known."

Will and me at MIB Headquarters. MIB3.

CHAPTER 36

The Captain's Table

I was flying from New York to Los Angeles to have a meeting with Robin Williams. It was my audition to direct him in *RV*.

Before in-flight entertainment, one of the few methods I had to take my mind off the plane losing a wing at 33,000 feet was the SkyMall catalog. It was the Amazon of the era. Not only did Sky-Mall offer items you never realized you needed, but they often used unfortunate photographs to sell them—my favorite was a woman who seemed to exist only from the waist up, thrilled that the door to her asbestos filled attic was now insulated.

SkyMall's "The Attic Tent."

My life took a huge turn for the better on that flight when I discovered an ad for Allen Brothers' mail-order steaks. Although I could buy six flash-frozen steaks and have them delivered overnight to my home, what excited me was the SkyMall photo of the cooked NY strip. It was a perfect image of exactly how I like my steak prepared. I folded and scored the page, carefully ripped it out of the catalog, and placed it in my wallet. This image, I knew, was going to have a very positive effect on my life.

Robin Williams was a jazz musician of comedy. With the possible exception of Jonathan Winters, no one has ever computed faster, been more spontaneous, or been more able to work at such a high level of comedy without a net.

Robin was so fast and talented that asking him to impersonate someone was an insult. You had to give him two names—Ethel Merman and LBJ. George Clooney and Marilyn Monroe. His Ethel doing an impersonation of LBJ was subtly but audibly different from LBJ impersonating Ethel.

One day on the set of *RV* while the camera crew was reloading the Panaflex camera, Robin did a ten-minute advertisement for Director of Photography action figures, using every cinematographer he had worked with and their quirks.

"Act now and you'll also receive the Allen Daviau. He's slow. He doesn't have a driver's license. But boy, can he make beautiful pictures."

Robin had a need to be "on" all the time. At night after a long day on the set, Robin would make unannounced appearances at local comedy clubs. We had the dubious pleasure of filming part of the movie in the Canadian Rockies, at a place called Lake Kananaskis. For a week, five times an hour, we would hear a different iteration of "Feeling weak? Feeling put upon? Open up a can an ass kiss!" or "Can an ass kiss? You bet it can!"

Robin was incredibly well read. He was an expert on geology, astronomy, religion, chemistry, local politics, and history. Like almost every comedian I've known, he collected watches and fountain pens. He substituted the third of the comedian collectables—cars—for custom built bicycles.

Sitting at dinner one-on-one—which I did only once at Cin Cin, an Italian restaurant in downtown Vancouver—was enlightening. It was like having a meal with your favorite professor—Neil deGrasse Tyson meets the Dalai Lama. I learned more about the kabbalah in the first ten minutes of our meal than I ever cared to.

Then the waiter came to take our order.

It was as if the MC at Madison Square Garden had announced, "Ladies and gentlemen, Robin Williams!"

Not only was Robin giving a stand-up for the waiter, he was performing for the entire restaurant. That was the end of any serious discussion for the evening. Robin went from table to table, using props, sitting on laps, dancing with patrons. For a half hour, the restaurant came to a standstill.

A dozen years later Sweetie and I were filming *A Series of Unfortunate Events* in Vancouver. The first time we showed up at Cin Cin, the maître d' walked up to our table, introduced himself as Richard, reminded me he was my waiter a dozen years ago when I ate there with Robin, and told me he had PTSD for several years after that night, as did many of the restaurant's regular customers. When he saw I had made a reservation, he came in on his day off to tell me it was one of the most thrilling and scary evenings of his life. I knew exactly what he meant.

* * *

I landed in Los Angeles with the steak photo in my wallet. I met Robin at Lucy Fisher and Doug Wick's offices. Lucy and Doug were married and the producers of *RV*. Lucy had been my boss during the first *Men in Black*, when she was the president of production at Columbia. Doug is one of the funniest people I have ever met.

Doug is to dry as Robin is to wet.

Robin and I shook hands. He did five minutes of stand-up about Jews. When he stopped to take a breath, I took advantage of the micro-second lull.

"Hey, Robin. Finish the following punch lines."

"Got it," said Robin, rubbing his hands in anticipation.

"The light lunch..."

"Was my idea," laughed Robin.

"Hell. If you help me find my car keys..."

"We can drive out."

"And then the old man says, 'If only I had known...'"

Robin grinned. "I could have saved Eleanor Roosevelt."

Mom would have been upset by that one.

"Too hot?"

"Too sweet!"

I went with a very obscure joke with very little for him to work with. This time, I would stump him.

All I said was, "P.S...."

"Your vagina tastes great with bacon and onions," Robin screamed as he jumped on the couch in victory.

I was flabbergasted. He knew the joke but had a totally different punch line. My version ended with,

"Your vagina is in the bathroom sink."

At this point, although I was there to be interviewed by Robin, Doug, and Lucy, I announced to Robin, "You're hired."

Robin didn't enjoy working with me, and in some ways, I don't blame him. His jazz, his tightrope walk without a net version of improv comedy, is very different from the controlled, visual, specificity of how I work. I was always willing to let him "try a few his way" after we got what was written, but more often than not he would do the same words but in the voice of a Korean or Mr. Howell from *Gilligan's Island*.

Robin was a tortured soul, but I would only learn that firsthand once we started to film.

After meeting Robin, I tested my SkyMall photo in West Hollywood at the Palm Steakhouse. I ordered a brutally shaken Belvedere in a martini glass, the crabmeat cocktail, and a New York strip. I was anxious with anticipation. The waiter came through.

"And how would you like that prepared?"

Handing him the SkyMall ad, I asked, "What do you call this at your restaurant?"

Staring at the photo, never seeing anything like this before, he offered, "I'm going to call that our medium rare plus."

"Okay. I'd like a medium rare plus New York strip, please."

A week later, now in New York, I was having dinner at Lure Fishbar.

Oxymoronically, Lure Fishbar had a great steak. I showed my Allen Brothers photo to the waiter.

"I'd call that medium."

"I'll have a medium New York strip, please."

Josh Capon, the executive chef and a friend, was schmoozing at our table when this event happened.

"What the fuck is that?"

"It's a photo of how I like my steak cooked."

"Give me that."

Josh took my little SkyMall photo, held it over the table's candle, and set it on fire.

"Hey. That's not fair. I'm using a photographic aid to communicate with your waiter. I'm not giving your chef a line reading. I'm not saying, 'Cook it like this.' I'm just trying to find out what I should call a steak cooked like this photo at your restaurant."

Josh realized I was right, put out the fire, took the half-burned image back to the kitchen, and came back with it laminated.

"Here," he said.

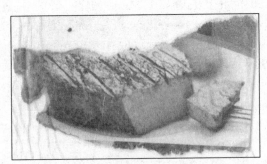

The STEAK DONE-NESS card is still in my wallet. Note burn marks on left side of the steak from Josh's candle.

For eight years I had a column in *Esquire* called "The Digital Man," where on a monthly basis I would test and review gadgets, cameras, cell phones, headphones, GPS units—whatever I felt like learning about. In mid-September 2009, I was getting ready to do my annual Christmas issue, which meant testing dozens of gift ideas—perfect for a road trip. Departing Telluride, Sweetie and I had four GPS tester navigation units/apps suction cupped to our windshield, which drove Sweetie nuts since not only did it impede visibility, none of the units were muted.

Sweetie takes pride in her navigation skills and is threatened by even one GPS. She also hated my recently purchased squishy steering wheel cover.

Four navigation units/apps, a radar detector, and a squishy steering wheel.

Deciding to spend the night in South Dakota, we were surprised to find what seemed for Custer to be an upscale bistro called "The Sage Creek Grille." It looked like a Tribeca transplant.

Modern decor.

Big wine list.

Tablecloths.

The waitress took our order. Glasses of wine. Appetizers. Sweetie ordered the trout.

"And I'll have the New York strip."

"How would you like that prepared?"

I thought she'd never ask. I took out my wallet, pulled out the laminate, and said:

"What does your restaurant call this doneness?"

"Oh my God," the waitress exclaimed. "I have to show this to Chef."

"Please don't."

"He's going to love this."

"Actually, he won't."

She was confused.

"It will be better if you tell me what your restaurant calls a steak cooked to this doneness, and then I'll say those same words back to you."

"Chef is going to love it," she said, as she skipped away.

The maître d' brought us our wine. Forty-five minutes later I said to Sweetie,

"I wonder where our appetizers are."

"I wonder where our waitress is," said Sweetie.

Her view corridor included the entire restaurant, and Sweetie hadn't seen our waitress since she took our order. At that moment, the maître d' approached. With a theatrical presentation worthy of Custer's finest dinner theater, she handed back my laminate, which had disappeared with our waitress.

She then said:

"Please finish your wine and leave. We will not be serving you tonight."

"It's about the steak photo, isn't it?"

"This restaurant has a chef. Not a cook. Please leave."

"Hey, listen. I told your waitress it was a bad idea to show you . . ."

"Please leave."

I picked up the Allen Brothers steak photo and gingerly placed it back in my wallet. Sweetie and I walked across the street to the Captain's Table, where we had the house specialty: prime rib and fried shrimp, which is really, if you're out for dinner in Custer, South Dakota, what you want in the first place. And since they carved the meat from the prime rib carving cart tableside, no photo was required.

CHAPTER 37

CM the CM, Part 2

The Child Molester

Mike Laurence, CM the CM, was born Max Levine. Mike was my mother's cousin on the Levine—her mother's—side, as opposed to Kellerman, her perhaps epileptic father's side of the family. CM's father, Mel, a major piece of shit, was the brother of both Bertha—Mom's mother—and Sam Lewis, born Sam Levine, a somewhat successful songwriter.

Mike was an erudite, charming, smart, cultured, violent, lying thief, and a pedophile. Like my mother, his lies and truths were seamlessly merged into one coherent—to them—story line. When confronted with evidence refuting their untruth, they would deny ever saying such a thing. The difference was my mother would cry. Mike would turn Ferrari red and throw things.

The most public of his outbursts occurred while waiting in line one cold fall night outside the Second Avenue Deli. Until he was murdered, the owner of the deli was a gregarious Jewish fella who would bring trays of open sandwich bites out to the diners waiting for a table.

Mike, my parents, and I along with a half dozen other hungry people were in the inner vestibule protected from the bitter November winds of the Lower East Side when a grinning Abe Lebewohl arrived, holding a tray of small open faced chopped liver sandwiches.

"Make yourself useful," he said, as he handed Cousin Mike the large catering tray.

We all reached for a piece of heaven. Mike balanced the tray with one hand as he took a piece for himself. A woman with too much makeup and aggressive perfume took a second, third, and fourth piece, hoovering them into her mouth as Mike, starting to turn the color of a cooked nonkosher lobster, held the tray.

"Here," Mike said, handing the large serving platter in her direction.

"Serve yourself."

"No, thank you. I like being served."

"Well, I don't like serving," he said as he shoved the tray at her pancaked face.

"Well," she said, not knowing the kind of rage Mike was about to volcano, "I only eat at restaurants where I am served."

"Get served this, CUNT."

Mike then threw the tray of chopped liver at her head—a distance of eighteen inches. Of course, the woman ducked, and of course my mother was standing behind her, so inevitably Kelly got covered—her face, her hair, her brown suede jacket—with chopped chicken liver. A melee broke out. The husband of the accused cunt attacked Mike. Mike happily started to punch the husband. Thrown back in the fracas, my mother found herself on the ground.

For some reason the wife kept screaming "homo" at Mike, which was true, but beside the point. As my father finally restrained Mike, the husband started to call my father "homo."

Abe came out from behind the cash register and calmed everyone down. I helped my mother to her feet. The brown of her suede jacket and pants camouflaged most of the liver, although parts of her hair and face were speckled with a riot of the stuff.

Then the cops arrived. The Sonnenfelds, Mike, and the Homo Haters offered various interpretations of the event. Whenever my father said anything, the offending husband and wife team would yell "Homo!" which would prompt Mike to scream, "Shut the fuck up, Cunt!"

I think the homophobic couple realized that Mike was certifiably insane, which is why they hurled insults exclusively at Sonny.

One of the cops, realizing there was no good outcome to this tribal skirmish, pretending to hear something in his walkie-talkie, said "Hey, Joe. We've got a 501 on Avenue A and 5th," which my father later claimed meant,

"The pizza is ready. Let's get the fuck out of here."

The cops made us all promise to behave and fled the scene.

Abe sat the two warring parties on opposite sides of the restaurant, and we ate in peace, although my mother smelled fowl.

I noticed that the homophobic screamers stood outside the restaurant after finishing their meal. This feud was not yet over.

We finished our dinner and stepped outside.

"Homo!" they screamed in our direction.

Dad, meanwhile, was bodily restraining Mike, who was screaming, "I'll kill both of you fucks! Let me at them, Sonny."

A police car slowed to a crawl in the parking lane. The feuding parties knew better than to continue this insanity and went their separate ways.

Although Mike called himself a vice president at NBC, his real job—and position of power within the family—was as the network's event planner. That meant whenever NBC was having a convention for their O&Os—owned and operated stations—or coverage of national political events, he was in charge of hotel rooms, catering, entertainment, and other associated amenities surrounding the event.

He'd show up at our apartment with swag like NBC-branded all-transistor radios and pens. We would be invited to NBC events, like the live studio broadcast of the Huntley-Brinkley presidential election coverage from Studio 8H in Rockefeller Center.

The fact that occasionally their O&O conventions were held at Miami and Los Angeles hotels where Mike would put us up at the expense of NBC also kept him in good graces with my parents—his penchant for sexually abusing their son notwithstanding.

Mike had two things that gave him a jumping-off platform for his molesting of children.

First, he was an absolutely terrifying bully. And second, through the manipulation of his expense account, which according to my mother, is what eventually got him fired from NBC—*Wait! It wasn't the fact that he was a child molester*—he got various family members dinners and hotel rooms that he traded for young flesh.

It makes absolutely no sense unless Kelly and Sonny truly hated me or didn't care about my welfare that they would let Mike take me unattended to some of these local events. It also made no sense in retrospect that I was willing to go. But the night of the 1964 presidential elections NBC was broadcasting election results from Studio 8H and I wanted to go. Dad was with a "client," and Mom, well, she:

"Had a splitting headache and felt an angina attack coming on and needed to lie down with a wet towel across my face."

I was always interested in politics. I ran for student president in junior high school and gave one of the worst speeches in the history of worldwide junior high school elections, having dropped my index cards on the way to the stage. I gathered up the 3x5s and read them in a William S. Burroughs postmodernist order. I got a lot of laughs but not a single vote. Even I couldn't vote for me.

In addition to politics, attending the live broadcast was exciting. I was fascinated by the lights, scaffolding, cameras, and human resources it took to put together a live show.

According to my mother, she had been the stage manager of the Stage Door Canteen in Times Square during World War II, which might have instilled my interest, but like all utterances from Kelly, I cannot speak for its veracity.

My father had surely sold NBC many of the lights and dimmer equipment for Studio 8H, since at one point in his career, he was the top theatrical lighting salesmen in New York, which seems paradoxical considering how often we had no electricity.

Perhaps I felt safe, since CM the CM and I would be in a very public place surrounded by many layers of NBC brass, all of them in one form or another his boss.

The clients' booth—a twenty-by-twenty-foot glass room that looked down upon Chet Huntley and David Brinkley's Gulf Oil branded podiums—was reserved for the sponsors of the election night coverage. The corporate heads of Gulf Oil, their ad agency Young & Rubicam, various NBC executives, me, and Mike were gathered in the room. I was eleven.

There was catering, although mercifully no chopped liver sandwiches.

Mike's slightly hyperthyroidal eyes bugged out as he spotted a "clients' phone" on the far side of the couch. He stared at it, surveyed who was in the room, slithered along the green leather sofa toward the magic phone, and picked up the receiver. Without having to press a 1 or 9, he heard a dial tone. This meant he had found a phone with free long distance set up for the elite clients.

Mike called his mother in Miami.

The highly combustible combination of a man with a very, very short temper and a Jewish mother who had not heard from her son in weeks created the firestorm you would have expected but desperately hoped would not occur.

The conversation quickly became heated, and to the shock and dismay of everyone in the glass atrium, Mike, turning rage red, started to scream at his mother. Wives of CEOs were cringing. NBC executives were silently appalled. I headed for the catering table and pretended I didn't know Mike as he spat into the phone what a CUNT his mother was, that her new husband was a putz, and no he wasn't going to visit anytime soon. Mike was going to quickly get fired if I didn't intervene.

"Hey, Mike," I whispered, as I pointed to the studio below. "Look at the big board."

A few months earlier I had seen *Dr. Strangelove*, which remains my favorite movie. "The Big Board" reference was to the movie's nuclear threat board projected on a large screen behind George C. Scott, Peter Sellers, and others.

In this case, I was trying to direct Mike's rage away from his mother and toward the floor below.

Mike waved me away.

"But Mike. Check it out," I frantically pointed.

"Not now!" Mike screamed as he pushed me away.

"Right. But Mike. You might want to talk to your mother later." I said as I indicated with a slow head nod the various well-dressed important people starring at CM the CM.

The guests, relieved that Mike was no longer yelling "fuck" and "cunt," were still pretty put out by a grown man screaming at a very small 11-year-old kid. Even Mike realized he was the center of attention at the wrong time in the wrong room with the wrong people. Mike screamed one last vindictive "CUNT" as he slammed the phone into the cradle.

Shockingly, he still had a job.

Between the time he was fired by WMCA radio, "The Good Guys," a phrase that Mike claimed he coined, and hired by I'm sure the now regretful NBC, Mike lived with us—sleeping on our living room couch and getting free petting privileges of various young boys and, if prepubescent, girls.

Mike was incredibly transparent in his molestation. A field day for Mike were the Jewish holidays where various neighbors, uncles, aunts, and cousins—my father was one of seven—from the Sonnenfeld side of the clan were at our apartment eating burnt brisket and candied yams with carbonized marshmallow topping. After we were sated, sitting around the living room, Mike might say to any of a half dozen of us, as he patted his lap,

"Come over here."

The sorry kid who made eye contact plank-walked toward Mike. Placing the scared child on his lap, he'd proceed to unzip his zipper and put his hand into the opening, at which point my mother or father—none of the other adults were willing to even meekly stand up to Mike—would say *"Miiiiike,"* which would force CM the CM to zip the kid up and send him or prepubescent her on their way.

I seem to have made it through Mike's molestations relatively emotionally unscathed, although thirty-five years of anxiety and sciatica might suggest otherwise. Someone very close to me, perhaps a Yucca Beauty, wonders about my definition of "relatively."

Although I knew my parents were aware they were housing a pedophile, the first time I confronted them was over thirty years ago, when they invited Sweetie, who was not yet my wife, her two children, and me over to their house in Hampton Bays for Jewish holiday brisket.

Sweetie's two daughters, Sasha and Amy, were nine and six at the time—perfectly ripe for Mike's taste in children. I asked my mother who else would be coming, and she responded,

"Just Mike."

"Just Mike?" I screamed.

"You want to put Susan's kids in that kind of danger?"

"I'll police Mike," my mother insanely replied.

"You were going to let me bring Susan and her children to your house without telling me Mike would be there? Are you nuts?"

"You're nuts, Barry. We'll be careful."

"Careful the way you were when Mike lived with us? The way you were careful with Raul and me and all the others."

"Barry. Stop it. Come over for brisket. Leave. See if I care how long you stay."

"Mom. We are not coming to fucking Shit Hampton. You are insane to have even suggested it. You are insane to have let Mike live with us. And molest me. How could you and Dad let that happen? You should all be in fucking jail."

My mother, with no irony, said the words that my father would parrot thirty years later.

"Barry," she wept. "Back then child molesting didn't have the stigma it has now."

"Mom. We're going to pass on the bitter herbs. And if you ever put me in a room with Mike Laurence, it will be the last time you see me in your life."

Weeping, Kelly managed to get out:

"You're crazy. You know that. Absolutely craz..."

I hung up.

Back at the night of the '64 presidential election, having cursed one last "cunt" as he hung up the phone, Mike said, "Let's get out of here and get some Chink food."

Since Mike was now gainfully employed by NBC—he called it the National Biscuit Company—and was no longer camped out on our living room couch, Mike took me in a cab back to his apartment and ordered Chinese takeout.

This was not the plan for the evening—being alone with Mike. My heart started to pound as I stood silently in the elevator on the way up to his apartment.

He led me into his bedroom, where he had a very cool Tandberg stereo tape recorder that had iridescent green-blue recording meters. He showed me how they worked, talking into a microphone, while he stood behind me, his erect penis pressing against my 11-year-old body as he unzipped my pants.

He pulled me over to his single bed, where he laid me down. He snuggled behind me into a spooning position, where he reached around and unbuttoned and spread apart the waist area of my pants. I told him to stop. He shushed me and started to stroke my penis. I begged him to please stop. He continued to stroke. He was breathing onto my neck in a slow, moist repetition. I was in psychic pain, and incredibly scared.

An hour earlier he was screaming at his mother in Miami in front of dozens of powerful people, yet his rage went unchecked. Now I was alone with no one to protect me.

I was very alone.

I started to silently cry. I laid there while he did what he wanted. I also knew that in a profoundly guilty way—in a confused and horrified way—my penis was erect. Did that mean I was somehow okay with this?

A year earlier, when he was living with us and knew that I only had a half day of school, I came home to discover that Mike had traded in his Thunderbird for a new Mercedes and wanted to take me for a ride. We drove all the way to Grossinger's Hotel in the Catskill Mountains. Mike was going to teach me how to swim.

We started by having a late lunch in the restaurant, where Mike signed the check with a fictitious room number. He then bought us each swimming trunks, also signing them to the fraudulent room.

After the "swimming lesson," which consisted of some discomfiting underwater hand moves by Mike, he took me into a single shower stall, closed the frosted door, pulled down my swimming trunks, and started to touch my penis.

I begged him to stop. He continued, his body behind me, his arms wrapped around my waist.

Loudly, I said, "Hey, Mike. Please stop."

"Shush."

And then a voice from the bathroom: "What's going on in there?"

"Just giving the boy a shower," Mike said.

"Is that true, boy?" said the voice.

"I'm actually done," I said.

"Then why don't you come on out?"

Mike turned me around and gritted his teeth as he glared at me and pulled up my swimming suit.

We both stepped out.

The man stood there and made sure I dried off and got into my street clothes, then followed us out. Mike, having illicitly signed for our lunch and swimming suits, was in no position to make a scene.

It was a very long and silent ride home from Sullivan County to Manhattan.

Now, a year later, I found myself in a very similar position but much worse, since we were alone in his apartment. He started to stroke me harder, his breathing becoming faster, deeper, and more desperate. Tears silently flowed from my eyes. My mind took a trip, leaving its body. I knew I was about to be raped but was terrified of Mike's rage if I resisted.

Suddenly there was a knock at the door.

The Chinese food delivery.

Mike warned,

"Stay here!"

He got up from behind me and left the room. As soon as he walked out, I jumped off the bed and pulled up my pants as fast as I could.

I listened as Mike opened the door and I mercifully heard my father's voice,

"Is Barry here?"

"Hi, Dad."

I rushed from Mike's bedroom to the front door.

"Ready to go?"

"You bet."

"Thanks for taking him to the elections tonight, Mike. You got everything, Barry?"

"Yeah, Dad. I'm ready to go."

Sonny had gone to NBC. We weren't there. He came to Mike's apartment to get me. He knew what was going to happen and got there, on one level, before the worst of it. On another level, the fact that he and Mom entrusted me to Mike's care for that evening and others is impossible for me to reconcile.

On the drive up to Washington Heights Dad didn't ask me about the night, I didn't volunteer, and Mike continued to be a presence in our lives for many more years, until, according to my mother, CM the CM died of AIDS.

Additionally, according to my mother, he contracted it from the boy that John Guare's *Six Degrees of Separation* is based on. Mike picked him up one night on Columbus Avenue.

The only part of Mom's story I can personally attest to is that Cousin Mike the Child Molester is dead.

CHAPTER 38

Burying the Lede

On April 1, 2009, my father called to give me his version of a happy birthday greeting.

"You know if your mother was alive it would be her birthday too. Your mother gave birth to you on this very day."

"Thanks, Dad. Yes. I know. But I'm still holding out hope I was adopted."

Ignoring me, he continued,

"So in many ways, it is as much her birthday as yours. If she were alive."

"What else is up, Dad?"

"Well, the reason I'm calling is because your birthday reminded me I'll be ninety this September."

"Yes, you will."

"You should throw me a party."

"Okay, Dad. Thanks for calling and wishing Mom a happy birthday. I'll talk to Sweetie and get back to you."

"Wait. Barry..."

"Yes, Dad?"

"A big party."

★   ★   ★

Although she would never call it hate, over the years Sweetie came to dislike my parents almost as much as I insisted she should. But Sweetie is a much kinder and more loving and giving person than I'll ever be, so she agreed with Dad. Yes, it will be painful, but not everyone gets to not only be ninety but be a very lucid, healthy, happy ninety. We agreed to throw Sonny a party.

Sweetie did some research and came up with Bayard's, a catering restaurant located at Hanover Square in the financial district. We could take over their entire second floor.

"Hey, Dad. You win. Sweetie and I will throw you a birthday party Saturday night, the last weekend in September. Send me an invitation list."

Sonny never knew if his birthday was September 27, 28, or 29. His mother said it was on the last day of Rosh Hashanah, but that date changes since the Jewish calendar does not line up with the Gregorian. Rather than pick a day and stick with it, Sonny always celebrated for three days a year.

A week after agreeing to the party, I received Dad's list of 250 names.

"Dad. You're 90 years old. Your friends should all be dead. We can't invite 250 people to your birthday party. It will bankrupt me."

"You're not serious."

"You're the one who isn't being serious. You surely cannot have that many close friends."

"I shortened it from 400."

"Well, good work, Dad, but you can invite 150 people. Tops. And even that number sounds insane to me."

"Does the 150 include you and Susan and Chloe?"

"No. You can call it 153. In fact, if you want, you can have 153 of your friends, and Sweetie, Chloe, and I won't come."

"Let's call it 153, plus you, Susan, and Chloe."

Always the salesman.

Dad made the invitation calls. If he felt he needed to invite someone, but resented them cutting into the 150, he'd say,

"Listen. My cheapskate son is throwing me a 90th birthday party, but he's only letting me invite a hundred and fifty people. You're invited since you're my favorite second cousin, but since I'm only allowed a measly hundred and fifty people, I'd rather you didn't come. There are a lot of lighting reps and theater designers I'm very close with and would rather have them."

Sonny tried several times for a bigger party, but I held my ground.

"Dad. With booze and flowers, we're talking about a $25,000 birthday party. I'm not that rich, I promise. It's a hundred and fifty people."

"Not including you, Susan, or Chloe."

"Yes, Dad. Not including us three. Although as I've mentioned..."

"How much are the flowers?"

"What?"

"What if we didn't have flowers? How many additional people does that get me?"

"None, Dad. We're having flowers."

"Cheapskate."

I arranged for a microphone and some sound speakers in case anyone wanted to make a toast. Old people, young people, relatives, and business associates started to stream and dribble into Bayard's.

An old person I had never met cornered me and demanded to know if I had arranged for toasts.

"Yes, I did. There is a podium and a microphone and speak..."

"When do the toasts start?"

"We'll have cocktails, dinner, and then there'll be time for toasts."

"You're not leaving enough time. Everyone's going to want to make a toast."

"Okay. Let's see how it goes."

"I'm going first. Call on me first. I have a lot to say, and I don't want these old people falling asleep while I'm talking."

"Well, actually, sir, I'm going first."

"Second then. Call on me second. Saul! My name is Saul!"

Getting ready for the party.

Cocktails went fine, although way too many people smelling of perfume, talc, and saliva would pinch my face and say a version of, "You don't remember me. Do you?"

"Nope. Sorry. I don't."

"You're kidding me. You don't remember me?"

"I'm sorry. I don't."

"Thelma! Come over here and tell Mr. Bigshot who I am."

Once I greeted everybody I huddled in a corner with 16-year-old Chloe.

"Who *are* these people?" Chloe asked, as if we were being invaded by aliens.

Saul found me and demanded we get started on the toasts.

"Saul, people are just sitting down for dinner. Let's give them twenty minutes. Then I'll make a toast and call on you."

"You're not listening to me. You're going to run out of time. These people don't want to be here till two in the morning listening to toasts. Everyone is going to want to speak. You have to start now. If you don't, I will!" Saul screamed at me.

"Okay. Okay. I'll make a toast."

"Now. Right now. And then call on me."

Standing at the microphone, I clinked my glass for quiet, announced that due to popular demand and a death threat from Saul, we were going to open the toast process way too early. I gave a short toast thanking Sonny for my sense of humor. That I was sorry I didn't get more of his traits, like his ability to be a perpetual optimist although rarely having electricity and phone service. Or his ability to instantly fall asleep.

I made fun of Mom, who although dead, was still a strong presence in the room. I joked that I had gotten my pessimism and fear of everything from her. It was a nice kind toast to both my parents, considering how much I disliked them for their years of neglect.

"Okay, for what it's worth, I am opening up the mike to anyone who wants to say a few words about Sonny, and if they are mean, they get bonus points."

Saul stood up.

"Yes, Saul. You get to go first."

"Second," he corrected.

As he came forward others lined up to speak. People on canes, crutches, my cousins, theater designers, lighting designers, Broadway musical producers...The line kept growing. Saul was right.

And now I'll come clean.

I buried the lede.

My parents were loved by hundreds of people. Speech after speech after speech talked about how Kelly and Sonny changed their lives. Many individuals, based on talking to Sonny, or Sonny and Kelly, had literally switched careers, gone back to college, started their own firms, told off their boss and got a big raise, divorced their spouse, or come out as gay.

Several people went on in emotional detail about how Sonny had given them money in their time of need. One of Sonny's brothers went on about how Sonny had given him twenty thousand dollars when he was in the financial dumps.

WHAT?

Without exception, every speaker said that Sonny, or Sonny and Kelly, had been the most important people in their lives or, at a minimum, their careers.

Sonny was truly beloved.

The same speeches would have been made at Kelly's party if we had thrown her one. People constantly told me she had changed their life. That they always sought out her wisdom before making big decisions. Or that she was their favorite teacher. Ever.

Here's the truth I've been keeping from you:

My parents were good people.

They were just horrible parents.

Sonny and Honey Rose at his 90th birthday party. Dad insisted on name tags.

"A Miracle Is What Seems Impossible but Happens Anyway"

Sweetie asked if I wanted to include an epilogue.

"Maybe something of value at the end of the book. You know, sum up what you learned in life so far."

She continued:

"Something that would make parents buy your book for their child graduating college."

"I think the porno chapter will queer that deal, Sweetie."

"That's why I said college. Not high school.

"I think there's a lesson to be learned from your life," she said.

"You know how you advise young people to go ahead and declare themselves what they want to be? How you bought a camera when you got out of film school so you could call yourself a cameraman? It worked. You would not be where you are today if you had worked your way up as a camera assistant, camera operator..."

I agreed with Sweetie that declaring myself a cameraman and bypassing all those intermediate steps was a way to go. But what Griffin the Archanan also taught me is that a life is an amalgam of so many billions upon billions of arbitrary decisions—not only by me but everyone around me—that you can't put your finger on a single decision and say,

"There. That's the one."

I shudder to think how many close calls, how many muggings, car collisions, and airplane crashes, I accidentally avoided.

Will Smith joked that he wanted to take me to Philadelphia public schools, point to me, and say,

"If this guy could end up as a successful film director on big-budget films, anyone can."

He's right. If I could end up as a successful film director on big-budget films, anyone can.

My advice: be what you want to be and don't blame your parents.

Acknowledgments

Sweetie: Without you I'd be an insufferable disaster of a human being. You have brought me love and family and a life worth living. You make others willing to spend time with me.

I watched you shake the bed with laughter (the ultimate compliment) as you read "An Actress Short, a Cum Shot Behind," which I wrote as a lark more than a decade ago.

You helped me believe I could be a writer. You give me confidence and strength and, hard as it is to admit, a happy life.

Thank you to David Granger who as editor in chief of *Esquire* magazine published "The Digital Man," a column I wrote for many years. Over lunch, more than ten years after I gave up the gig, you asked if I had a book I'd like to write. Your encouragement and intelligence have been mother's milk to me (though the idea of my mother nourishing me with anything other than formula is an absurd concept). Without that lunch, I never would have written this book.

Thank you to Hachette for agreeing to publish this memoir based on three prototype chapters. Thanks to Mauro DiPreta and Michelle Aielli, who convinced me to come to Hachette, and to the very patient Brant Rumble, who took over editing duties partway through this endeavor.

Finally, thanks to my friends and family who have put up with my large personality and neediness. I am so grateful you are in my life.